The State and Human Services

MIT Studies in American Politics and Public Policy
Martha Weinberg and Benjamin Page, general editors

The State and Human Services:
Organizational Change in a Political Context

Laurence E. Lynn, Jr.
with the assistance of Timothy C. Mack

The MIT Press
Cambridge, Massachusetts, and London, England

This book was set in VIP Optima by DEKR Corporation and printed and bound by Murray Printing Company in the United States of America.

Library of Congress Cataloging in Publication Data

Lynn, Laurence E   1937–
    The state and human services.
    (MIT studies in American politics and public policy; 7)
    Bibliography: p.
    Includes index.
    1. Social work administration — United States — Case studies.
2. United States — Social policy — Case studies.   I. Mack, Timothy C.,
joint author.   II. Title.   III. Series: Massachusetts Institute of Technology.
MIT studies in American politics and public policy; 7.
    HV91.L95   361.6'1'0973   80-10851
    ISBN 0-262-12084-4

Contents

Series Foreword

Social scientists have increasingly directed their attention toward defining and understanding the field of public policy. Until recently public policy was considered to be a product of the actions of public institutions and as such was treated as the end point in analysis of the governmental process. But in recent years it has become clear that the public policymaking process is infinitely more complex than much of the literature of social science would imply. Government institutions do not act in isolation from each other, nor is their behavior independent of the substance of the policies with which they deal. Furthermore, arenas of public policy do not remain static; they respond to changes in their political, organizational, and technical environments. As a result, the process of making public policy can best be understood as one that involves a complicated interaction among government institutions, actors, and the particular characteristics of substantive policy areas.

The MIT Press series, *American Politics and Public Policy,* is made up of books that combine concerns for the substance of public policies with insights into the working of American political institutions. The series aims at broadening and enriching the literature on specific institutions and policy areas. But rather than focusing on either institutions or policies in isolation, the series features those studies that help describe and explain the environment in which policies are set. It includes books that examine policies at all stages of their development — formulation, execution, and implementation. In addition, the series features studies of public actors — executives, legislatures, courts, bureaucracies, professionals, and the media — that emphasize the political and organizational constraints under which they operate. Finally, the series includes books that treat public policy making as a process and help explain how policy unfolds over time.

In *The State and Human Services,* Lawrence Lynn analyzes one of the most pressing problems facing all levels of government, the problem of planning for and delivering services designed to help the many different kinds of persons who turn to government in times of need. Lynn looks at the intent and results of federally mandated human service reorganizations in six states and analyzes the political and bureaucratic consequences of these reforms. He shows that all government reorganizations are affected by the political climate in which they are set and by the political actors who are charged with planning and executing these plans. Lynn provides important insights into the nature of the reconfiguration of power that accompanies these reorganizations both within states and between states and the federal government. His study increases our understanding of human services organization and delivery and raises important questions about the design and execution of human services policy.

Lawrence Lynn is Professor of Public Policy at the John F. Kennedy School of Government of Harvard University.

Martha Wagner Weinberg

Preface

The idea for this book took shape in 1975 as I was completing a study for *Evaluation* (now *Evaluation and Change*) magazine on human services in Florida. The purpose of the study had been to assess the consequences for human services of several recent administrative reforms in the executive branch of Florida state government: the "Government in the Sunshine" Act, program budgeting, the beginnings of a management-by-objectives (MBO) system, and commitment to planning and evaluation.

My interest in this subject was kindled during 1972 and 1973 when I was assistant secretary for planning and evaluation in the U.S. Department of Health, Education and Welfare under Secretary Elliot Richardson. The federal government's limited ability to plan and coordinate hundreds of categorical programs made Richardson want to increase the role and competence of state governments, especially governors, in overseeing these programs. Many of his associates were skeptical; after all, the federal role in human services had been growing in part because the states could not be counted upon to deal effectively with the problems of needy and disadvantaged people. Was state government becoming more capable of coping with such problems, or could it be made to do so with judicious pressure from the federal government? Florida's experience might give some clues.

The final study was quite different from my original intent. At the time of the study, the Florida legislature was reorganizing the state's human services agency. The objective was to decentralize program administration and streamline services delivery by "integrating" services, i.e., by bringing independent and scattered services activities into a single management system. This type of reorganization was one of the reforms that Richardson and his staff had been advocating. However, the legislature was sponsoring the change, not the governor. In fact, the governor had serious reservations about it. Since governors usually sponsored reform of this sort to increase their control over program policy and administration, the legislature's role in Florida was surprising.

Closer investigation revealed that the entire lawmaking environment in Florida was changing. Reapportionment had increased the power of young, aggressive legislators from the cities and suburbs. The legislature had begun meeting annually, maintaining records of its activities, and providing full-time staff to its committees. The Health and

Rehabilitative Services Committee of the Florida House of Representatives, for example, was developing a capacity for independent program evaluation, and bright young people with graduate degrees were being recruited as committee aides.

In contrast, the executive branch reforms I had set out to study were proving to have little bearing on policy. The state's program budget was an artifact that fulfilled no purpose in budget making. Management conferences between the governor and his human services advisors, which had been started as part of an MBO process, were discontinued when top officials became preoccupied with reorganization. The "Government in the Sunshine" Act was partly responsible for the demise of these conferences; participants did not want to discuss sensitive reorganization matters in front of the press and public. The program evaluation office in the Department of Health and Rehabilitative Services was facing stiff competition from the legislature's evaluators and an uncertain future.

In short, the significant story of Florida was not executive-branch administrative reforms. Rather, it was the reconfiguration of political power within the state and, in particular, the growing interest, involvement, and competence of the legislature in matters concerning the content and administration of human services programs. By enacting the reorganization in 1975, the legislature challenged the governor's prerogatives and policies concerning human services administration and considerably enlarged its sphere of influence in such matters. It did so, moreover, despite intense opposition from organized interest groups fearing that reorganization would greatly reduce professional control over programs.

If developments similar to those in Florida were occurring elsewhere, conventional views about relationships among federal, state, and local governments would have to be revised. An important strand of reformist thinking concerning intergovernmental relations — the Nixon administration had labeled it "the New Federalism" and Richardson was perhaps its ablest exponent — stressed the role of elected chief executives, namely, governors and mayors. In this view, responsibility for setting priorities and designing programs should devolve from federal agencies to state and local chief executives. The authority of governors, mayors, and other "general purpose government" executives over program administration could be increased through such devices as revenue sharing, block grants, and executive review and approval of state agency applications for federal funds.

The Florida experience suggested that it would be naïve to expect that the power of governors and mayors could be increased without provoking a challenge from legislative bodies. The challenge, moreover, might be more than simply blocking executive proposals. Legislatures could develop real competence to deal with complex budgetary, programmatic, and administrative matters. They might become initiators and innovators, especially if the political stakes were high.

The meaning of such developments for human services was not clear. Services integration was the outcome in Florida, but quite different outcomes could occur elsewhere, and subsequent Florida legislatures could just as easily resegregate services. Much would depend on the political situation. In Florida, moreover, key legislators were interested in how other state legislatures were grappling with similar problems. Perhaps, then, services administrators were becoming more vulnerable to pressures from all directions: from the federal government and the governor's office as well as from state legislatures and, through them, from other states. Human services policymakers and administrators might have to adapt to a more complex political environment. More specifically, administrative concepts such as services integration, coordination, planning, accountability, and efficiency might have to be analyzed in terms of their political significance as well as in terms of their implications for organizational functioning.

One could not make such a case solely on the basis of developments in Florida. Hence, with the generous support and encouragement of the National Institutes of Mental Health — specifically, Dr. Howard R. Davis, chief of the Mental Health Services Development Branch, and Ms. Susan E. Salasin, chief of the Research Diffusion and Utilization Section — I undertook a study of human services organization and administration in five other states. A fillip to this effort was the emergence of Jimmy Carter as a serious presidential candidate. If he was elected, it was expected that his experience in reforming Georgia state government would have a major influence on his administration, so it seemed worthwhile to investigate the nature, extent, and implications of these reforms. Thus studies of human services reform in

Georgia and Florida, along with studies of Arizona, Washington, Minnesota, and Pennsylvania, are the bases for this book. The work has been supported by NIMH Grant No. MH27738-02.

The primary purpose of the book is to help further our understanding of one of the most socially consequential domains of public management: human services organization, administration, and delivery. My hope is that it will also contribute to more effective action and advocacy by people in government dedicated to improving governmental competence in meeting human needs. In the process of completing the research for this book evidence indicated that many administrators dedicated to effective government are often their own worst enemies because they act as if politics should have no place in designing the government organizations and programs. This attitude exacerbates conflict with elected officials who are bound to feel otherwise and is usually counterproductive. Effective government is more likely to be achieved if proponents of beneficial change, or opponents of destructive change, develop an understanding of the political dynamics whereby decisions are reached and tailor their designs and strategies accordingly.

This study could not have been completed without the invaluable assistance of my colleague Timothy C. Mack. He conducted most of the field interviews over a period of nearly three years, prepared extensive accounts of organizational change in each state, conducted a correspondence with many of our primary sources, assembled a bibliography, and helped me throughout with the design of the analysis. We are both grateful to the more than one hundred people who agreed to be interviewed, most of them on the record, many of them more than once. Kathleen G. Heintz assisted me in my original study of the Florida reorganization. Edward F. Lawlor assisted me in the research and thinking for chapter 2. Martha Wagner Weinberg has provided perceptive advice and steady encouragement concerning the focus, organization, and content of this book. I received valuable comments on the penultimate draft from Michael S. Dukakis, William Roper, T. McN. Simpson, and Guy D. Spiesman. Marci Hazard and Emily Chatfield typed numerous drafts; Marci provided valuable editorial assistance, and Emily prepared the final manuscript. My wife Pat gave me the will to continue.

The State and Human Services

1
Organizing to Meet Human Needs

Throughout our history, whenever serious problems of social welfare have arisen, we have turned to government for help. As these problems have grown in extent and variety, so has the role of government. The federal government now outspends the state and local governments in every social welfare category except education, but all levels of government support and administer social programs of almost every type. The allocation of program responsibility to the different levels of government has been haphazard, however. The result has been confusion and disagreement over the proper role of each. In particular, the federal role in human services has provoked conflicts with state and local officials who, while welcoming federal grants, have been increasingly unhappy with the elaborate restrictions on how federal funds can be used. Though favoring continued federal financial support, governors and other elected officials would like many of the strings removed. Some state officials go so far as to argue that many federal restrictions on how programs shall be administered are unconstitutional.

This issue has its origin in the passage of the Social Security Act in 1935. Prior to that time, responsibility for assisting people to obtain services and relief rested primarily with state and local government and with private charitable organizations. In addition to creating a federally administered retirement program, the Social Security Act authorized federal grants-in-aid for state-run programs of maternal and child health, child welfare, and crippled-children's services and for income assistance to the aged, the blind, and children of families deprived of a male breadwinner. In the decades since, the federal system of categorical grants-in-aid has expanded to include mental health and retardation, health and medical care, employment assis-

---

Throughout this book, the terms *human services* and *human service programs* will refer to government (or nonproprietary) efforts to deal directly with people in such a way as to improve their functioning and general well-being. The term *agency* will refer to the organizational unit that administers a service. The term *human service organization* will refer to an organization with administrative responsibility for more than one type of service or agency.

The terms *human services, human resources,* and *social welfare* are used interchangeably in the literature, though some writers draw various distinctions for purposes of policy analysis. The term *human services* is employed throughout the book, and the occasional use of other terms for variety does not imply any substantive distinctions.

tance and training, new forms of income maintenance, all levels of education, and criminal justice. By 1978, states and localities were eligible for approximately 270 different human service grants.[1]

State and local governments have been given relatively little say in how these grants are to be used, however, especially in recent years. Professor James Q. Wilson has noted that

the 1960s mark a major watershed in the way in which the purposes of federal aid are determined. Before that time, most grants were for purposes initially defined by the states, such as highways, public works, public health, and aid to the deserving poor. . . . Beginning in the 1960s, the federal government . . . increasingly came to define the purposes for these grants not necessarily over the objection of the states, but often without any initiative from them.[2]

These federal purposes are predominantly in areas related to human needs and include expanding the level and types of service available, encouraging innovation and reform, improving access to services by the poor and otherwise disadvantaged, and rectifying geographical imbalances in service availability. To ensure that federal purposes are carried out, grant programs are administered in accordance with detailed guidelines on the use of funds. Furthermore, as federal program administrators face unforeseen problems, and as pressures for accountability from Congress, auditors, and judges mount, program regulations tend over time to become even more numerous and detailed.[3] Thus the steady growth in the number of federal grant-in-aid programs and in the specificity of the rules governing their use has led to substantial federal involvement in state and local decision making.

In the late 1960s, governors and other general-purpose government officials (that is, officials whose responsibilities are not restricted to specific programs) viewed federal controls as insulating categorical and specialized interests from state and local judgments about need, as severely restricting their ability to respond to changes in priorities and budgets, and as too burdensome. Dissatisfaction with the categorical grant system generated political support for returning authority over program priorities and administration to the states. Revenue sharing, grant consolidation, state agency review and sign-off on federal grant applications and awards, and similar measures were proposed as devices for giving the states and their elected and appointed officials greater freedom to set and carry out program priorities.

With strong backing from the administration of Richard M. Nixon, several decontrol and decentralization measures were adopted in the early 1970s. Congress authorized general revenue sharing and passed three bills — the Comprehensive Employment and Training Act (CETA), the Community Development Act, and an amendment adding Title XX to the Social Security Act — that gave states and localities more flexibility in using federal funds. The Office of Management and Budget issued several management circulars designed to standardize, simplify, and coordinate grant application and administration, and ten regional councils were created to decentralize federal decision making on issues directly involving state and local governments.

Despite these measures, Congress, federal program administrators, and state and local officials who are direct beneficiaries of the current system have been reluctant to cut the strings that have been tied to federal grants over the years. Their support for any kind of revenue sharing or block grants has always been shaky, and evidence suggests that, as the Advisory Commission on Intergovernmental Relations (ACIR) notes, "the tendency for Washington to tighten controls over block grants seems to increase as the program ages."[4] Repeated Nixon administration proposals to decategorize HEW grant administration were greeted with indifference by Congress, as was Nixon's proposal to create a Department of Human Resources to further unify federal administration. Moreover, court-enforced federal commitment to such goals as guaranteeing the rights of women and minorities, citizen participation in program administration, and equal opportunity for the handicapped have, in ACIR's view, "brought us into a new era of national regulation" of state and local politics and administration.

Among the many explanations for the reluctance of Congress and of federal and nonfederal program officials to loosen controls over state and local actions is skepticism concerning state and local capacities to withstand pressures for tax reductions, debt retirement, or unwarranted subsidies to local interests. This skepticism is expressed most often in connection with controls that have been created to insure specific services for needy, dependent, and vulnerable groups who may not have strong political representation in the states, or to protect essential but less visible programs that might be sacrificed by governors or mayors who have other priorities. A participant in federal discussions concerning consolidation of elementary and secondary education grants, for example, recalls a visit by representatives of several state commissioners of education, who

warned us against too much grant consolidation. Their commissioners, they said, were under severe pressures from statewide teacher groups for general salary increases. As long as federal programs were covered by sufficient strings, the program funds would be out of bounds for wage negotiations. But if too many of the strings were removed, the funds might fall into the category of general aid, despite the commissioners' desires to the contrary.[5]

Similar views are often expressed by advocates for the poor and by supporters of public health, vocational rehabilitation, nutrition, mental health, and retardation programs, who fear dilution of program quality, loss of visibility, and reduced control over program administration by trained professionals.

The main counterargument to this viewpoint is that distrust of state government is no longer appropriate. One close observer of developments in state government argues that such views

ignore the essential revolution that has taken place in most state and local governments over the past fifteen years or so. . . . Albeit in unequal measure, the states have replaced their constitutions, assigned more clear-cut authority to their governors, reorganized their executive structures, moved to more professional budgeting systems, and made their legislatures far more efficient and democratic.[6]

As an author and proponent of decentralization and decategorization measures, former Massachusetts lieutenant governor and HEW secretary Elliot Richardson regards predictions that such measures will lead to poor quality and inadequate services as "implausible." "State and local governments are gaining in competence almost everywhere." "One is forced to conclude that the real reason for interest group opposition [to decategorization] is the familiar reason — preservation of their own control over a federal funding source."[7] Indeed, he goes on to develop a diametrically opposed thesis. Opponents of decategorization and decentralization, he believes,

simply do not understand the limitations on the federal capacity to meet human needs. . . . Excessive grant proliferation results in *less* benefit to any given national interest than it would receive from its proportionate share of a block grant. Why less benefit? Because the value of the categorical grants has been diminished by ballooning overhead, prolonged delays, and endless aggravation.[8]

Focus of the Study

The debate over appropriate federal, state, and local roles in human services raises several questions concerning the political economy of state decision making. How much and what kind of power do governors, legislators, local officials, program personnel, and professional associations have over human services policy and administration? What are their goals? Who is likely to initiate changes in the status quo, and who is likely to oppose them? How does the institutional setting in a state — the extent to which authority over resource allocation and services administration is centralized, the way the executive branch and the legislature are organized, the responsibilities of local government in human services delivery — shape human services policy and administration and affect the prospects for change? In contrast to structural or institutional factors, how do personalities and personal relationships shape policy outcome? How much leverage does the federal government have over state and local actions? Does each state represent a unique story or are generalizations possible? For example, does recent experience suggest that the states in the aggregate are gaining competence or are more likely to pursue national goals in responding to human needs? Because answers would be valuable in the making of decisions concerning the role of the states in human services policy and administration, these questions are the central concern of this study.

As posed, the questions are too broad to be investigated with any precision using existing methods of inquiry. To bring them into sharper relief and obtain sufficient variance in state experience to make generalizations possible, this study focuses on the specific issue of how decisions are made concerning the organization and administration of state human service agencies.[9] This issue is well suited to the concerns of this study for three specific reasons.

First, the major themes of advocates for loosening federal controls over state actions have been (1) the need for comprehensive planning and administration of state programs and (2) the desirability of "services integration," that is, the common location of related service activities, a single intake system for new clients, and delegation of authority to supervise and coordinate services to local, nonspecialist administrators.[10] Both themes imply extensive organizational restructuring in the states. Thus, the study of decision making concerning organizational issues is directly related to the question of the appropriate state role in the federal system.

Second, organizational issues arise at various times in every state. With explicit or implicit federal encouragement — but often without it — states and localities have been trying alternate approaches to human services organization, including those advocated by "new federalist" reformers. A number of states have attempted, following the example of the Department of Health, Education and Welfare, to integrate top-level policy and program administration by consolidating separate agencies into a single department,[11] and a few have attempted services integration in the field. At the opposite extreme, other states have rejected innovation in favor of retaining the more traditional organization of services under virtually autonomous boards and commissioners of categorical services such as public and mental health, corrections, education, and public welfare. A few states have attempted major organizational changes, then abandoned them. Thus, a wide variety of recent and relevant state experiences is available for study.

Third, a study of how individual states deal with the issue of organizing and administering human services is bound to reveal interrelationships between political processes, organizational structures, and policy priorities. Reorganization is a classic reform issue in which the expressed goals are usually improvements in responsiveness, efficiency, or quality of services. The real goals, however, are almost always partly or wholly political, and a study of decision making concerning organizational issues must take into account the political context.

Proposing a reorganization may, for example, represent a declaration of intent by a governor or legislator to challenge entrenched interests, to shake up the system. It may represent a more direct political challenge to specific vested interests — welfare bureaucrats, hospital administrators, county commissioners — designed to erode their power. It may represent an effort to gain greater control over an existing organization and its resources by mandating change and then controlling the steps necessary to carry it out: the filling of new

positions; geographic reallocation of payrolls, construction, and purchase of services; the redefinition or refocusing of organizational
missions. Depending on the form it takes, reorganization may be seen
as a way to enlarge both the scope of an agency's responsibilities and
its budget and personnel; as a way to weaken, eliminate, or take over
competing organizations; or as a way of gaining visibility for an
agency's mission and programs. Reorganization may signal a desire
to "do something" about a problem when it is not clear what should
be done.

The reactions of parties affected by a proposal to reorganize can be
expected to depend in large measure on whether they perceive a gain
or loss by it. Further, the actual resolution of the issues raised by a
specific proposal will depend on the relative political power of the
parties to the decision making. Indeed, a proposal for organizational
restructuring is unlikely to become a serious issue at all unless a
sufficiently powerful political actor sees enough advantage in it to
warrant sustained advocacy. Changes in the configuration of power
and influence at the state and local levels brought about, for example,
by court-ordered reapportionment or constitutional revision, are likely
to affect human service agencies because they will alter the extent to
which political officials see advantages or disadvantages in the status
quo.

Finally, decisions about human services organization are, at bottom,
decisions about human services policy. Human services programs and
organizations are created to deal with specific social problems. However, achieving social goals such as putting welfare recipients to work,
preventing child abuse, and rehabilitating offenders, and doing so
efficiently, is exceedingly difficult, if not impossible, and disagreements over both means and ends abound. It is not surprising, then,
that human service agencies are beset by administrative problems and
controversies and are the frequent targets of critics charging that they
are not performing according to expectations.

A problem-ridden or controversial agency is an invitation to political
action. Faced with public criticism, interest-group pressure, or media
attention, the governor, legislators, or an agency head may feel they
must do something. Officials may also view a problem-ridden agency
as a political opportunity, a chance to show that they are competent,

decisive, or responsive to public or interest-group concerns. The program administrators who are the objects of this attenton may resent what they regard as political interference, but their resistance may only enhance the justification for political officials making a decisive move.

The appeal for reorganization and administrative reform in such circumstances is not hard to understand. The root cause of the department's problems may be the unattainability of program goals, inadequate funding or staffing, or political conflict over what should be done and how. Dealing directly with such causes may be politically unfeasible, however. Proposals that involve abandoning goals, revising budgets, or resolving conflicts of purpose are apt to be full of political pitfalls and thus unattractive to governors, legislators, or politically ambitious appointees to executive jobs. In contrast, reorganization may seem to avoid such pitfalls because it sidesteps divisive issues and aims at goals with which no one can disagree without appearing parochial. It often seems the easiest thing to do when something must be done. Not infrequently, officials in human service agencies find themselves immersed in organizational issues, even when its problems seem to be the aftermath of previous organization reshuffling.

Thus, to shed light on the character of state decision making with respect to meeting human needs, this study is concerned with the process of organizational change in a political environment, with how human service organizations are shaped by and interact with political processes in the states.

Study Approach

The kinds of questions that constitute the focus of the study are most fruitfully approached through an analysis of particular cases drawn from these experiences. Case studies can readily assimilate the information that must be used in studies of this kind: material from both primary and secondary sources and from formal analytic studies, subjective assessments obtained through interviews, journalistic accounts, and the like. They can explore the variety of interactions that comprise the process of change. Thus, in providing a detailed yet systematic "feel" for how things work, the cases will advance the kind of understanding of policymaking processes that is the aim of this study. Cases that show how the processes of deciding on human services organization work in different states would be valuable even if powerful generalizations did not result.

Because the phenomena to be investigated are exceedingly complex, because a rigorous study design is virtually precluded, and because investigators must be selective in gathering information, case studies are vulnerable to the criticism that they are self-validating; investigators may unconsciously find what they set out to find or be drawn to information that is consistent with a priori views, with the result that such views are never submitted to disconfirmation. Significant factors may escape documentation, elude interviewers, or have their effects in ways that are not directly observable. Investigators may tend to identify with participants to whom they have access or, for that matter, with anyone with a strong, articulate, or well-informed view.

Distortions of this kind have been minimized by careful and repeated cross-checking of information obtained through interviews and by the repeated circulation of drafts among participants and observers with diverse perspectives on the events being studied. Equally important, however, is the organizing context or framework used to guide the selection of information and provide the answer to the questions: What is this a case of? What is the investigator looking for? For the findings to be credible, the framework must be explicit and as carefully developed as possible.

How should organizational change in a political context be studied? What are the questions and variables of interest, and from what theories or conceptual bases should they be derived? The framework for the present study builds on ideas from the literature on human service organizations,[12] on organizations in general[13] especially studies of the relationships between organizations and their environments, and on public-policy determination. Unfortunately, little of this literature bears directly on the present study. For example, though much has been written on how interactions between business firms and their environments affect organizational structure,[14] little has been done of a similar nature on government organizations. Thus, the framework for this study synthesizes and extends ideas and approaches in the literature that seem most germane to the kind of understanding that is the study's goal. This framework can be summarized as follows.

The process of organizational change begins with political or economic demands that may originate either inside or outside the organization. The stimulus for these demands may, for example, be unmet needs or newly discovered problems such as a rising rate of alcoholism or divorce, poverty among the elderly, or malnutrition among children. It may be evidence of organizational malfunction such as inadequate treatment, administrative incompetence, or inertia in responding to a political mandate. Basic value conflicts may also motivate change. The people-processing character of human services, the value orientation of service providers, and the key role professionals play in human service agencies and organizations may lead to conflicts between levels of an organization (administrators in the central office and professionals in the field), between the organization and its clients, or between the organization and outside interest groups representing service workers (physicians or county welfare directors) or suppliers of fund (taxpayers). Thus value conflicts may underlie proposals to consolidate separate agencies, centralize planning and budgeting, or reallocate administrative authority.

Demands for change will be given concrete expressions by participant-sponsors when an opportunity for a decision that can produce the desired change arises or can be created. Such opportunities are continuously provided by the political process through elections, budget reviews, the actions of legislatures, and so forth. The decision-making process will be fundamentally political, and it may be protracted and accompanied by considerable conflict. To be successful, originators of change must gain enough support, by aggregating enough preferences or by appealing to enough people with ideological sympathies, to gain a favorable decision. Usually this will involve bargaining and compromise to reconcile diverse interests and views. The resulting change, if any, will take the form of alterations in such organizational dimensions as the allocation of authority, the character of the services to be delivered, and the value orientation of the organization's service delivery (e.g., whether welfare recipients shall be "put to work," "aided to become self-sufficient," or "provided with a check").

The cases, then, will focus on the originators of organizational change proposals and what they were seeking, the processes of debate and deliberation, and the results. While the primary aim is to gain insights into this kind of decision making in the states, the analysis of the cases will also address the following questions: Are various classes of actors — governors, legislators, service professionals, bureaucrats — consistent in what they are seeking? Are certain classes of actors more successful in initiating or opposing change than others? Are certain kinds of changes more likely to be adopted than others? Do structural variables such as the powers of the governor, the organization of the legislature, the role of local governments, or the degree of centralization of the principle human service organization affect the likelihood and character of change proposals, the processes of deliberation, or the results? Are certain kinds of change more durable than others? Are there any factors that can be systematically associated with either the likelihood of change or its durability? Does the federal government have any consistent influence on organizational arrangements adopted by the state? Are any trends detectable?

The Cases

Six states were chosen as the subjects for case studies. In four (Arizona, Florida, Georgia, and Washington) extensive reforms of human services departments have been attempted; Minnesota has proceeded deliberately but cautiously in promoting organizational and administrative reforms; and in Pennsylvania state officials have shown only limited interest in revising human services organization. In Georgia and Washington the governors were the initiators of change; the legislature was the change agent in Arizona and Florida. The extent and durability of the changes also varied in these states — some undertook modest changes that have lasted, while others embarked on more radical changes, then retreated. This selection thus facilitiates comparisons and contrasts among states that have diverse experiences in reorganizing human services.

The cases focus on changes in the organization that include the state's public welfare and social services agencies. Because so many recipients of public assistance need various kinds of help, these organizations are typically the focal point for debates over whether, why, and to what extent service agencies should be combined or integrated at the policymaking level or in the field.

An analysis of six other states might produce quite different conclusions. The states chosen for this study include a disproportionate number that have been involved in far-reaching organizational changes. Had the study included instead states such as Illinois, New York, and Texas, where experience with change in the last twenty years has been far less extensive, another picture might have emerged. The purpose of this study, however, is to understand the dynamics of change in order to provide insight concerning the policy implications of an important type of policy proposal: giving more power to the states. These six cases should be effective for that purpose.

2
The Changing Shape of Federalism

State human service organizations are a product of 360 years of American history. A reading of this history suggests that a fundamental tension has shaped the processes of change in state-aided human services. As the demands by reformers, service providers, and interest groups for expansion, differentiation, and specialization of services for the needy have grown, they have met resistance from elected and appointed public officials demanding coordination, efficiency, and economy in tax-supported public programs.[1]

At the root of this tension is the fact that "need" is an imprecise and often controversial concept. It is based on the ideal of the physically, psychologically, emotionally, and materially self-sufficient individual, family, or community. Need arises when people are not self-sufficient and require help from "external" agencies for any of several reasons: temporary or permanent physical impairment such as sickness, blindness, or other handicapping conditions; the inability of fit individuals to find enough work to support self and family; inability to work because of age or because of psychological or emotional impairment; and, some would add, unwillingness to assume responsibility for self-support. At all times, numbers of people need at least minimal outside help for physical and material survival.

Needs in this essentially quantitative sense will vary continuously as the size and age structure of the population change. Growth and aging of the population, for example, will increase the numbers of dependent people, especially the elderly. Needs will also change as people congregate in or migrate to areas that lack the capacity to provide enough jobs or as both temporary and permanent shifts occur in the quantity, nature, and location of employment opportunities. Social and economic changes associated with the transition from agriculture to industry and commerce and the recurrence of economic depressions have dramatically altered the nature of dependency, creating a large urban work force vulnerable to economic and social change.

But need also has a qualitative dimension. Needs have grown as society has gained greater understanding of the nature and causes of dependency and of remedies for it. The advancement in knowledge of how to control the epidemics that plagued the Colonies, for example, created a need for the public health services that could prevent them. As the belief grew in the late eighteenth and early nineteenth centuries that the insane could be cured, a need for appropriate treatment facilities emerged; subsequent developments in knowledge of the causes and treatment of mental illness have affected perceptions of the magnitude and character of needs for mental health services, leading, in particular, to demands for readily available community-based care. The prolongation of life and greater understanding of the causes of and treatments for illness have increased the need for organized and specialized medical care as well as for facilities such as skilled nursing homes. As technology for enabling people with physical handicaps to increase their mobility has developed, a need for making it available has arisen.

Thus, need has an open-ended character. As we learn how to do more to assist dependent people, the "need" to do more grows. Moreover, the articulation of need is predominantly done by the program specialists, professional care givers, and organized interest groups who are closely identified with the people for whom they feel responsible.

While making possible a higher quality of life for people in need, the progressive specialization and professionalization of human services has at the same time widened the possibilities for political conflict over both the ends and the means of government-assisted human service programs, especially in the states. Human service professionals and other advocates tend to want to render all possible assistance to needy individuals regardless of cost. They are apt to define need in absolute terms: a person who can be helped should be helped. As ideas about who can and should be helped and about what constitutes appropriate help have become more sophisticated, the demands for public programs to meet human needs have grown in size, variety, and cost. Elected officials who must come up with the funds for public programs are thus faced with the necessity of determining the merits of these demands and responding in an appropriate way while at the same time controlling the costs of government and acting in accordance with the traditional values of their constituents: work, self-help, charity for the deserving, and social control of deviants. State officials are apt to define need in relative, not absolute, terms, and weigh the claims of advocates for services expansion against the availability of resources and the preferences of the larger community. As government increases in size and costliness, the questions of elected officials concerning efficiency and appropriateness of service tend to become more insistent and legislative involvement in the organization of the service system more frequent and detailed.

The evolution of this tension is evident in the history leading up to recent developments described in the case studies. The remainder of this chapter outlines this history, stressing (a) those developments which produced shifts in the character of need, and which thus shaped the demand for government-assisted human services; and (b) the evolution of the state role in human services provision, i.e., of the supply of state-assisted or state-provided services.[2]

The Colonial Period

The complex combination of factors affecting demands for state-assisted human services have been evident since Colonial times. Population grew steadily in the seventeenth century — a few hundred quickly became a few thousand and, by 1700, a quarter of a million people — and with it, the number of poor and otherwise dependent. Throughout the seventeenth and eighteenth centuries problems of dependency created by the hardships of Colonial life were exacerbated by the British policy of exporting undesirables such as paupers, vagrants, and convicts to the Colonies and by the influx of refugees driven from frontier settlements by the French and Indian Wars. By as early as 1650, seaport towns were becoming crowded, with the poor tending to congregate there, and problems of dependency grew throughout the eighteenth century as the population swelled to over five million. In a population of this size, of modest means to begin with, the number of poor, sick, aged, widowed, orphaned, or otherwise dependent constituted a problem for town officials, especially in the Northeastern and Middle Atlantic states.

Inevitably, early local efforts to meet these needs bore the mark of English traditions. When informal supports proved inadequate, towns or parishes provided relief (Plymouth in 1642, Virginia in 1646, etc.), using the model of the Poor Law of 160l. This model defined categories of the needy; assigned financial responsibility to the community if family resources were inadequate; made "settlement," that is, residence in the community, a condition of eligibility; and authorized care in central places such as almshouses (indoor relief) and income maintenance in a residence (outdoor relief).

Before long, resources were strained in many larger towns. The influx of refugees from King Philips' War, for example, led Boston to apply to the General Court of the Massachusetts Bay Colony for aid in providing for them, and in 1701 relief to people with contagious diseases was provided from the general treasury. The role for Colonial administrations, however, was limited to providing relief for the "unsettled" or "state poor," people whose residence in a town could not be established. For them, the Colonies bore no administrative responsibility; that was left to local poor-law officials.

Throughout the eighteenth and most of the nineteenth centuries, public outdoor relief was the rule and took the form of providing sustenance to the needy in their own homes or contracting with householders (perhaps following an auction) to care for them on a per diem basis. Children could be "bound out" to a foster family or apprenticed for training. The feebleminded, insane, and handicapped were in general treated in the same manner as the poor and the destitute. Dependent individuals who were not residents were "warned out," that is, sent elsewhere, often with an official escort. Thus, the needy were aided in a manner that did not unduly disrupt either their lives or the functioning of the community. Institutionalizing people was an infrequently used last resort.

As Colonial America grew, however, the problem of what should be done with the able-bodied poor became troublesome. Religious views stressing the duty to give charity to those in need were diluted by the increasingly popular belief that virtue resided in the accumulation of wealth and property. Pauperism came to be regarded as a vice and a symptom of moral defect, and aiding the able-bodied poor became in the view of many a subsidy for idleness which might undercut the incentives to work and accumulate that were the basis of the modern industrial state. Even in the seventeenth century, legislatures passed laws authorizing the binding, jailing, whipping, or indenturing of the voluntarily idle, and a few towns would place them in workhouses to earn their relief.

In general, the growth of need in the Colonial period was largely shaped by population growth, the characteristics of those immigrating to America, and the harsh conditions of life, including frequent epidemics and wars. The transition from self-sufficient communities dependent on farming to more urbanized settlements based on commerce, fishing, shipbuilding, and other industries not only increased the number of transient and dependent poor but also increased the stigma associated with pauperism and idleness, thus introducing an enduring element of controversy into public policies toward the needy.

The New Republic Before the Civil War

The nineteenth century prior to the Civil War was marked by continued population growth, by the steady migration westward of the able-bodied population, and by the influx of impoverished immigrants (over 350,000 annually in the early 1850s) mainly from Germany and Ireland. Often employed at subsistence wages, unskilled immigrants were especially susceptible to illness, unemployment, and other misfortunes. The problems of industrialization and urbanization were becoming serious, particularly along the Eastern seaboard, as the number and size of cities grew. The immigrant populations of these cities were vulnerable to the frequent and prolonged economic depressions such as those of 1815–1821, 1837–1843, and 1857–1859.

The growing numbers of needy people in special categories — the deaf and dumb, lunatics and the feebleminded, the sick, the blind, orphans — aroused educated middle- and upper-class reformers, assisted by a few experienced professionals, to become advocates for better identification and treatment of the dependent and to demand improvements in how the state provided for them. Reformers of the Jacksonian era fostered the idea that deviant and dependent behavior was caused by "faulty community organization" and that society required specialized institutions — asylums — to care for the dependent and the deviant. The first political movement for human services expansion and reform was born.

Reform was not the only motive for institutionalizing the needy. Because of abuses and rising costs, general opposition to outdoor relief was growing, both in England and America. According to the English Poor Law Amendments Act of 1834, passed largely in response to rising taxes for the upkeep of the poor, aid to the able-bodied poor and their families was henceforth to be given only in almshouses. In America, the states began authorizing towns, cities, and counties in the new republic to establish almshouses, poor farms, and asylums run on a contract basis by a private superintendent. The institutions served as residences for the indigent sick, the feebleminded, the mildly insane, the crippled, and able-bodied poor men, women, and children. Children might be bound out as apprentices by county commissioners, and the violently insane could be jailed. Beyond these exceptions, no efforts were made to classify and differentiate inmates. Segregation, not therapy or rehabilitation, seemed to be the main purpose of care.

Deplorable conditions and abuses in the local welfare programs contributed to the impetus behind the reform-oriented movement to establish state-run asylums in the decades preceding the Civil War. Reformers believed that an asylum could, as David Rothman has put it,

fulfill a dual purpose. . . . It would rehabilitate inmates and then, by virtue of its success, set an example of right action for the larger society. . . . The well-ordered asylum would exemplify the proper principles of social organization and thus insure the safety of the republic and promote its glory.[3]

Through the early middle decades of the nineteenth century, state institutions of all kinds proliferated, initially buoyed by the advocacy and optimism of their supporters. Moreover:

Whatever their shortcomings, almshouses were humanitarian as compared with the irresponsible, cruel systems of auctioning the poor or contracting for their care with persons who were often on the edge of dependency themselves. Not infrequently, in the larger cities at least, affluent citizens pointed to the almshouse with pride as the place their community's generosity had provided for its unfortunate citizens.[4]

The almshouse became the temporary haven for many poor immigrants, often in ill health, who were by then arriving in America in unassimilable numbers.

The state sponsored institutions were largely autonomous. Interest groups would persuade governors and legislators to create politically visible special purpose institutions, the director or boards of which would be appointees of the governor. Though nominally responsible to him, the superintendents would be subject to virtually no oversight or supervision.

At this time, both Connecticut and Kentucky received federal land grants to facilitate the establishment of asylums for the deaf and dumb. A significant federal role was not to be, however. In a landmark application of the Tenth Amendment, President Franklin Pierce in 1854 vetoed legislation that would have authorized federal land grants for insane asylums. Congressional support for such a measure never materialized again, and Pierce's interpretation of the Constitution prevailed with few exceptions until the Depression, guaranteeing that state and local activities would shape the history of government-assisted human services until that time.[5]

By the 1850s, the institutions had lost their reformatory purpose, and they were increasingly used as dumping grounds for society's outcasts, including immigrants. David Rothman notes:

As the community increasingly utilized asylum facilities to confine the hardened criminal, the incurably insane, and the decrepit poor, the recently insane from comfortable households or the able-bodied poor in need of temporary relief avoided them as best they could. In turn, the chronic and the helpless filled the vacancies and the institutions became even less attractive to anyone else.[6]

Another significant change was occurring. The first asylums were designed and run by idealistic lay reformers, but, in the case of insane asylums, physicians had taken over their administration by the mid-nineteenth century. In contrast to the optimism of the Jacksonian reformers, these physician-administrators had a pessimistic view of the curability of insanity and preferred the primitive medical therapies of the time to the environmental therapies of the early reformers. In 1844 they formed the Association of Medical Superintendents of American Institutions for the Insane to further their interests.[7]

Thus the processes of change were being irrevocably transformed. The identification and definition of need were being undertaken by non-governmental advocates organized for that purpose and by groups with specific institutional and professional interests. Moreover, these needs were being defined in categorical terms: children, the mentally ill, paupers, and criminals were being viewed as groups with special problems requiring specialized forms of care and custody.

From One War to Another

The Civil War brought order of magnitude changes in the problems of dependency. Suddenly states and communities were faced with large numbers of poor and suffering war victims, veterans (nearly two million in 1865) and their families, and orphans. Additional needs were created by the emancipation of black slaves, who numbered nearly four million at the beginning of the War. Those needs were viewed as temporary and the needs generated by the Civil War were compounded in the decades following by continued migration and immigration, the accelerated pace of industrialization, and the effects of recurring depressions, all of which created near crisis conditions in the larger cities by the turn of the century. By 1910, for example, one-third of the population in the eight largest cities was foreign born. Moreover, the poorer quarters of America's larger cities were the most densely populated areas in the world. The deteriorating urban conditions, violence, and class conflicts of this period, the heyday of American laissez-faire capitalism, aroused concerns for the stability of American institutions.

Because institutions were useful for segregating and controlling the deviant and dependent, legislatures continued to create and support them. The proliferation of nonaccountable, problem-ridden institutions prompted Massachusetts in 1863 to set up the first Board of State Charities to advise the institutions and the legislature. Five unpaid board members were assisted by two paid staff members. Their duty was to investigate and oversee conditions in the institutions and offer recommendations in the interest of economy and efficiency. Over the remainder of the century, state legislatures appointed committees on efficiency and economy, and their reports invariably recommended central control, especially of administrative functions such as purchasing and accounting.[8] Other states formed state boards to integrate welfare functions and administration.

A variety of structures emerged: administrative boards, policymaking boards, and, closer to modern structures, single executives. To an increasing extent these boards were staffed with full-time employees. They led a trend away from catchall almshouses toward more specialized facilities for the mentally ill, physically handicapped children, and other dependent children. They insured some break with the patronage traditions of the first half of the century by occasionally persuading governors and other elected officials that institutional administration required qualified, competent people, not merely party loyalists. Not all states favored central boards, however; and in the ones that did, changes were less than dramatic. Major changes in human services administration had to await the adoption of merit-based personnel systems and the professionalization of public administration in the first part of the present century. The period from the Civil War to the turn of the century is significant nonetheless because contemporary themes and tensions surfaced in legislative deliberations over state aid to the needy: coordination, economy, professionalization, specialization, centralization, and integration. Furthermore, over time legislative concerns with economical administration of aid on behalf of the deserving needy would influence the character of advocacy. Advocates for children or the mentally ill, for example, would work hard to differentiate their interests from the undifferentiated interests of the poor so as to avoid the stigmatization increasingly associated with pauperism and the almshouse, as well as the economy moves to which they were subject.

The strongest force bearing on the evolution of the state role in human services in the period between the Civil War and World War I was the proliferation of mutual aid societies and other private charities, especially in the cities. Philadelphia had more than eight hundred such groups in 1878. That the response was predominantly private was due to several factors: evidence of governmental corruption, leading to widespread distrust of publicly provided relief; the writings of Herbert Spencer, William Graham Sumner, and other social Darwinists, which reinforced the prevailing laissez-faire ideology; and the emergence of upper-class charitable activities motivated by a desire to insure great social control over potentially dangerous classes of society. All these factors came together in the rise of the charity organization societies (COS). Beginning in 1877, COS were formed in city after city by members of the wealthy classes acting out of both a fear of social unrest, charitable impulses, and a determination to discourage indiscriminate giving in favor of selective aid offered in the spirit of moral uplift. They sought to foster cooperation among local charity organizations, to maintain information on the population in need of assistance, to conduct investigations of need and direct resources to the most worthy cases, and to discourage pauperism.

One result of the urban, class-based COS movement and its emphasis on private activities was that public institutions and public outdoor relief came to be viewed by most people as services of last resort. In the COS view, those individuals and families most easily redeemed or saved from pauperism and dependency were best dealt with through private charitable arrangements tailored to their needs. Only the irredeemable should be referred to public institutions, a view which furthered the tendency to use these facilities as warehouses for the hopeless.

Another outcome stemmed from the COS use of "friendly visitors" to investigate need and advise the needy. The visitors, most of whom were women, sought specialized training to help them advise their destitute clients. This desire formed the basis for the formation of schools and a profession of social work. Indeed, the COS movement provided the model — careful investigations of need by qualified specialists whose goal was rehabilitation — for publicly provided relief programs, especially the growing number of municipal outdoor relief programs of the period.

The predominance of the conservative COS movement, with its emphasis on a minimal, last resort role for the state, eroded as the Progressive movement gained in strength. This movement represented a fundamentally different reaction to social distress and the concentration of economic power. The government was seen as protector and guarantor of individual rights and equality of opportunity. The Progressives' emphasis was on poverty, not pauperism, and on prevention through social insurance and attacks on the causes of poverty, not relief and stigmatization. Its troops were the social activists associated with settlement houses, not the patrician friendly visitors with their caretaker mentality.

Progressive era reformers were defeated in attempts to win widespread state adoption of the unemployment and health insurance programs already popular in Europe. However, they singled out two traditionally deserving categories of needy people — the aged and widows with dependent children — and fought their treatment as paupers or relegation to almshouses. President Theodore Roosevelt convened the first White House Conference on Children in 1909, and by 1912 Congress had authorized creation of the Children's Bureau, to gather and disseminate information on the welfare of children. Demands for specialized services for mothers and infants were spreading in response to health-related draft rejections, the feminist movement, and new knowledge concerning maternal and infant mortality. Contributing to the strength of mothers and infants as a categorical interest were such antecedent developments as the formation of societies for the prevention of cruelty to children in the 1870s, of the American Pediatric Society in 1889, and the American Association for the Study and Prevention of Infant Mortality in 1909.

Under pressure from such groups, most states adopted mothers' aid programs providing pensions to needy widows. COS leaders opposed such aid as "merely" public outdoor relief, though they convinced most jurisdictions to administer them according to the social work model, i.e., with a caseworker assigned to investigate and give advice. In 1911 Missouri enacted the first widow's pension law. By 1919, thirty-nine states had them. Similar success, albeit ten to fifteen years later, was achieved with respect to pensions for the aged.

Children's Bureau director Julia Lathrop, basing her arguments on infant mortality data collected by her bureau, persuaded Congress to pass the Sheppard-Towner Act in 1921. This act authorized federal matching grants to states for programs to reduce infant mortality, and thus it stimulated further state involvement in human services. In 1907, no state had a bureau of child health; in 1927, forty-seven states had them. The Sheppard-Towner program was intensely controversial, and opposition from the private charities, the American Medical Association, and states' rights legislators fearing socialistic invasions of private and local prerogatives blocked its extension beyond 1929.[9]

In 1917, the first contemporary state human services organization appeared when Illinois created a Department of Public Welfare. The new department was headed by a director appointed by the governor, and its responsibilities included state institutions, parole administration, old age assistance, and child welfare services. Creation of the department, initiating a general movement that continues to this day, was part of a statewide reorganization designed to reduce the number of persons with whom the governor had to deal regularly and to integrate similar functions under a single departmental director. New Jersey created a Department of Institutions and Agencies the following year, and other states followed suit in adopting departmental administration of human services.

Thus, in the twenty-five years preceding the Social Security Act, states were both taking on new social welfare responsibilities in the form of categorical programs and centralizing and integrating their administration. Moreover, the federal government had begun to play a role in encouraging state programs for the needy, and federal categorical grants had been shown to be an effective way of stimulating organizational change in the states.

The Depression

The Depression devastated all classes, races, ethnic groups, and areas of settlement. The need for insurance against economic calamity, widely recognized in Europe, finally was recognized in America. As relevant to the future of human services as new programs, however, was the engine of change created by President Franklin D. Roosevelt and the Democratic Party. The coalition of interests that formed during the next four decades would, from vantage points both inside and outside of government, reliably articulate the demands of the human services constituencies for enlarging and revising social welfare programs. Though they would not always prevail against conservatives representing traditional distrust of big government — despite evidence of continuing need, for example, federal support for the system of day care centers authorized by the Lanham Act in 1941 was cancelled by Congress in 1948 — the programmatic and political base for expansion was now permanent, its power waiting to be ignited.[10]

The states responded to the Depression by enacting temporary relief programs, both assisting local government relief efforts and in many cases assuming more direct responsibility for the relief function. As the Depression deepened, state and local resources were simply not enough. Under pressure from reformers, and drawing on Progressive ideas, the federal government created numerous relief and assistance programs under a variety of legislative authorities. Federal relief policy stimulated significant changes in state social welfare administration. Federal emergency relief was channeled through state agencies, which were in turn obliged to guarantee the proper use of the funds. Thus, the states were propelled even more directly into a program that was traditionally a local responsibility.

The major development of the period was the Social Security Act of 1935, which authorized grants-in-aid to the states for aiding dependent children, the blind, and the aged and for programs for crippled children, maternal and child health services, child welfare services, vocational rehabilitation, and public health services. The administration of the federal grant-in-aid mechanism transformed state human services organizations and intergovernmental relations. "The greatest impetus to a permanent state structure with primary responsibility for social welfare was given by the provisions of the public assistance provisions of the Social Security Act."[11] The Act required administration of the programs by state agencies, planning, the matching of federal funds from state sources, and the availability of public assistance in all political subdivisions. Thus the public-assistance and social-services provisions of the Social Security Act drew state government permanently to the center of social welfare administration.

The New Federalism

Demographic, social, and economic changes following World War II continued to alter thinking about need, though the changes have been more subtle and less induced by crisis. For example, when women drawn into the labor force during World War II stayed there, demands for supportive child care services grew more insistent. The number of families headed by women profoundly affected perspectives on the need for public assistance and supportive social services. Stimulated by the civil rights movement, advocates for disadvantaged groups articulated a wide variety of needs associated with equalizing opportunity and promoting human development. Categories of need became steadily more refined, and included, for example, mentally retarded rape victims, unwed teenage mothers, elderly victims of physical abuse, and functionally unemployable young adults.

During an intense decade, the administrations of President John F. Kennedy and President Lyndon B. Johnson greatly accelerated the process of program growth and change that began with the New Deal. Existing legislation was amended and new legislation was passed which expanded the governmental role in human services. The Manpower Development and Training Act and Social Security Act Amendments of 1962, the Mental Retardation Facilities and Community Mental Health Construction Act of 1863, the Economic Opportunity Act and food stamp legislation of 1964, enactment of Title XIII (Medicare) and Title XIX (Medicaid) of the Social Security Act, the Elementary and Secondary Education Act, and housing assistance legislation in 1965, the Social Security Act Amendments of 1967 creating the Work Incentives (WIN) program, and dozens of other legislative enactments and policy developments during the 1960s and since transformed the size, scope, and complexity of the federal and state roles in social welfare, and created the political circumstances to which President Richard M. Nixon was responding in 1969.

In proposing general revenue sharing in August 1969, President Nixon announced that it was a goal of his administration "to so strengthen state and local government that by the end of the coming decade, the political landscape of America will be widely altered, and states and cities will have a far greater share of power and responsibility for solving their own problems." This idea was a product of traditional Republican opposition to expansion of federal authority and pressure from governors and mayors for more control over program priorities and implementation. Its origins, however, are traceable to administrative developments that began with the New Deal.

Prior to passage of the Social Security Act of 1935, though perhaps half of the states had state boards of charities, few had boards with authority which went beyond visitation, reporting, and inspection, and fewer still had departments with administrative controls over state institutions and agencies.[12] Even the large-scale relief requirements of the Depression failed to promote rapid change. In most states, relief was administered through existing state structures or by "emergency" agencies. The incentives generated by the 1935 Act were more decisive in providing the impetus for creation of integrated state departments of public welfare with varying combinations of functions and measures of control over institutions and programs.

These developments were in part a product of the impetus for administrative reform that had been initiated at the federal level. President Franklin D. Roosevelt's Committee on Administrative Management (the Brownlow Committee) stated in its 1937 report that efficient administration required "the establishment of a responsible and effective chief executive as the center of energy, direction, and administrative management [aided by] appropriate managerial and staff agencies."[13] The committee then drafted an implementing reorganization plan that, in addition to creating the Executive Office of the President, created in 1939 the Federal Security Agency (which Brownlow and his associates would have preferred to call the Department of Social Welfare), comprising the Social Security Board, the National Youth Administration, the Civilian Conservation Corps, the Public Health Service, the Office of Education (which then included the vocational rehabilitation program), and the United States Employment Service. The committee also articulated the philosophy of reorganization as an executive function, part of the executive's administrative responsibilities, and constituting a "continuing process of internal distribution of activities."[14]

In 1950 the first Hoover Commission had recommended creation of a cabinet level Department of Social Welfare, and in 1953 President Dwight D. Eisenhower followed this recommendation by renaming the Federal Security Agency as the Department of Health, Education and Welfare (HEW). Though the programmatic developments of the 1950s and 1960s aggrandized numerous federal departments, HEW emerged as the largest and most visible of all federal departments. Many states followed suit by creating and enlarging state departments administering human service programs. The terms Comprehensive Human Resource Agencies (CHRA) and "superagencies" have been coined to characterize the largest of these state departments.

As the federal role grew in importance, the question of the proper relationship between the different levels of government was raised by state officials and by conservative legislators on behalf of states' rights and economy and efficiency in government. President Eisenhower took up the theme of "returning to the states some of the vast powers now exercised by the Federal Government."[15] The Advisory Commission on Intergovernmental Relations was created by Congress in 1959 to insure a continuing focus on intergovernmental issues. Throughout the 1960s governors and mayors of both parties expressed dissatisfaction with the extent of federal control over state decision making.[16] By the time President Nixon translated the issue into a Republican program, decentralization of federal authority over program administration had bipartisan support at the state and local levels.[17]

A corollary to the New Federalism theme was services integration. As programs proliferated in the 1960s, several federal efforts, including the Community Action Program, Model Cities, and Pilot Neighborhood Centers, were set up to coordinate program administration. With the goal of improving the organization and delivery of services, the Nixon Administration in 1972 proposed the Allied Services Act, the provisions of which would have given states substantially greater latitude in deciding how federal funds for human services were to be used. The Allied Services Act never received serious consideration in Congress. However, HEW funded a number of services integration demonstration projects — including Services Integration Targets of Opportunity Grants — to test ideas for service delivery reform. In subsequent years, the goal of the administration shifted from redesign of services delivery to the achievement of planning and management reforms and enhanced authority for general purpose government officials. A new set of HEW funded demonstration projects, called partnership grants, was created in 1973 to further this objective. Thus at least three purposes for reorganization were being pursued during the Nixon administration. The first was improved program and resource allocation planning, which is the primary goal of Title XX. The second was improved delivery of services along lines envisioned by Elliot Richardson. The third was improved management of services and greater control of programs by general purpose government officials.

During the 1970s, then, several strands of organizational evolution intertwined: the movement toward strengthened executive control over state programs that began early in the century; the growing resistance of governors to federal restrictions on executive autonomy; and an interest in services integration resulting from the administrative experiences of the 1960s. The precise result in any given state depended on its politics, and these varied widely, as subsequent chapters make clear.

3
One Became President: The Other Did Not

Few governors achieve national prominence. Jimmy Carter, Georgia's governor from 1971 to 1975, and Daniel J. Evans, governor of Washington from 1965 to 1977, did so in large measure because of their efforts to reorganize state government. Their experiences differ in significant respects. Carter, a Democrat, made a bold and decisive bid for change. Evans, a Republican, initiated a more halting and protracted process. Both, however, are classic examples of the chief executive, in the manner advocated by the Brownlow Committee, seeking administrative changes designed to enhance the governor's ability to manage the state. As part of their reform programs, both governors sought to achieve greater coordination and integration of human services administration and delivery.

In limited respects, Carter might be judged more successful. His general concept of a Department of Human Resources survived the election of a successor more or less intact. Evans's concept of a Department of Social and Health Services was partially dismantled by the legislature before he left office in 1977, and a major internal reorganization had taken place that appeared to be a retreat from Evans's original intent. For the most part, however, his concept, too, survived his successor's election. Thus, both governors created a new status quo that appeared to enhance the role of the governor in human services policy and management by centralizing and integrating the administration of formerly autonomous agencies.

In both states, change in central administrative functions proved easier to accomplish than changes in the administration of service delivery in the field. In this regard, experience in the two states highlights the kind of role a legislature may assume in the face of executive-initiated reforms. A governor and the legislature, even if they are of different parties, may unite behind reforms in central administration because, as elected officials, they have a shared interest in achieving greater economy and efficiency in state administration. Legislators, however, are in a good position to exploit politically the local dissatisfactions that administrative changes are likely to create and, in effect, to have it both ways: "The governor botched the job we authorized him to do." A governor embarking on major reorganization thus takes up a politically vulnerable position. The risks can be reduced to the extent that the governor and his or her subordinates avoid management mistakes that the legislature can exploit.

The Governors' Proposals

Carter and Evans each sought to reorganize his state's human services as part of an across-the-board reform of the executive branch. Both won legislative support for creation of so-called superagencies for human services: a Department of Human Resources (DHR) in Georgia and a Department of Social and Health Services (DSHS) in Washington. Moreover, in addition to bringing several human services divisions into a single department, the appointees of both governors sought to integrate the management of service delivery in the field under regional administrators, who were to report to a state official responsible for field operations. Thus, they were seeking to restructure previous arrangements whereby the field administrators for each type of service reported to their respective state program officials. In this latter objective both governors failed.

The Georgia legislature authorized the creation of a Department of Human Resources in April 1972, fifteen months after Carter assumed office. Carter had not promised reorganization during his campaign. It soon became his number one priority, in part because balancing Georgia's budget was a constitutional imperative, and reorganization was viewed as an economy measure. "I want to be able," Carter said at one point, "to take any section of the plan and defend it by showing specifically where it will save the state money or by showing that . . . it represents a better way of doing something."[1] The majority leader of the Georiga House of Representatives, George Busbee (who would succeed Carter), argued that without reorganization "we're going to have to raise taxes in this and every other session."[2] In general, Carter saw the achievement of executive branch reorganization as a test of his administration's strength.

The new governor was also seeking greater control over the executive branch by cutting the number of officials reporting directly to him and by reducing the power of bodies, such as the State Board of Health, that could be expected to oppose him. His first victory was obtaining, despite a struggle with opponents in the Georgia Senate, legislative majorities granting general authority whereby his reorganization proposals would automatically be approved unless vetoed by the General Assembly. With this authority, Carter initiated the design of proposals to reorganize state government.

Carter's initial DHR proposal was the product of an intense, year-long study and consultation process, superintended by a private consulting firm and hastened by political imperatives. Because of subsequent constitutional revisions, Carter was Georgia's last governor who could not succeed himself. Expectations were that Lieutenant Governor Lester Maddox, who bitterly opposed Carter, was likely to succeed him four years hence. The administration believed, therefore, that reorganization would have to be authorized and implemented quickly before Carter's lame-duck status inhibited change.

A Department of Human Resources was one of the consolidations recommended by this study effort. It was to bring together nine existing administrative units and their boards: the Department of Public Health, Department of Family and Children's Services, Office of Rehabilitation Services, Board of Corrections, Board of Pardons and Paroles, Board of Probation, Commission on Aging, Cooperative Area Manpower Planning Systems, the Economic Opportunity Office, and all functions and programs relating to housing, plus the Drug Treatment program. Moreover, instead of relying either on the existing county boards or on officials in Atlanta to administer local programs, the new leaders of DHR would soon propose an administrative structure whereby local administration was managed by twenty-three area network directors (ANDs), with oversight by four regional directors who reported to the Deputy Commissioner. The ANDs were to integrate services then administered through the 159 county boards of health and an equal number of boards of family and children's services, fourteen health districts, thirty-four mental health catchment areas, eight vocational rehabilitation districts, ten family and children's services districts, and forty-two Juvenile Court circuits.

Evans, who was to serve three four-year terms, proceeded more deliberately. Following his 1965 election, he had asked the consulting firm of Warren King and Associates to study the management of state government, but the management orientation of the recommendations had limited political appeal at the time, and few of them were implemented. Following election to a second term in 1968, Evans created a task force headed by Brewster Denny of the University of Washington School of Public Affairs to study the possibilities for executive reorganization. In its November 1968 report, the Denny task force pinpointed the problem: "The Governor is not the boss."

Executive authority is divided among eight other independently elected officials over whom the Governor has no control. . . . He has little to say about recruitment, development and assignment of the key executives of state government. . . . At the present time 28 departments and agencies report either directly to the Governor or through commissions. In addition, in excess of 60 other boards and commissions function within state government. Some of these manage line operations and many of them have significant policy-making functions. While the Governor appoints many of these commissioners and board members, and they expect to have access to him when they want it, he often has relatively little influence over their actions.[3]

By May 1967, in line with Denny's principal recommendations, Evans had consolidated the state budget and planning agencies into an Office of Program Planning and Fiscal Management (OPP&FM, now the Office of Financial Management). Recommendations for the creation of superagencies to administer state programs had a harder time of it. The largely Democratic legislature (Evans came in with a Republican House, but that soon changed) refused to give Republican Evans the kind of reorganization authority Democratic Carter had been given by Georgia's Democratic legislature. Each of Evans's reorganization proposals had to be submitted individually to the legislature as a governor-sponsored bill. Introduced in 1969, the bill to create DSHS passed in February 1970.

The intent of the legislature and the governor in creating the new department appears to have been more diffuse and less clearly expressed than in Georgia. Both governors were interested in economy and in improved delivery of services, but the emphasis they placed on each goal differed. Evans was interested in services integration as a means of improving services delivery. His office did its best to play down expectations of dollar savings, stressing instead that an integrated department could "contain" budget growth. The legislature was interested primarily in giving budgetary relief to the state. Legislative interest in economy became even more pronounced as the state entered a fiscal crisis at the end of the decade associated with the slumping fortunes of the Boeing Company and of the industry. Not all legislators viewed the human services reorganization as exclusively an executive initiative; many felt a sense of responsibility to improve coordination among the various service agencies. They were inclined to see services integration as a means of achieving money-saving reductions in the duplication of services and therefore were receptive to Evans's argument that services integration was a new idea that deserved a try. The legislation creating DSHS called for "a single department which will unify the related social and health services of the state government. The Department is designed to integrate and coordinate all those activities." Apart from these administrative considerations, both the legislature and the governor felt the need for a department that would enable the state to deal more effectively with HEW on issues associated with programs such as Medicaid and social services.

The new department consolidated the departments of Health, Institutions, Public Assistance, and Vocational Rehabilitation, and the Veterans Rehabilitation Council. For the most part, the legislature left it to the Evans administration to determine the internal organization of DSHS. After a lengthy period of study and deliberation three functional units within DSHS were set up: Program Development, comprising the Economic, Health, Social, and Vocational Rehabilitation Services divisions, with responsibilities for planning, monitoring, and evaluation of programs; Services Delivery, which handled day-to-day operations; and Management Services, which carried out budgeting, accounting, data processing, and personnel and training functions. As with the original AND concept in Georgia, services administration was to be decentralized; with administrative authority delegated to ten regional administrators. In addition, the Evans Administration actively sponsored several local services integration demonstrations to test the advantages of fully integrated field operations.

The Process of Change

The changes sought by Carter and Evans provoked sharp opposition from several quarters. The precise nature and intensity of the opposition varied with local conditions. Evans faced a legislature of the opposite political party, while Carter was opposed by a dedicated Democratic rival in Lester Maddox. Yet the general character of the opposition, principally from program people and legislators, was the same in both states. Moreover, the experiences of the two governors reveals the extent to which opposition can be blunted or exacerbated by the ability of the governor's administration to deal with it. Carter's reorganization began with strong momentum, which sustained it through political difficulties. Evans's reorganization was wobbly from the start and thus vulnerable to internal mistakes, which were numerous, and external exploitation of those mistakes.

The South Georgia Turtle

Following the legislature's grant of reorganization authority in February 1971, the Carter administration undertook an intense one-year process of designing and submitting for legislative review an executive branch reorganization plan. The process involved consultation with agency heads, legislators, and other individuals inside and outside of government, during which interim drafts of the reorganization plan were discussed, but the final details of the reorganization (which closely followed the discussion drafts) were not publicly released until shortly before Carter was to submit his proposals to the legislature. The reorganization statute required the governor, prior to submitting proposals to the legislature, to submit them to the state's other constitutionally elected officials, who could veto features affecting them which they found unacceptable. Then the two houses of the legislature had the opportunity to veto the proposals as a whole. Opposition was encountered throughout the entire process. Indeed, the DHR proposal became the lightning rod for Carter's entire reorganization plan. Those who opposed executive reorganization or Carter or both focused their discontent on DHR. Overt opposition came principally from four interrelated sources: the legislature, especially the political forces led by Maddox and state senator Culver Kidd, the state's powerful health board, the heads and personnel of many of the program agencies, and many county boards of health.

Despite reapportionment, rural interests remained powerful in the Georgia legislature, especially the Senate. Reapportionment had strengthened suburban interests, but according to Representative Sidney Marcus of Atlanta, suburban areas vote neither rural nor urban, having instead "a whole different agenda." The part-time, understaffed legislature tended to be conservative on human services questions and disposed toward the interests of the numerous county boards and of the state institutions in members' districts. Such was the orientation of Maddox and of Senator Kidd, whose home district, Milledgeville, contained the state's largest mental hospital. Maddox, the ex officio president of the Senate, could be counted on to oppose virtually any

Carter initiative. Kidd, a Maddox ally who became chairman of the Senate Committee on Economy, Reorganization, and Efficiency in Government in 1973, backed by Clarke County Board Chairman John A. Hunnicutt III, resisted all attempts to whittle away the influence and size of Central State Hospital and frequently voiced the views of Carter's opponents. He opposed DHR, by far the largest department in state government, from the start, later saying, "I was opposed to it due to size; to get anyone that's qualified in the many, many areas that DHR covers in services to people is an impossibility." Many believe that Dr. Gary Miller, the innovative director of the new mental health division, who had been appointed by Carter personally even before the new DHR Commissioner was appointed and who was a supporter of DHR deinstitutionalization policies, was fired by the Carter administration in 1973 to head off Kidd's threats to dismantle the department.

The strongest professional resistance to DHR came from the health community, which feared losing control over programs. (The criminal justice community also resisted the plan, and the legislature put Corrections, Pardons and Paroles, and Probation together in a new Department of Offender Rehabilitation.) Up to that time, health professionals ran the Department of Public Health. The Board of Health, before reorganization a board with full administrative powers, was composed of eighteen members, almost entirely medical professionals,[4] representing the views of the well-organized Medical Association of Georgia (MAG). MAG fears proved to be justified; as part of Carter's general reorganization plan, all state boards with administrative powers were reduced to policy status. (The decision not to abolish state boards completely was based on both the existence of some constitutionally mandated boards and the political popularity of boards in general.) The Board of Health had been intimately involved in the day-to-day running of the Department of Public Health, and reduction to a policy role was a definite loss of power.

The anxieties of program people surfaced during the study process preceding design of the reorganization plan. Along with management studies in technical areas such as data processing, cash management, and vehicle utilization, the entire governmental structure of the state was canvassed for problem areas by use of detailed questionnaires designed to pinpoint dissatisfactions or disfunctions. Such problem areas were then subjected to study by program teams. The study teams, however, were not primarily interested in soliciting suggestions from the various levels of state governments.[5] The questionnaire sent to the agencies had one page set aside for general recommendations, but it was composed largely of requests for data on agency, facilities, functions, and interrelations. Moreover, this was a one-time-only questionnaire, and except for problem area studies and personnel loaned to the study team, many individuals in the affected agencies of state government felt they had only limited access to the reorganization study. From the viewpoint of agency heads, the study was much more management than program oriented. Moreover, no one outside of the study teams knew the substance of Carter's proposals until the governor chose to release them.

Following DHR's creation, resistance of employees to change and of professionals to supervision by nonprofessionals became a major problem. Besides the resistance of health professionals to DHR in general and to a nonmedical commissioner, Richard Harden, nursing and vocational rehabilitation felt threatened by the proposed use of nonprofessional regional administrators — that is, the area network directors. At approximately the same time, DHR officials were considering the use of a generalist worker who would perform intake functions and then follow the client through the system, thus threatening professionalism in those areas.

The county boards consisted mainly of the largely county-funded and -supervised boards of health and the more state-oriented boards of family and children's services; as a rule, these services and their administrators looked unfavorably upon state-dictated change. The 159 counties in Georgia (only Texas, with 254 counties, has more) formed a strong power structure, and the existence of four of the most urban counties was mandated by the 1945 Georgia Constitution, thus reinforcing their political durability. Although the state's fiscal role in county services was growing steadily, the counties retained an administrative role of which they were extremely protective, especially in health. As one county health administrator noted, "Georgia once fought a war over the issue of local control."[6]

During the protracted struggle to win support for his reorganization plan, Carter's apparent stubbornness and determination earned him the soubriquet "South Georgia Turtle." He was never able to earn a reputation as a governor who could work with the legislature, despite concessions and compromises that he made. Several of his early decisions and actions resulted in later controversies for the creation of the new department.

A first year concession to the legislature, for example, made to gain approval for the general reorganization authority he wanted, permitted the head of each agency mandated by the Constitution — the commissioner of labor and agriculture, the secretary of state, comptroller general, attorney general, and superintendent of schools — and the five-member Public Service Commission to accept or reject those aspects of reorganizational proposals that affected their agencies before the proposals were submitted to the legislature. When given the reorganization plan ten days prior to its submission to the legislature, many officials exercised their veto powers to the fullest, with labor commissioner Samuel Caldwell alone vetoing twenty-nine separate sections of the plan. Carter was forced to react and to use political capital. He took the position that a majority of the vetoes went beyond the scope of the officials' authority — though no one was able to define clearly that authority. He publicly termed most of their vetoes "frivolous" and considered only seven out of the total forty-five "valid." These "valid vetoes" he submitted to the legislature as separate bills amending the reorganization plan. In reply, the constitutional officers charged without avail that the governor could not disallow the action of another elected official.[7]

The Carter study teams' decision to narrow the scope of changes to those which could be readily accommodated within the Georgia governmental system also affected the course of implementation. The study team hoped to develop solutions tailored specifically to Georgia concerns.[8] In retrospect, not all those connected with the study felt that this approach was a good one. The Georgia reorganization often involved the use of old administrative systems in conjunction with the new departmental structure, rather than the replacement of these old systems. Criticism of study personnel was directed in particular to the retention within DHR of the county boards' services delivery system from the old Department of Health and Department of Family and Children's Services.[9] Perhaps reorganization could not have succeeded otherwise. While commissioner of the Department of Family and Children's Services, Deputy Commissioner James Parham had attempted to have a bill introduced that would transform the county boards into state-administered units. The political reaction was so negative that Carter persuaded him to withdraw it, lest it ruin the chances of reorganization as a whole.[10] Subsequently, this failure to gain state control of the county boards of welfare and health was a major factor in the difficulties experienced by the area network directors in implementing services integration. As noted by William Wright of the Region IV office of HEW, while these proposals "may have appeared to some to be of no great significance, the opposite was demonstrated as implementation got underway."[11]

The decision to confront the Maddox forces head on also had serious ramifications. According to many in DHR management, the politically volatile conditions surrounding the birth of DHR, and not size, caused its problems. Maddox had sworn to dismantle DHR if elected to succeed Carter, and most Georgians, friend and foe, believed him. This belief contributed to the Carter administration's haste; the idea was that if ten steps could be implemented, maybe Maddox would only be able to dismantle four of them.[12] This haste, coupled with the ongoing resistance of factions within the new department, made the first two or three years of DHR's existence painful ones. The haste left its mark on the quality of the structure that was initially thrown together.

We were forced by circumstances to implement very rapidly without time to assess support services, without time to perfect an organizational structure in advance, and related types of problems. And as a result of these constraints on our implementation, we have experienced difficulties in establishing proper accountability at various levels, in securing timely decisions and in communications.[13]

The resistance to DHR from inside and outside continued through implementation and into full-time operation. What with a hundred-person administrative cut imposed by Carter to enforce his economy pledges, the new DHR administration was put under a good deal of strain. Another apparent shortcoming in early efforts with respect to DHR was the lack of attention given to retraining personnel. Parham admitted he did not "foresee the narrow, somewhat unenlightened approach that would occur as a result of professional jealousies, turf guarding, anxieties over role change and status." Although Carter made assurances that no state employees would be fired, few knew how their jobs would be affected by reorganization, to whom they now reported, or if their chances for career advancement had been altered.

The most visible personnel problems of DHR were in top management. The passage of his reorganization plans gave Carter the opportunity to appoint the heads of five new agencies.[14] The issue was that, especially in DHR, the demands of the job were relatively unknown. Whether Carter made his leadership choices wisely in the case of DHR is a matter of debate. The first commissioner was Battle Hall, former head of the State Budget Bureau, who resigned after six months and was replaced by Richard Harden. Harden had initially come into state government as a bookkeeper for the Carter campaign. Later he worked in the Governor's Office as liaison to the reorganization study. Originally appointed by Carter as director of the new Department of Administrative Services, Harden had administrative training, background in reorganization, and commitment to services integration.[15] Nevertheless, the twenty-eight-year-old Harden was, in the eyes of many, an inappropriate choice for commissioner, if for no other reason than his youth. "They looked and looked and they couldn't find anybody that they could agree on and finally in desperation they gave the job to Richard."[16] Harden admits to being a compromise choice, as no one with either the medical, social service, or administrative experience could be found who would accept both the salary and the grief. As Harden put it: "What they wanted was a 40-year old doctor who had administrative experience and who would be willing to work for $30,000 a year, and who was also willing to get into a very stiff political situation."[17]

Harden had little experience in the human services field and was perceived as an "idea man," issuing concept papers such as "Harden's Theory of Circularitivity," which illustrated the need for integration of services with the example of a hypothetical mother with a family which, suffering from numerous problems, was continually referred to different agencies. Instead of dealing directly with division heads and staff, Harden issued an agency-wide announcement series, entitled DATA, by which he informed the 22,000-plus employees of impending problems or position shifts. It took more than a year and a half into his term before Harden began dealing with other than top management as a direct result of the growing controversies over the network directors. Other employees expressed concern over the uncertainties of administration caused by the legislative budget cuts. In response Harden made a whirlwind tour from April through September 1973 to county offices throughout the state supporting the area network concept and listening to complaints. Unfortunately, the tour was much too hurried; Harden was not considered by many a personable man, and his "CPA" approach to human services issues deepened communication problems.[18]

Harden is often described as an aggressive administrator, protective of his prerogatives. Together with Parham and Jack Watson, chairman of the Human Resources, which had policy-making authority over DHR, Harden tended to function as a member of a triumvirate that ran DHR without local or program advice. Regardless of their validity,[19] such perceptions did not enhance Harden's effectiveness.

Deputy Commissioner Parham, a human services professional of long experience, balanced Harden's style by serving as administrative troubleshooter. As liaison for Carter with the General Assembly during the reorganization debate and former director of the always controversial welfare agency, Parham had been unacceptable to many legislators as commissioner. To block him, they wrote a provision into the reorganization act that no head of a constituent agency could become head of DHR until the end of Carter's term.[20] Carter may have intended that Parham run DHR from the deputy position, but neither Hall nor Harden was willing to accept that arrangement. After Harden retired at the end of Carter's term, Governor Busbee retained Parham as acting commissioner,[21] and was able to negotiate his confirmation as commissioner with the legislature.

Evans's Flickering Reforms

In retrospect, the prospects for governmental reorganization appear to have been better in Washington than in Georgia. Similar bases for conflict existed — program interests and legislators opposed to Evans could be expected to resist the changes — but initially the opposition was neither so virulent nor so well organized as in Georgia. Unlike Carter, Evans felt no political need for the kind of haste that could offend the legislature's sense of its own prerogatives. The creation of DSHS was a product of normal legislative processes, not an all-or-nothing, extraordinary confrontation, and as noted above, differences appear to have been ones of emphasis, not policy.

Before Evans left office, however, the legislature had already partly dismantled the department. An internal reorganization restored many of the operational responsibilities of the program divisions, a significant retreat from the original concept. The department's future stood for a time in doubt. This outcome appears to reflect mistakes of the Evans administration more than the initial height of the obstacles to be overcome. Evans's overall strategy for achieving change was less focused, organized, and decisive than Carter's. Though he continued to use his power to defend his idea, in the end he was worn down.

Though seemingly less numerous and problematic than those faced by Carter, the obstacles facing Evans were notable. Many program interests were predictably opposed to losses of autonomy or to being placed in the same department with welfare. The Department of Vocational Rehabilitation (VR) was to have been part of a new Department of Manpower and Industries. When the proposal for creation of that agency faltered in the legislature (due to opposition from the Washington State Labor Council and the U.S. Department of Labor), VR was included in DSHS instead. Though unsuccessful in opposing this move, VR interests obtained mandatory program division status in the new department. A last-minute effort by veterans' interests failed to prevent the incorporation of veterans' programs in DSHS, and interests representing Health and Institutions were even less successful in warding off reorganization. Nevertheless, effective leadership was essential to avoid igniting the discontent of these programs and provoking legislative attacks on the new arrangements.

Though the legislature shared many of Evans's hopes for the new department, the natural rivalry between the progressive, strong-minded Republican governor and the Democratic legislature was bound to affect the fortunes of DSHS. Washington's legislature was long viewed locally as a classic "amateur" legislature (much like that of Georgia), with meager staff resources, low pay, and a short legislative session every other year. It was not surprising that an energetic Governor Evans, like Carter, was able to take the initiative on executive reorganization and "make it his own."

Conflicts were inevitable for reasons other than partisan politics, however. Many of the "amateur" legislators are professionals or executives of the Boeing Company or other business firms who because of their business orientation, may have had less understanding of and sympathy with the complexities of managing bureaucracies. Further, many key legislators were from more conservative and rural eastern Washington. Their political orientation and attitudes toward DSHS were apt to be different than those of legislators from the western part of the state. As Charles Morris, who became secretary of DSHS in 1973, noted:

Dan Evans, the Dan Evans legislatures and the original concepts of DSHS were essentially western Washington phenomena. . . . The eastern Washington political style is more of an "old boy" system, wary of big government, government spending, bureaucrats, etc. Institutional policies tend to be more pro-institutional and anti-community care, partly for substantive reasons and partly because of the strangeness and potential disruptiveness of the community concepts.[22]

Evans saw the idea of east-west distinctions as somewhat dated, because after the redistricting of the late 1960s, 75 percent of the legislators were from western Washington state. There remained an urban-rural delineation in legislative reactions to human services questions. Rural legislators were usually less supportive of human services than those from urban areas, where such services were in greater demand.[23] Legislators soon envisioned an independent role for themselves with respect to the newly created Department of Social and Health Services, and a number of observers view the subsequent half-dozen years as a struggle for control of this agency between the legislature and the governor.

That opponents could actually succeed in frustrating achievement of many objectives of the reorganization is attributable primarily to executive failures during the department's first few years. As controversies over departmental administration multiplied, the legislature was able to keep Evans continually on the defensive and eventually to dismantle its structure. Internal changes of one kind or another were made constantly, with a major internal reorganization that restored much program autonomy occurring soon after the departure of its apparently dispirited first secretary.

Evans appointed Sidney Smith, then secretary of the Department of Public Assistance, as the first DSHS secretary, and Smith presided over the year-long formation of DSHS out of its constituent and change-resistant departments. Smith was popular with the public, the department, and even legislators (only one opposed his confirmation), and he became strongly identified with the new department. As budgetary and communications problems developed, they were more often attributed to the inherent difficulties of managing "superagencies" than to incapacity on his part. The press reported that "there are many who feel that the super agency has become so big that even Smith is incapable of controlling it." [24] Apparently Smith began to believe this himself. In late 1972, two and one-half years after he took office, Smith announced he could no longer do the job and would leave as soon as a replacement could be found.

The unsteady fate of the department during its first few years is attributable to the approach taken by the Smith administration in setting it up.

During its first year, DSHS remained an umbrella over the original departments, now called divisions, which were otherwise unchanged. Few details of how the new department was to operate had been worked out in advance, and the legislation creating it provided little or no guidance, stating merely that

the department is designed to integrate and coordinate all the activities involving provision of care for individuals who, as a result of their economic, social or health condition, require financial assistance, institutional care, rehabilitation or other social and health services. [25]

Therefore, it was business as usual while the Secretariat, as the Office of the Secretary was then called, developed the new structure. The outline for this structure was described in a *Concept of Organization,* approved by Evans a year after the department was created. The document was vague on many specific issues. Typical is the comment that "because of the numerous factors and inputs to be carefully considered, the boundaries of regions have yet to be determined."

Following approval of the *Concept of Organization,* all of the incumbent department heads were appointed as heads of new DSHS divisions, apparently because of their experience and status as exempt personnel and because "they just fit" the new administrative structure. However, the day the DSHS structure was decided on, deputy secretary William Conte resigned in what was generally seen as a dispute with Smith over control within the agency. Conte had been head of the former Department of Institutions, which included both corrections and mental health programs, and the resistance of these two disciplines to inclusion in a fully integrated structure continued throughout the Smith administration. Smith was not able to fill the deputy secretary spot permanently after that and ran the department largely on his own for one and a half years, while first Charles Brink, head of the University of Washington School of Social Work, served as acting deputy secretary, and later R. R. Rathfelder doubled as acting deputy secretary and personnel officer.

According to Rathfelder, no money was appropriated to put DSHS together and hire administrative personnel. In contrast to the division heads, many of whom brought their staffs with them, Smith had virtually no personal staff to help him build up the unified agency. Dr. Robert Shearer, then assistant secretary for social services, was forced to run social services program development with a staff of two. The Secretariat was overwhelmed with new, vaguely defined responsibilities, with no manpower with which to do the job. Seven major resignations in the first year of existence (including both the planning and management review chiefs) gave DSHS a reputation as a highly frustrating place to work.[26] The Integrated Services Delivery Project, the department's major services integration demonstration, had four directors in less than three years.

Thus, Smith found himself in a war of nerves with virtually no resources to wage it. Few changes were carried through. For example, a departmental operations manual promulgated by Smith in August of 1972 was only half completed, was never utilized, and has never been revised. Further, when confronted with opposition, the Smith administration was usually conciliatory.

The progress of regionalization typifies the department's performance during this period. Early in the development of the new department, ten planning regions had been designated. In July 1971, eighteen months after the department's creation, these regions were converted to administrative regions. However, the appointment of regional directors and their oversight of services delivery did not occur until January 1972. Moreover, each regional director had but one assistant and perhaps one or two additional staff. Given this halting start, it is small wonder that both the program divisions and the local service offices tended to ignore the regions. Smith was quoted as saying, "People are restless, and they are uncomfortable with change.

We made a mistake in not doing a better job of telling our people what we are trying to do." Shearer later said, "A serious flaw in the organizational structure . . . was a lack of clarity as to who was responsible to whom for what. Old lines of authority were dissolved formally but remained informally."[27]

The regional system never included all DSHS services. Vocational Rehabilitation, for example, resisted regionalization, and institutions within each region were also exempt from regional supervision. In characteristic fashion, Smith declared in December 1971 that "consideration of regionalization of major institutions is intended for a future date as soon as an appropriate schedule can be determined." The Services Delivery Division in the central office was expected to administer those services the department found it impossible to regionalize. Reporting relationships were confused, however. The problem with institutions, for example, appeared to be less their undefined status outside of the regional structure than the undefined nature of administrative arrangements.

Managers of institutions *did* know to whom they were *supposed* to report: service delivery regarding administrative problems, social services for program problems. The problem came as to which was which, and they sometimes solved it (or ignored it) by reporting to neither or to both.[28]

According to Marilyn Ward, citizen participant on the DSHS Advisory Board and a former member of the Evans citizen lobby team that worked for the reorganization, there came a time when Smith "had to begin to crack heads together in order to make the organization work, and/or to fire people who were in exempt positions that were unable to move into the new mileau." Smith was either unwilling or unable to do this, Ward felt, and "became very dispirited."

The expanding roster of internal problems invited intervention by the legislature. When legislative expectations for DSHS — including increased economy and lowered state payrolls — did not quickly materialize, the legislature began a long-term campaign to reduce costs and staff through budget pressures. The 1972 legislative session saw the first of a long series of initiatives to excise various divisions and programs from the department. The 1972 state elections proved a further setback for DSHS. Former governor Albert Rosellini, running against Evans, advocated the dismantling of DSHS during the campaign, arguing for a return to times when "government worked." He found sympathy in the legislature and in disaffected elements of DSHS. Although Rosellini was not reelected, the 1972 campaign provoked a showdown within the agency and a stop-DSHS movement within the Democratic legislature.

By this time, Smith had announced his intention of leaving. In its 1973 session, the legislature, citing fiscal and program mismanagement and sensing a leadership vacuum, initiated a number of bills to dismantle DSHS. At the beginning of his third term, Evans's power was still sufficient to ensure defeat of these bills, including one that would have removed Corrections from DSHS. However, the political and public reaction to several highly publicized incidents in the state prison system convinced the Evans administration to make Corrections a separate program division. Some legislators, such as Senator William Day, saw even a concession as a slap in the face. "He didn't want the legislature to do anything he had the authority to do by executive order." [29]

Immediately after Smith announced his resignation, Evans had formed a committee from the DSHS Advisory Board to search for a new secretary. Unfortunately, no replacement could be found for nine months, reportedly due to the position's low salary and the legislature's reputation for combativeness. [30] Added to these factors was the committee approach used in the search and disagreements over what constituted an "ideal" secretary. Both a secretary and a deputy secretary were finally selected in August 1973. The new deputy secretary, Milton Burdman, head of the California corrections system, arrived in August, but the new secretary, Charles Morris, was not able to leave the Manhattan welfare system until November. In the interim he was a long-distance consultant to Evans and Burdman.

Smith's resignation had thrown DSHS into a turmoil. Several long-term integration and regionalization projects that he had begun went into limbo. Division heads who fear that they would not survive a change in secretaries kept low profiles by making few decisions. When Morris started recruiting new personnel, he chose a number of staff from New York, and these, along with Burdman's California people, added to the apprehension among top managers that "outsiders" would take over the Secretary's Office.

Summing up the situation when he took over, two and one-half years after the department had been created, Morris recalls:

When I arrived at the agency in November of 1973, my perceptions were that the agency was badly adrift, that there was immense confusion up and down the line, and that the agency was being progressively nipped to death by a legislature and a press that was not so much hostile as merely aroused and smelling blood. The confusion throughout the agency ran to matters of both policy and practice: that is, there was confusion about the mission of individual services and the goals of service integration, as well as confusion about who was responsible for what and who reported to whom, about how much money was in the budget, and even about how one went about hiring staff.[31]

When Deputy Secretary Milton Burdman arrived in August 1973, he set up an ad hoc committee to study possible changes, and within two months he established a separate Division of Adult Corrections with authority over services delivery, following recommendations made by the committee and in accordance with the governor's promise. On November 1, with Morris's arrival, the rest of the recommendations of the ad hoc committee were implemented, constituting a major reorganization of the department.

According to Morris:

The first year objectives I set for myself were essentially 1) to restore relations with the legislature and the press in order to earn a breathing space for the agency, 2) to define clearly the program policy issues in order to focus internal policy debates, and 3) to clean up the agency infra-structure.[32]

The social and economic services division were combined into a Community Services Division, and health services program and delivery elements were reunited.

Further, the regional program was cut back. Probation and Parole Services were removed from regional jurisdiction, and the ten regions were reduced to six as of January 1, 1974. Economic Services, Social Services, Delinquency Programs, and Veterans Affairs remained under a regional structure within a new community services division, and Morris apparently intended that the administration of their activities be more decentralized than the other programs.

However, the philosophy had been revised. In his history of DSHS, R. R. Rathfelder states that this move

was not a change in thinking with regard to the degree of decentralization. Rather, it was a modification of the approach to integration of programs. The committee felt that the case-work generalist concept would be very difficult to implement. Instead, it was felt that other steps could be taken to bring about some degree of integration — e.g., co-location of staffs from several programs in field offices — without placing several programs under the operational control of single regional administrators. . . . While programs were still decentralized, the previous regional structure was no longer viewed as the key to effective integration. The current policy is to proceed slowly and cautiously toward more integration, but only where it can be clearly shown to be advantageous. On that basis, it is felt that many programs should never be integrated.[33]

Thus, the orientation of the top management shifted, and with it the goals of the department. Services integration per se was no longer the top priority. Accounts vary as to whether the new emphasis at the secretary's level represented opposition in principle to services coordination and integration or was a concession to reality: the original concept was not working. Morris states:

When Milt and I changed the previous organization back to a more traditional line structure we didn't view it as a concession to pressure groups — although it may have been viewed that way on the outside. We both thought it was the sensible thing to do.[34]

Despite these changes in direction, which should have proved appealing to the department's opponents, the adversary climate did not dissipate. Though the Morris administration was more politically and more managerially oriented than the Smith administration, both legislative and program opposition continued.

Morris immediately strengthened the planning, research, and management elements in the Secretary's Office in order to obtain more information on the issues facing him. He attempted to establish managerial accountability within the agency, develop reasonably accurate and rigorous budgeting and accounting systems, and tighten vendor and assistance payments oversight.[35] Although Smith is sometimes faulted for not having done these same things himself, staff within the Secretariat placed the blame for this failure on the legislature:

I think he [Smith] felt it was a priority. But there was really, when the law was set up, no money provided for it. Maybe we'd have to say that we weren't successful in convincing them they should kick in some money for it. We were so busy convincing them to let us . . . try some of these things. . . . Charlie came in, and, of course, being a new guy, he had some advantages. He had a honeymoon and also he was backing off the controversial concepts. But he did push and got some budget and staff and built some systems.[36]

Faced with a mandate to cut the budget during the last biennium of his administration, Morris cut back Social Service staff in some areas as much as 50 percent, while increasing staff in Corrections and Administration. One observer states: "In hindsight the effect on morale and the growing dissatisfaction with DSHS can be attributed in great measure to the loss of these 600 plus caseworkers."[37]

Morris was soon perceived within DSHS as more interested in efficiency and political accommodation than in program effectiveness.[38] He was also perceived by many as an administrator who could make sweeping decisions without considering their impact.[39] He was not without defenders, however. Said one:

I think Charlie Morris did care about the quality of the services. . . . If I found vendors that were not serving the state's priorities or were not meeting safety requirements, he said we could withdraw funding. Perhaps it was as much Morris's vigorous administrative style as anything that raised so many hackles.[40]

Morris himself speaks forcefully about quality of services considerations in areas like mental health, where quality of services proved difficult to measure. He talks of the

inflation of objectives that seems to plague social service programs. We have a tendency to adopt goals out of all proportion to the means we are prepared to expend, or indeed, the means that we know how to expend if we had them. When we don't achieve those ends, when we don't achieve El Dorado, we tend to indulge in bitter self-recrimination.[41]

The removal of Evans's power of line-item veto (except in appropriations matters) during the 1974 session weakened his ability to enforce his policies against a Democratic legislature.[42] The line-item veto had become the focus of some controversy between the governor and legislature, largely through Evans's use of it to veto

pieces and parts of a section [which would] scrub out a concept. We were very careful not to try to tip things completely over, but if the legislature tried to intertwine these kinds of things so it was difficult to veto, we just as carefully extricated them by line item veto.[43]

After several court battles with the legislature, in the course of which the State Supreme Court invalidated the line-item veto bill, the legislature acted to remove the power completely. This loss played a large role in Evans's declining influence. Evans had increasing difficulty getting through proposals or making his vetoes effective. Democratic

Senator Al Henry recalled that at times "the Governor's own party was helping to override his vetoes."[44]

For example, a bill to create a separate Veterans division passed both houses in the 1975 legislative session, only to be vetoed by Evans. By the 1976 session, sufficient votes had been amassed to override the veto, and the Department of Veterans Affairs was created. Thus, exactly six years after the creation of DSHS, the first actual splitting off of a part of the department occurred. Within one year, the budget request for Veterans Affairs went from $10 million under DSHS to $14 million, with nearly a 100 percent increase in staff, generating no small amount of legislative disillusionment with separate departments.[45] Disillusionment was not severe enough, however, to prevent the removal of the program for the blind from DSHS in the 1977 session.

Moreover, the legislature's interest in economy was having its effect. The 1976 DSHS staffing level of approximately 13,000 was a result of constant cutbacks by the legislature over the previous three years from a high of 14,000. One influential legislator long critical of the department said of the DSHS experience:

All I know is that we've got too many people, we've got too many departments, and you're not getting the services for the amount of bodies that you have. . . . We've got more employees in the conglomerate now than we ever had in a separate agency. And I don't think the needs are that much greater.[46]

Another, expressing his sense of the legislature, stated:

The thing that we've got to have is a Department that recognizes they have a responsibility to do more than just chase the federal dollar and do the whims of the Governor, that they have a responsibility to the legislature in formulating policies and programs. . . . Department people are promoting their own political philosophy, not trying to implement the directives of either the legislature or the Governor.[47]

Finally, Morris's change in direction on regionalization also came under legislative attack. Many legislators, who had seen services integration as the key to cutting costs, were unhappy with Morris's apparent retreat from that goal. In December of 1975, a Legislative Budget Committee audit of the regional system found that the division of responsibility had still not been clarified and that promises of "greater efficiency and effectiveness through integrated and coordinated planning and operations have not materialized."

There are disagreements over Evans's personal role in the development affecting DSHS. In the eyes of many, the governor was the best thing to ever happen to human services programs in Washington State:

Governor Evans on both sides of the aisle was considered to be a very progressive, intelligent individual who had outstanding ability to identify and grapple with major issues and who on a national basis was considered to be one of the most outstanding governors in the country. . . . I don't believe anyone who really was part of the development and enactment of legislation that created DSHS, nor who was involved within or without the system, ever felt that Dan Evans did not give wholehearted support and attention to DSHS.[48]

Not all those involved within or outside the systm were so positive about the governor's support for DSHS, especially after the 1972 elections. Specific issues, for example services integration, were seen as strongly tied to support from the governor. "He initiated it and got it going. . . . But then other things came up and he just didn't push it anymore . . . and it just died naturally."[49] Whether services integration did in fact "die" in Washington remains a matter of controversy, but according to most observers the relationship of the governor and DSHS varied noticeably between Evans's second and third terms.[50] Evans himself, while admitting that no executive can give constant, ongoing attention to all initiatives, denied that DSHS was ever abandoned:

There wasn't any time in the whole administration where a week went by when there wasn't some considerable contact with the Director or with one of the elements of the Department. . . . I'm talking about my own personal involvement.[51]

The Ambiguous Fate of Services Integration

The plans of both governors called for services integration. The Carter administration made the more ambitious attempt: regionalization and decentralization of services administration. Despite internal opposition, the Carter administration never abandoned its support for the idea, but Carter's successor did. The intention to integrate services state-wide in Washington never took definite shape. Smith's concept of departmental administration called for regionalization of services supervision. A complementary set of services integration projects was created to demonstrate the effectiveness of integration of field operations. In the face of intense opposition, the Evans administration retreated on regionalization and abandoned the services integration demonstrations. The experiences of both states reveal in sharp relief the character of the conflicting demands on the managers of human service organizations.

Services Integration in Georgia

The Area Network Directors program was not included in the formal reorganization budget. For the first six months of its existence, DHR paid for AND from funds drawn from other parts of the organization's budget. In the 1973 General Assembly this practice ran afoul of several legislators, including James H. "Sloppy" Floyd, chairman of the House Appropriations Committee. Floyd's concern was that a program existed for which funds had not been specifically appropriated by the legislature. Thomas Murphy, at that time a member of the House Appropriations Committee, complained that if the agency had surplus funds, they should be taken away and used elsewhere in the state. Newly appointed DHR commissioner Richard Harden felt differently. When Harden told Floyd in 1974 hearings that if the legislature would not fund the AND program, he would have to find funds for it from elsewhere within the agency, he was candidly stating DHR priorities — that the area network director was believed to be essential to both integration of services delivery at the local level and state-local coordination. The legislature, however, saw this statement as defiance of legislative intent, and the war over the area network directors was on.

Much of the conflict over AND funds reflected sharply different perspectives on budgeting. Executive agencies, especially DHR, wanted to raise as much money for their programs as possible. The DHR administration attempted to "free up" state funds for the AND program by using federal funds obtained under Title IV-A and Title XX of the Social Security Act to finance activities that were formerly paid for by the state. The legislature was interested in retaining control over the allocation of budgetary resources and they wanted to pin down the uses of all funds within DHR. Instead of receiving acclamation from the legislature for manipulating programs to obtain additional revenues, DHR was suspected of having a padded budget.

In response to charges from the legislature of illegality, Harden obtained approval from the attorney general for his shifting around of funds. He consistently maintained that the funds had been for administrative uses to begin with and were not taken from services. Carter soon added his support to the program and found Governor's Office funds for AND in 1974. With his influence, DHR managed to stave off the legislature's efforts to kill the AND program until the end of Carter's term as governor.

Despite this holding action, the AND program never had a chance. It became a focus of dissatisfaction with DHR at all levels. This dissatisfaction, especially on the local level, was intense. At the same time that the state was seeking increased control over local service systems, the counties wanted more flexibility and autonomy. In a published letter to Harden in June 1973, the Clarke County Board stated that there had been no liaison between the state and the county for over a year, that the Clarke County staff had been subjected to unreasonable work loads and anxiety about their future, and that at least fifteen staff had quit because of these conditions. The chairman of the Clarke County Board, John A. Hunnicutt, III, wrote:

It is apparent to board members that the state staff gave little thought to local staff workloads, and they show little willingness to accept advice, suggestions, or input from the board. Morale has gone to the devil. Never in my years of public service have I ever experienced a proposed state plan that has been totally unexplained, constantly changed, and after one and one-half years still not implemented.[52]

In every service area, there were some local government officials who viewed the AND program as an attempt to destroy county government, and many line professionals saw it as resulting in network director fiefdoms. Less-threatened services, such as mental health, generally ignored the ANDs. Dr. James Craig, superintendent of Central State Hospital, contended that the duties of the ANDs were ill defined and did not address mental health programs. Craig's approach was that if the ANDs wanted to coordinate services, it was their responsibility to make the liaison.[53]

Program people contended many of the area network directors were unqualified for the responsibilities of the position. Although the program divisions were partially involved in choosing the area network directors, only about seven directors were chosen with advice from program officials. The rest, it was maintained by at least some program officials, were chosen to mollify the critics of DHR.[54] The AND positions were filled before job specifications could be drafted, without approval from the state's merit system of personnel administration. Merit system officials noted that some of the new directors did not even meet state qualifications.[55]

The merit system question became a particular sore point in the AND controversy, as DHR vigorously defended itself against merit system criticism. The Commissioner's Office accused merit system officials of responding to political and personal pressure from DHR opponents. This was vehemently denied by one merit system official:

It's my observation and opinion that these wild allegations are nothing but a smoke screen to conceal the confusion in the DHR administration and the gross violation of merit system rules and regulations that have already occurred.[56]

While Harden wanted the greatest political mileage out of the AND appointments, he considered the appointments not as political patronage but as steps in the building of an integrated system: "One of the things we tried to do in setting up the Area Network system was identify the leadership people in a given area, and, in effect, give them the additional responsibility of pulling everybody together."[57] In this effort, Harden admits, they were not entirely successful. "We made some good choices and some bad choices." According to Parham, the effort was as much an attempt to appease elements within the department as at the local level. "We were trying to balance the placements within the divisions that had been created or merged. We tried to get some from Health, some from VR, some from Mental Health, Social Services, and Benefits Payments." Outside observers indicate that the success of individual ANDs depended on their ability to work with existing systems, for example, where the AND "attempted to become a facilitator and coordinator instead of establishing a new control point."[58] Nevertheless, the job remained an exasperating one, as few guidelines for it had been developed, and service workers remained responsible to both the AND and their own program directors.

The area network directors were expected to break down the compartmentalization of services delivery. One former AND recalls:

There was the idea that there would be facilities developed meshing various agencies at the local level, and we were instructed as Area Network Directors to develop those facilities in any way we possibly could, and mesh as many people in human services under one roof in a county as we possibly could.[59]

However, at least from the state level, things did not appear to change much. One observer noted:

They continued, at several levels in the Department, to prefer to go their own respective ways, although we had pretty strong leadership in the front office and this was contained beyond a given point. But . . . at the field and county level, it's almost impossible to control and direct to the extent that you can eliminate these feelings of, first of all, insecurity, and second, professional jealousy.[60]

From the commissioner's point of view, the internal battle reflected in part the resistance of professionals at odds with one another. "The Rehab people, the Health people, the Welfare people, and the Mental Health people — they all thought that they had the answer and they all thought that other people were less qualified."[61] Resistance to the ANDs reflected an unwillingness of program people on the county boards and in the district health director's office to be supervised by a generalist and dissatisfaction by program directors who felt they were not consulted sufficiently on development of the AND system. Outside perceptions of this sort of DHR infighting apparently affected merit system decisions.

These two classifications, Regional Administrators and Area Network Directors, were unanimously denied by the State Personnel Board at our December meeting, because it was the considered opinion of the Board that the organizational structure of DHR was uncertain, unclear and the subject of much conflict and disagreement among members themselves in the DHR administration.[62]

In 1973 and again in 1974 the legislature voted down funds for salaries for the area network directors and their staffs. The relatively high salaries[63] of the ANDs, in contrast with their reputed low qualifications, contributed to the dissatisfaction with the program and with DHR in general. When the legislature finally funded the substate management structure in 1975, it was only on the basis of Governor Busbee's promise to review and streamline its management.[64]

Busbee had run on a platform of dealing with the DHR and the AND "problems." In the 1975 session, the General Assembly granted

Busbee powers to remodel DHR. Its stated purpose was to "authorize the Governor to direct and implement such internal reorganization of the Department of Human Resources as he may find necessary to improve the management and administration of the functions assigned to the Department."

In May 1975, Busbee exercised his new powers by terminating the AND program, citing "a lack of clearly defined responsibilities for the Network Directors."[65] In its place he substituted a coordination network utilizing ten planning and coordination districts, headed by area coordinators.

Many area network directors were caught in the middle by the reversal. Since the program managers weren't rewarded for coordinated activity — in fact were penalized, because coordination took time away from their basic programmatic tasks — this coordinative effort had only limited impact. Because the commissioner met with ANDs only every few months, counties and service delivery personnel that had been supportive of the AND and integration efforts began complaining that the commissioner had abandoned them.[66] One former AND tied subsequent ineffectiveness to the loss of line authority by coordinators:

Without authority, the coordinators' influence in problem solving was minimized dramatically. Where before I had been called virtually every day by Senators, Representatives, County Commissioners who needed assistance, within a very short time they realized that I could not coordinate that sort of assistance because I didn't have the authority to do so.[67]

Though these coordinators were without administrative authority, having instead more of an ombudsman and communications role, factions in the counties and the General Assembly suspected collusion between the governor and DHR in order to continue AND under a different name, and resistance to the new system persisted. On December 22, 1976, the governor abolished the Office of State and Local Coordination and vested the coordination activities in the Office of the Commissioner of Human Resources. Dr. Douglas Skelton (previously Mental Health Division director), who replaced Parham as commissioner of human resources when the latter joined the Carter presidential administration in Washington, D.C., phased out the coordinators' positions altogether as an approach that had become too politically tainted to be useful (though he vowed commitment to services coordination per se in other forms).

It would be incorrect, however, to characterize the failure of the AND program as a result of local self-interest alone. Many DHR employees were unhappy with the changes, and the turmoil at the district level was probably as much internal conflict within DHR as conflict between the state and the counties.[68] Loss of status in the physical and mental health areas generated much resentment of the new structure, especially at the local level. One psychiatrist's letter of resignation stated, "If a physician has to answer to a non-medical person, he is no longer a free agent or able to practice medicine."[69] Of program people's objections, a former AND said:

They had been operating little fiefdoms that made them essentially their own bosses. They worked for, say, thirteen county governments, who had joined hands to employ them. And while they were paid by the state, they insisted that they worked for all thirteen of those counties. It would have taken a majority of those counties to remove one of these medical directors. So they were very secure. When we came in and the Department started indicating that these MDs were state employees, there was a lot of anxiety.[70]

Not all integrative efforts in Georgia were unsuccessful. In 1975, DHR introduced a provision that "the district director of health and other executive staff of district health and welfare organizations shall hereafter be appointed by the Department of Human Resources" subject to the veto of the county boards of health in that district. This arrangement increased DHR control over the district health officers, who had previously been appointed by the county boards of health, and had frequently been strong critics of the new department. The powers of the county boards of family and children's services had already been eroded by a series of federal rulings which required state control.

Therefore, instead of aiming for line control of counties and clear-cut services integration, the impetus was now for state appointment of personnel on county boards and collocation of services. While the employees of county health departments remained county employees, the district health staff became state employees and the executive director of the county health board is the district health officer. Services integration in Georgia ultimately involved at most a generalist management for collocated services in a few counties (e.g., Clayton County).

Whether this approach has had any actual effect on the services delivered is not clear. A 1976 U.S. Health Resources Administration study found:

With regard to the reduction in duplication of care services, there appears to be no apparent reduction evident. Although several of the state level people perceived a major change in this area, the majority felt that this was not true and this, in fact, was substantiated by local staff.[71]

Services Integration in Washington

The progress of services integration in Washington is more ambiguous, because the means of achieving it were never crystallized. The functions of the regional directors were never so specifically spelled out as were those of the ANDs in Georgia, nor was it clear what priority should be given the services integration demonstrations. To the extent that regionalization was intended as a step toward services integration, movement in that direction had been partially arrested but not altogether halted by the Morris administration of DSHS.

The regional system remained in controversy after Morris's departure. Critics maintained that it had little to do with services delivery. Neil Peterson, who directed the regional program under Morris, believed that a decision was needed either to delegate "more authority, more staff at the regional level, or junk it." Yet others in DSHS asserted that the regional system was expanding, that Morris had strengthened it, and that resentment toward it was a combination of its earlier ineffectiveness and its new, stronger intrusion into the local offices. "We're more decentralized that we have been in years, and it seems to be working pretty well."[72] The future of the regions was hard to predict, however. In June 1977 Dr. Harland P. McNutt, who replaced Morris when Dixie Lee Ray succeeded Evans as governor, said, "I lean both ways on regionalism vs. centralization. There are some strengths in regionalism and some in the central office."[73]

The services integration projects in Washington were discontinued soon after the arrival of Morris as secretary. In the eyes of a number of people, both inside and outside of DSHS, the services integration projects had constituted the basic intellectual thrust of the department.

The original idea was first to bring most programs under the control of a single administrator in each region. It was planned that later, further integration of most of the similar programs could be brought about at the client level. For example, it was hoped that a single intake and eligibility process could be developed for many programs. Serious thought was also given to the feasibility of making a portion of the casework staff into generalists who could handle counseling and referral of clients in any of several programs. . . . Specialists in each of the programs would be available as needed, but the generalists could handle a major portion of the workload.[74]

The most visible loss was the Olympia Center in Bremerton, a one-stop services project in the old Naval Hospital. According to some, the project was operating realtively well when seriously shaken by the removal of Corrections to the status of a separate division, which of course made impossible the integration of Parole and Probation at the services level. Parole and Probation staff resistance to the program had been apparent before this, and there had been friction with the staffs of Corrections and Public Assistance as well, so perhaps Morris's actions did no more than accelerate the center's demise. According to one source, the project director did not forcefully advocate his program with Morris, and it was abandoned as nonproductive.

A program within the Integrated Services Delivery Project (which monitored the Olympia Center) located in downtown Seattle was also experiencing difficulties with integrating Public Assistance and Vocational Rehabilitation. As noted, VR had been removed from the integrated system earlier. According to a report of the Integrated Services Delivery Project, only within the support services was any degree of services integration achieved.[75] The report (dated November 26, 1974) charges, "possibly the greatest detriment to full administration implementation of the project goals is the federal requirement for a single organization unit for vocational rehabilitation." In March of 1974 the Integrated Services Delivery Project was also forced to close by the Morris administration.

In retrospect, Evans himself viewed the aforementioned services integration projects as not entirely representative of the integrative thrust of the department. They were delivery experiments, essentially unrelated to the day-to-day delivery of services, which in Evans's opinion has consistently improved under the DSHS structure. He felt "current integration of services is so significantly more than it was before the advent of the Department" that to take the political fate of one or two projects as an indicator of the level of integration through-out the department would be a mistake.[76]

Departmental officials made other claims of success, though they related more to integration of managerial functions and policy making than to integration of services delivery.

Centralized planning, budgeting, and purchase of services were claimed to have resulted in better vendor oversight, lower error rates, and better management review. The new building, where 80 percent of the DSHS management could finally collocate (after five years of being scattered throughout Olympia), was universally acknowledged to have improved internal communication, effectiveness of problem solving, and access to decision makers. In fact, some DSHS officials believed that the political controversies had stimulated management review and a more rigorous budget process, that is, created a necessity to "get our act together before we go outside." Evans is more positive about the success of the DSHS concept: "Sure, the Department has evolved and changed and gone in some different directions, but the end result . . . is a significantly more integrated approach than we had before the Department, and one which I think does a better job." It was Evans's opinion that those shifts made away from a classical integrative format were political necessities, essential to the survival of the department as a unit, and without critical effect on its initial thrust.

The Aftermath

In both Georgia and Washington, the processes of change were tur-bulent. In their campaigns, the successors to Carter and Evans were able to exploit the controversies associated with the new departments by promising to do something about the problems opponents were complaining about. The dismantling of both departments was a dis-tinct possibility, and George Busbee, who succeeded Carter in 1975, and Dixie Lee Ray, who succeeded Evans in 1977, might have profited politically if they had done so.

Neither did, however. After an initial period of deliberation and troubleshooting, both acted in such a way as to calm anxieties that existed on all sides while avoiding being placed on the political defensive by departmental opponents. Equally interesting were the changes occurring in the legislatures of the two states. During the period of intense controversy over reorganization and its implementation, each legislature appears to have taken steps to increase its capacity to deal in a systematic and competent way with the kinds of issues that were arising.

Georgia's DHR had come to be viewed as "Carter's folly." A popular view was that it had barely gotten through the legislature, survived only through his influence, and would probably cease to exist when his term was over. Critics of the department, within and without, were encouraged by its narrow squeaks and funding cutbacks. Upon taking office, Busbee was faced with a budget crisis in a state whose constitution mandated a balanced budget and the residue of his predecessor's increasingly poor relations with the legislature, including Carter's remark about 1974 being the "most unproductive of all General Assembly sessions." [77] As Busbee consolidated his position, however, he generally supported DHR, and hopes of its demise dimmed. Although Busbee initiated some DHR remodeling, as noted above, legislators grumbled that Busbee did nothing for over a year and a half, and hinted at deals with Carter. [78] Yet by his actions Busbee defused what appeared to be a legislative mandate to dismantle DHR, and this gave critics time to settle into a new relationship with the department. Busbee's actions also had a positive effect on DHR itself, an agency torn with both external and internal strife. "He took his time and made studies, analyzed the situation, and then he took a series of actions. . . . The Governor came off looking strong, the agency internally looked better, and . . . morale improved." [79]

In addition to Busbee's actions, the Georgia legislature also played a direct role in promoting administrative changes in the department. Busbee separated the Medicaid program from DHR by executive order, but the impetus to do so came in part from a legislative investigation that publicized the crisis in the program. Some legislators viewed DHR's poor management as an indication that a department the size of DHR could not be run by a single commissioner. Moreover, according to Senator Kidd, those departments least affected by reorganization — for example, Veterans Services — remained the most efficient. [80] The Georgia legislature did not wrest control over departmental organization from the governor, however. The legislature was able to modify and even frustrate executive aims, but Georgia's reorganization remained centered in the Office of the Governor.

Changes in the Georgia legislature were also expected to affect the future. Representative Sidney Marcus noted the essentially conservative nature of the General Assembly and observed that with DHR now the status quo, more stability could be expected. In addition there was a growing practice, especially in the General Assembly, of insuring cross-membership on both human service committees and appropriations and rules committees,[81] thus facilitating a broader understanding of agency problems by individual legislators. The legislature was also taking steps to get more professional staff, and thereby better advice. Not only are there as many budget analysts (seven) within the legislative Budget Office as within the Governor's Office of Planning and Budget, but the General Assembly now actively utilizes the Governor's Office of Planning and Budget.

We've gotten into political negotiations and discussions, relative to appropriations, in a very decisionmaking kind of environment. The top leaders in the Senate and House call regularly on our budget people for information, in addition to their own budget people.[82]

Evans's successor, Governor Dixie Lee Ray, had appealed in her campaign to both Republican and Democratic conservatives, who were advocating the breakup of DSHS, promising them immediate and radical change. Ray's only initial move — other than the appointment of a new secretary, Dr. Harland McNutt — was the convening of a Governor's Select Panel on DSHS to conduct a thorough review of DSHS problems. Dismantlement bills, which received committee endorsements in the 1977 session, were held up until the governor's report was released.[83] In the agencies and legislature, this was interpreted as a sign that Governor Ray, regardless of her rhetoric, would hold off on any action until she had studied the issues.

Because Ray appointed former Governor Rosellini to the panel, there was some anxiety about the objectivity of its findings. However, the Select Panel also included a number of knowledgeable health and social services professionals, and it initiated an intensive subject-oriented task-force approach. While the panel's final report criticized DSHS administration, it also advocated its continued existence (overriding a minority report by Rosellini, which favored dismantlement).

Gradually, even persistent critics of DSHS, such as Senator Day, began to soften their criticism.

The Washington legislature had been taking a variety of steps to increase its staff capacity. In 1977 the House Appropriations Committee initiated a program that would enhance its budgetary control over social and health services. Utilizing a data system designed by Boeing, Inc. designated Legislative Evaluation and Accountability Program (LEAP), the House appropriations staff produced a document that incorporated, by program, all historical and present daily population (ADP) of clients, expenditures, budget requests, and percentage of growth, presented in graph/printout format. With the advent of such tools as LEAP, the House Appropriations Committee was able to get a more detailed assessment of the validity of DSHS budget requests.

The LEAP system also operated in a subtle manner to bring the actors in Washington state government together on human service issues. Because it represented the local state-of-the-art in fiscal analysis, the LEAP system put the legislature in an advantageous position. Later, both the Office of Budget in DSHS and the Office of Financial Management in the Governor's Office began to utilize the new semi-independent LEAP facility, supplying the data and drawing upon this in-house capability to draft their own budget requests or recommendations. This mutual information pool did much to narrow the previous communications gap.

The legislature's growing expertise was due in part to the initiation in 1973 of full-time legislative staffing. For example, the Senate Social and Health Services, which started with a staff of two in 1973, had a full-time staff of eight by 1978. In addition, both the Senate and the House set up research centers on which the small committees could draw for staffing. Several professional studies were done under contract with the legislature that aided legislators in dealing with DSHS issues. One example was a series on the state's health delivery system by the Health Policy Analysis Group of the University of Washington Department of Health Services.

The organizational issue became quiescent in both states as the governors and their legislatures settled into routine relationships with each other on human services matters. However, both departments harbor employees who are unhappy with the present status quo, and both legislatures have members who remain skeptical of large welfare-oriented bureaucracies and who would be quick to exploit evidence of administrative malfunction. Moreover, there is an unsettled issue in both places: services integration. Stresses could mount to the point that reorganization would again have political appeal. But the agenda of possibilities is now constricted. Creation of a "superagency" has, of course, already been accomplished. Proposing wholesale dismantling of these agencies has nuisance value; it is a good way for a legislature to fire a warning shot across a governor's bow. It is doubtful that legislative majorities could do much more than move program divisions around to alter their reporting relationships.

Whether services integration is likely to be achieved in either place is problematic. Can such a disruptive change be achieved if not benefiting from the momentum of a high-energy reorganization effort? The recent experience of Florida, analyzed in the next chapter, may provide an answer.

4
The Ambitious Legislatures

State legislatures do not have reputations as effective agents of change, especially when it comes to an issue as broad as the organization of the executive branch. They grant or withhold from the governor discretion to reorganize. They amend, limit, or turn down (some would add emasculate) the governor's proposals on behalf of particular interests or out of determination to control or reduce costs. In the absence of an executive initiative, they are ineffective in such matters. Or so the conventional wisdom has it.[1]

In contrast to Georgia and Washington, where determined governors fought legislative and bureaucratic inertia, the legislatures of Arizona and Florida fought their governors' indifference or reluctance in an effort to achieve comprehensive reorganizations of their states' human services agencies. The legislature's success in Arizona was no less than Governor Evans's success in Washington. Florida's legislature, never hesitating before obstacles, produced a model of politically successful services integration. These states' experiences raise interesting questions. Are they exceptions that prove the rule of executive dominance in organizational issues, or do they represent an altogether distinct model of the change process? Is it, rather, that the cause of services integration is compelling no matter who decides to take it up?

Experiences in the two states do not suggest the same answers. Once its initiative was launched and a Department of Economic Security was created, the Arizona legislature resumed a role similar to that implied by the conventional model: monitor, critic, and political opportunist. In sharp contrast, the Florida legislature has fought successfully to retain ownership of its reorganization: the decentralization and integration of services administration in the already existing Department of Health and Rehabilitative Services. Its unwavering protection, all the more remarkable because the initiators are no longer in power, was a sine qua non of effective change. However, both states' experience demonstrates the importance of how the governor uses his or her power. Florida's governors maintained as much control as possible over the execution of the legislature's initiative, becoming advocates for the change and minimizing their vulnerability to legislative criticism. Arizona's governors seemed to take little interest in the new department, leaving the department's leaders in a vulnerable and relatively powerless position. Implementation there was much more at the mercy of program bureaucracies with no commitment to making the new department work, and the reorganization faltered.

The Legislatures' Initiatives

The legislatures' initiatives in Arizona and Florida differ from each other, and from the reorganizations in Georgia and Washington, in significant respects. Florida's Department of Health and Rehabilitative Services (DHRS) had been created in 1969. The 1975 reorganization was internal and aimed at finishing what the legislature regarded as the unfinished business of decentralizing and integrating services administration — changes which neither the department nor the governor had shown any indications of implementing, despite continuous legislative pressure. The heart of the Arizona reorganization was the combining of welfare programs and employment assistance programs, a relatively uncommon arrangement. The Arizona legislature saw it as an ideal match, but the marriage was bound to be trouble filled.

The creation of the Department of Economic Security (DES) by the Arizona legislature in 1972 was the climax of a long, steady buildup of legislative interest in the executive reorganization. The postreapportionment 1967 legislature — younger, more urban, and more liberal than previous legislatures — set up a Council on Organization of Arizona State Government, a combined joint legislative committee and citizens' advisory board with a university-based staff, to consider ways of reorganizing state government. Membership turnover in 1969 interrupted continuity, but interest in and awareness of reorganization possibilities was growing, and a few legislators such as Representative Sam A. McConnell became consistent advocates of reorganization.

Momentum increased in 1971, when the House Government Relations (now Government Operations) Committee, drawing on the work of the Reorganization Council, prepared a report to the legislature on government reorganization. Action was to come the following year. The reorganization effort was aided by the formation in January 1972 of the legislature's Human Resources Services Staffing Demonstration (HRSS), a federal technical assistance project — of which the staff was active in writing and passing two major reorganization bills. HRSS was funded by the Social and Rehabilitation Service of the U.S.

Department of Health, Education and Welfare, in order "to enable a State Legislature to effect program innovation and innovation in human services."[2]

Twenty reorganization bills were introduced in the 1972 Arizona legislature. Seven passed and five were implemented, among them bills creating the Department of Economic Security, transferring the Office of Economic Planning and Development to the Governor's Office, and creating a Department of Administration to centralize personnel, finance, and other administrative functions. The House Committee on Government Operations then released a second report outlining the reorganization gains to date and recommending further changes.[3] As a result of this report, the legislature in 1973 created the Department of Health Services and, in the same bill, changed the status of the mental retardation program from that of a freestanding department to a component of the Department of Economic Security. Throughout this period, Arizona's governor played virtually no active role; power, as it were, was thrust upon him by a legislature imbued with the spirit of modernizing state government. For example, during the 1972 reorganization, numerous boards and commissions that had authority to appoint agency heads subject to the governor's approval were abolished, with the appointment authority transferred to the governor. Neither Governor Jack Williams nor his successor, Raul Castro, was considered to have used these powers to full advantage.[4]

When created in 1972, DES was one of the few human services organizations in the country to combine welfare and employment services. The department initially comprised seven agencies: Employment Security Commission, State Department of Public Welfare, Division of Vocational Rehabilitation from the Department of Education, Veterans Service Commission, State Office of Economic Opportunity, Apprenticeship Council, and State Office of Manpower Planning. Mental Retardation became the eighth, bringing the new department to a total of four thousand employees and to a total budget, including federal grants, of $250 million.

A popular conception at the time was that employment assistance programs could be effectively utilized to reduce or perhaps eliminate the dependent population in Arizona. A proposal to create a Department of Human Resources without the employment programs had failed in the previous session. In the original Senate bill, the new department resembled the Employment Security Commission with expanded authority. Welfare programs were only mentioned to say that they were to be included in the new department. The House Health and Welfare Committee, under the chairmanship of Representative McConnell and aided by HRSS staff, drafted amendments to the Senate bill that altered its orientation.

The House amendments, with the assistance of HRSS staff, redirected the thrust of the bill to the reduction of dependency through rehabilitation and integration of services . . . both contemporary perspectives of the U.S. Department of Health, Education and Welfare.[5]

The final DES bill was neither as manpower oriented as the Senate version nor as detailed as the House version. It was both vague and liberal in the discretion it gave to the DES director.

The Director may establish, abolish, or reorganize the positions or organizational units within the Department to carry out functions . . . subject to legislative appropriation, if in his judgment such modification of organization would make the operation of the Department more efficient, effective, or economical. The Director or his Deputy shall enforce cooperation among the divisions in the provisions and integration of all functions on the district and local level.

Some features of the DES structure were spelled out in the bill. The bill required six uniform districts to be responsible for services planning, programs, and intra- and interagency coordination. Each district office was to be staffed by a representative from each major organizational service unit of the department, one of whom would be designated to coordinate the district office.

At the time DES was created, officials of the U.S. Department of Labor, who would later have a decisive influence on the department's fate, believed it could evolve into "an agency that would be manpower-oriented and [that] clients would be funneled from the social/welfare program into jobs and self-supporting institutions."[6] HEW regional officials, too, were hopeful about the new agency and saw its creation as an opportunity for reform.[7] In their view, prior to DES, Arizona's welfare case loads had been handled by inadequate numbers of trained staff and welfare programs had been hampered by complex laws and regulations, with the result that the public had been unsympathetic, if not hostile.

The legislative leadership in both House and Senate, if not completely conversant with all the implications of their creation, certainly had an idea of what they hoped to gain. Timothy Barrow, then Speaker of the House, and his fellow urban Republicans in the legislature were in pursuit of efficiency and economy through the remodeling of state government.[8] The Republican leadership's commitment to the reorganization helps explain why the 1972 reorganization effort succeeded where earlier ones had failed. For example, when House/Senate disagreements threatened to hold the reorganization bills in joint conference committee past the end of the session, both times the legislative leadership informally entered negotiations and "dynamited" the bill loose.

The Florida experience, too, begins with the actions of a postreapportionment legislature. In 1968, the legislature approved (and Florida voters ratified) a constitution that required simplification of the state government's structure through the consolidation of overlapping, duplicative, and overly fragmented functions and agencies. The following year the legislature created the Department of Health and Rehabilitative Services (DHRS). Human services agencies, many of which had originally been independent and had reported directly to the governor and an elected cabinet (which also sat as the Board of Commissioners of State Institutions), were combined under a secretary appointed by the governor and became divisions of the new department.[9] The new divisions were Corrections, Family Services, Health, Mental Health, Retardation, Vocational Rehabilitation, and Youth Services. In 1973, two more divisions were added: Aging and Children's Medical Services.

The legislature apparently intended to establish a fully integrated human services delivery system. Its objectives were both better services and efficiency — getting maximum value for dollars spent. However, the legislature made two key compromises when creating DHRS. First, under pressure from provider groups and from the agencies themselves, the Tallahassee-based program divisions were permitted to retain line authority over local program administration. Second, the division directors were to be appointed by the governor, subject to Senate confirmation, not by the secretary of the department. These two compromises helped guarantee that the program divisions would retain substantial autonomy within the new department, thus jeopard-izing the integration goal.

Impatient with the lack of progress toward services integration by DHRS and with opposition from special interest groups, both houses of the Florida legislature passed major DHRS reorganization bills within days after convening in April for the 1975 legislative session. Basically, in the view of legislators, DHRS lacked the motivation to reorganize. Only the legislature could alter the status quo. In the view of the House Health and Rehabilitation Services Committee chairman Barry Kutun, "They could never do internally what we could do externally." The Governor's Office, including Governor Reubin Askew himself, appeared to concede that the legislature would have its way, and chose to work toward a reorganization bill that would preserve as much as possible of the governor's and the secretary's discretion over departmental management.

The matter was not settled without considerable controversy and compromise. The House and Senate versions of the reorganization differed in several important respects, and these differences had to be resolved. For example, the House bill retained program officials at the state level to oversee policy and program development and had the regional administrators report directly to the secretary; the Senate bill eliminated program officers altogether and had the regional admin-istrators responsible to an assistant secretary for operations. Both the House and Senate bills created a new department centered around corrections and offender rehabilitation. However, the House version transferred that portion of the Division of Youth Services dealing with juvenile offenders from DHRS to the new department, whereas the Senate left all youth services in DHRS. In general, the House bill was quite detailed in providing statutory specifications for DHRS manage-ment. The Senate bill was less detailed.

The governor chose to negotiate with the Senate over its version of the bill and seek its passage by the entire legislature. The final bill specified that hard-core delinquents accused of specific crimes such as rape, murder, or robbery were to be tried as adults and retained in a Youthful Offender Division of the new Department of Offender Rehabilitation, while youths charged with lesser offenses were to remain under the jurisdiction of the Division of Youth Services in DHRS. It established three assistant secretaries — for program planning and development, administrative services, and operations — with regional administrators reporting to the assistant secretary for operations, in line with the Senate bill. It retained program offices at the state level, in line with the House bill, and retained from the House bill a provision for state and district Human Rights Advocacy committees. And it mandated regional budgeting, also in accordance with the House version.

Thus, in 1975, the Florida legislature, convinced that the Askew administration would take no further actions to integrate services unless forced to do so, passed a bill requiring DHRS to integrate and decentralize human services delivery. The act called for the delegation of line authority over the delivery of DHRS services to eleven district administrators, who would report directly to the newly established assistant secretary for operations. The categorical service divisions were abolished, along with their operational control over service delivery. Categorical program identity was retained only in the form of program offices reporting in strictly a staff capacity to the assistant secretary for program planning and development; functions of the program offices included program planning, monitoring, and evaluation.

The district administrator would appoint a district manager for administrative services and possibly district managers for social services and health services. He or she was to set up district programs that paralleled statewide programs and were based on statewide objectives and policies, but client support services were to be consolidated and managed by the district administrator.

A significant revision mandated by the act related to how departmental resources were budgeted. Formerly, resources were allocated to the program divisions and within them to program activities. For example, the Division of Mental Health budget was further apportioned to mental hospitals, drug-abuse programs, community mental health programs, and the like, and, within community mental health programs, to community mental health services, public education services, development of mental health manpower, and the like. The act budgeted for four entities: the Office of the Secretary, the assistant secretary for program planning and development, the assistant secretary for administrative services, and the assistant secretary for operations. The latter's budget was to be further broken down by district, thus structuring a district-oriented, rather than a program-oriented, budget system. Within each district, funds were budgeted by program, with the programs defined in the traditional way. The secretary would approve and could amend all budgets, and he or she could transfer up to 5 percent of an approved district operating budget. The district administrator, with the prior approval of the secretary, would be able to transfer up to 10 percent of the district operating budget among the various programs of the district.

Former state senator Louis de la Parte of Tampa, who played a key role in the evolution of the state's human services, summed up the situation in the legislature:

The postreapportionment period brought about a radical realignment in the balance of legislative and executive powers and rising expectations among legislators as to what constitutes the proper exercises of legislative responsibility. Frequently programs enacted and funded were not properly implemented. This prompted the legislature to spell out its intent, in the most exact terms conceivable, and subsequently to hold those executive agencies accountable for implementation. To do less, from the legislative perspective, is to abandon its responsibility. Who is a better articulator of state needs and the means available to meet those needs?

The Process of Change

The pace and character of the change process was quite different in the two states. Arizona's deliberations were less substantive, detailed, and well informed than those in Florida; the issues in Arizona were framed in simpler terms, the alternatives under discussion were less numerous and complex, and fewer actors were involved in their resolution. One explanation for these differences is that the role and competence of state government is not nearly as well developed in Arizona. Though the politics in both states have been relatively conservative, state-supported human services, especially those that are welfare oriented, are far less well developed in Arizona than in Florida, with its larger, more urban population. Arizona, for example, was still the only state without a Medicaid program in 1979. Another explanation is the relative inactivity of Arizona's governor during reorganization. This, plus the absence of controversy, meant that proponents of change in Arizona had to do less homework. The years of debate in Florida produced greater expertise on the issues.

The Rise and Fall of DES

The story of change in Arizona has two distinct phases, corresponding to the administration of Governor Williams and DES director William Mayo from 1973 to 1975 and the administration of Governor Castro and DES director John Huerta from 1975 to 1977. Mayo, with the apparent (though passive) support of Governor Williams, aggressively pursued the goals of the reorganization, including integration of services. Opposition to his efforts came primarily from the program interests that were threatened by these changes and from their legislative supporters. Huerta, whose governor appeared less interested in organizational questions than in increasing the amount of federal funds flowing to Arizona, abandoned the central operational goals of the reorganization in the face of a sharp, federally backed attack from employment service and manpower interests and the militant opposition of vocational rehabilitation interests. The department under him became more like a loose confederation of programs.

This turnaround, similar to but more complete than the turnaround in Washington, highlights the continuing character of the change process in Arizona. With the governor playing a passive role, the director of DES became the focal point of all the controversies such reorganizations stir up: federal versus state interests, nonwelfare versus welfare services, the legislature versus the executive, and field-oriented program people versus generalist administrators. This experience suggests that an appointed official who seeks to accomplish changes will be in an untenable position unless actively protected by the governor, the legislature, or federal interests. The head of a state organization lacks the power to withstand intense pressure from opposing interests.

With carte blanche from the legislature, William Mayo, who had been head of the Employment Security Commission, undertook the thankless task of assembling what he saw as unwilling participants in the new department. He recalls:

We literally had to bring these people kicking and screaming. . . . There was tremendous pressure from political insiders and outsiders and [they said] nothing was going to work. Well, it was clear that it would work if somebody literally took a two-by-four to it. And I assumed that was my role.

He initially divided the department by function (somewhat as in Washington) into three divisions: field services, to which district officials would report, program services, and administrative services. Five Program Services bureaus — Income Maintenance, Vocational Rehabilitation, Employment and Training, Aging, and Social Services — were to serve as staff to the Division of Field Services, assisting with such matters as program quality control, planning, technical assistance, and the training of field workers. Administrative services consisted of four bureaus: Research and Statistics, Accounting Services, Electronic Data Processing Services, and Support Services. Its primary responsibility was to generate the uniform fiscal data needed for a fully integrated services system. (The following year, a Resource Planning Division was added.)

Under the broad powers granted him by the statute, Mayo expanded the duties of the district coordinators, calling them district managers. They were given the mission "to plan, organize, direct and coordinate the provision of direct services through field offices to clients of the Economic Security Department." The directives of the district managers were to be implemented by several area managers in each district who would supervise actual services delivery. As in Florida, Georgia and Washington, the intent was full services integration. Mayo's plan of implementation was more radical than contemplated when the bill creating the department was enacted.

The six DES districts were modeled after the governor's previously designated state planning districts (created under the federal Intergovernmental Relations Act), and the headquarters of each district was placed in the city where the local council of government (COG) had its headquarters. This move was an attempt to reduce long-standing resentment by local officials to direction from Phoenix and increase local involvement in program delivery.[10] Initially, the COGs remained in a purely advisory capacity; later they became the local Title XX planning agencies under contract with DES.

Mayo's prior relationship to manpower programs was immediately evident in the staffing patterns of the new agency. He appointed a number of his staff from the Arizona Employment Service and Unemployment Compensation division (later to be called Job Service and Unemployment Insurance) to management positions in the new department. Much of the DES support staff was drawn from the Administrative Service Division of the Employment Security Commission. Both the deputy director and five of six district managers were former Employment Security Commission employees. This staffing pattern, coupled with the fact that the program representatives in the districts were reduced to the status of program "consultants" more responsible to the district managers than to the program services directors, intensified the dissatisfaction of many program people with the new arrangements.

Mayo's appointments did not necessarily indicate that he prized loyalty or familiarity above all else. In many quarters, the Arizona Employment Service was the "crack" department in Arizona state government. It had one of the highest efficiency ratings of the fifty state employment services, the most up-to-date data services, and some of the most highly regarded administrators. However, the Employment Service also had a reputation for insularity. Its officials were relatively unfamiliar with the financing and politics of other human services and not altogether sympathetic to the problems of welfare administration. Many former Employment Service officials came to be viewed as "fish out of water" and mutual resentments grew. DES harbored an intensifying rivalry between so-called "economic" and "social" interests.

In retrospect Mayo is viewed as having "crammed together" DES[11] but he also appeared committed to bringing along those within the department willingly, or at least knowingly. "My own personal mission is that nothing should be done in a reorganization unless the highest to the lowest employee knows what's going on."[12] Mayo disseminated information to all personnel describing the goals of DES, its organization, and the missions and coordination of the various components. He made assurances that all competent employees who wanted to work toward these goals would have a job somewhere in DES. He instituted orientation and job training programs. He established and announced timetables of movement toward services integration.[13] He attempted to accommodate the interests of local government.

From the outset, however, there was conflict. Program Services Division personnel saw the district and area managers as building fiefdoms. The area managers resented the interference of program officials in services delivery. Vocational Rehabilitation complained to

HEW that the DES structure violated the single organizational unit requirement of the federal rehabilitation statute. The result was a long series of negotiations between federal rehabilitation and DES officials, including threats of a lawsuit by the National Rehabilitation Association.

Also dissatisfied with the new structure were former Employment Security Commission employees now forced to work with welfare workers and clients, which they considered a loss of status. Their resentment at being quartered in the same department with "welfare people" was intensified by Mayo's interpretation of the statutory requirement that DES "provide a coordinated system of initial screening, evaluation and referral of persons served by the Department" as meaning a common intake procedure at a one-stop program office. Employment and manpower officials asserted that the common intake procedure caused long lines and that cross-training of employees in the requirements of various programs lowered the quality of specific program services. The 1974 recession had brought sharply increased case loads and with them long waiting lines and greater error rates. DES critics argued that neither backlogs nor waiting lines starting at 2:00 A.M. need have happened and were a result of the single intake procedure. "If you're going down to get your unemployment check, you know what you want and you don't want to be hassled and spend a half a day filling out forms and having somebody examine your condition."[14] The efficiency rating of the job services plummeted.

These complaints invited public criticism and legislative intervention. Further, Mayo had become unpopular with certain legislators because of his supervision of a new federal food stamp program for native Americans. Critics charged that he was the left-wing champion of "Indians who did not even pay taxes." Mayo defended himself by noting that he was merely following federal guidelines. Native American enrollees in the already unpopular food stamp program exacerbated both one-stop center congestion and Mayo's failing fortunes. Finally, Mayo was a tenacious administrator who stuck with his services integration goals and who grew impatient with what he regarded as legislative interference.

In 1975, Democrat Raul Castro replaced Republican Williams as governor. The new governor asked the Department of Administration, in conjunction with a Blue Ribbon Management Committee, to investigate charges that DES was not doing a good job. Their report, the *DES Management Survey,* released in April of 1975, was preceded two weeks earlier by Mayo's resignation. Indeed, the report was generally perceived as designed to elicit that resignation. Mayo himself notes that although he was not asked to resign, Castro seldom communicated with him (in contrast to his almost daily contact with Governor Williams), and he felt unable to work well with the new administration.[15]

In his letter of resignation, dated March 24, 1975, Mayo castigated the legislature.

What I find truly disconcerting and, often, totally disappointing, is the low ebb in the quality of criticism laid upon this department by so-called professional lawmakers and other policy makers of equal importance. Very generally it seems their real intent is to "grandstand" in order to gain public support. Their understanding of the problems confronting agencies like DES often [shows] an abysmal lack of comprehension of what these service agencies are up against in trying to implement many, often conflicting, federal regulations and laws [while] still striving that services will continue to have relevance to the unique problems confronting a young state like Arizona . . . with its limited industry and very limited resources in general.[16]

Much of the interference that Mayo complained of was a result of the conviction among critical legislators that the services to Arizona's rapidly growing population were not being administered as sponsors of DES had promised. At least one Arizona observer contended that few of the legislators really understood in 1973 what DES was all about or the complexity of the problems DES had to face. "Legislators often fail to recognize the complexity of issues they confront and, thus, do not consider it necessary or appropriate to formally mobilize staff information gathering efforts to provide better options for the legislation they pass."[17]

One division administrator noted (in a manner reminiscent of observations in Georgia) that a major characteristic of the Mayo administration had been the hurried manner in which the agency was put together:

For whatever reasons, it became necessary to hurry — we hurried and didn't plan appropriately for the whole thing to take place. We ended up literally smashing together the administrative services part of this thing. As a result, particularly in the fiscal area, even though it's under one roof, the fiscal area still treated the program areas differently.[18]

As expressed by another program administrator, this weakness in support services was built into the DES structure from the outset:

The mistake that the legislators make all the time is that they don't view the funding mechanisms at all. This is what has really hurt us, because when you amalgamated all the agencies that come together, there was no such thing as a DES budget. There was no money, in other words, for DES *per se*. The monies had to be ripped off from each one of the other programs and that caused a lot of problems.[19]

John Huerta became director of DES in July of 1975. Huerta, formerly an employee of the Planning and Evaluation Office in the Office of the Secretary of HEW, was not the hard-nosed administrator that Mayo, a former British commando, was. Huerta's goals were to reconcile disaffected elements within the department and involve the community in its actions. He and his new staff considered the previous administration's approach counterproductive and inefficient. In retrospect, Huerta viewed the responsibility of the district manager for *all* programs as functionally equivalent to leaving district managers responsible for none. "Each district manager had his own little fiefdom out there. We had six welfare programs, six job services. . . . It just had no relationship to anything, no manual material that was uniform."[20]

In the eyes of the new director and his deputy, Dr. Arlyn Larson, program integrity was more essential, at least at that time, than decentralization. "The problem . . . was total unequivocal and extended management diffusion. There wasn't anybody except the director accountable for anything in terms of program operations."[21]

In Huerta's view, Mayo had attempted to coordinate ninety-eight programs that had been authorized by a generally incompatible series of old categorical and newer integration-oriented legislation. Huerta favored instead a "target population" orientation. In addition, the DES integrative structure, criticized by VR for several years, soon gained new adversaries. Shortly after Huerta arrived, the U.S. Department of Labor (DOL) protested DES practices on several fronts, including use of buildings formerly owned by the Employment Security Commission for the delivery of a broad spectrum of services. The Region IX office of DOL had chosen to raise such issues only after Mayo's resignation. Mayo's deputy, Hal Brown, noted: "Huerta and Larson have the problem that Mayo and I had, in reverse. Mayo and I both came out of DOL. DOL talked our language, we knew their programs. . . . HEW we didn't know that well."

When DES was formed in 1972, the Employment Security Commission owned thirteen buildings through Arizona that had been purchased with DOL funds. In contrast, the Arizona Department of Public Welfare was located in space provided free by the counties — space not always of the best quality. In a move to consolidate services, Mayo had moved the welfare offices into the only space over which the new DES had full control, those owned by the Employment Security Commission. At the time, the leadership position of Employment Services Commission people in the DES administration made this an obvious move. After Huerta's arrival in 1975, DOL demanded not only modifications in the method DES used to calculate rent, but also reparations for both back rent and rent paid by DOL-funded programs that were forced to rent space elsewhere. DES had calculated rent on the basis of the number of full-time employees (FTEs) rather than by square footage. On the average, DOL programs had more people working in the same area than HEW programs, and in DOL's view an inequity existed.[22] DES responded with partial rent payments, a move toward greater use of state-owned buildings, and new policies on building utilization. Several Employment Service offices now have entirely separate locations, and one-stop centers presently under construction are divided into separate DOL and HEW program wings.

[DOL] regulations . . . said there must be a director of employment service who would have charge of his field offices. There's also a provision that the Department authorize other forms of organization where programs wouldn't be adversely affected. So [DES] was authorized by Labor on that loose structure. But there was also a provision that if the programs were going to be adversely affected, we were to raise objections, which we ultimately did.[23]

DOL's apparent purpose was to reverse the integrative trend adopted by DES and put an end to Arizona experimentation in services integration. Shortly after John Huerta arrived in Arizona, the DOL regional office had informed him that they hoped to see a DES structure that would "maintain the identity of the statewide system of public employment offices as part of the nation-wide system of public employment offices."[24]

The Department of Labor, both at its regional offices and among workers at DOL-type services within the state, tended to see the shortcomings of DES as centered within the integrated approach taken by Mayo. Besides the usual complaint that associating with welfare types was insulting to Employment Service workers, job seekers, and UI recipients, DOL argued that multiservice centers were inefficient and discouraged employers in the business community from submitting openings to Job Services.

We look at the programs from completely different vantage points. We see the employment service as a labor market exchange and the unemployment insurance operation as an anti-cyclical device. They see them as social programs; they are helping someone get a job. [To them], income maintenance and UI are the same thing, helping people with money. This makes a difference in how you administer the program.[25]

The complaints of the Bureau of Vocational Rehabilitation about the DES structure were similar. The administrative centralization required VR in effect to support the administration of other programs, with what they believed to be a concomitant loss of quality in its own programs. In their view, while VR contributed to DES administrative overhead on a pro rata basis, the VR program had a low priority when it came to actual administrative outlays. Their illustrations were as esoteric as DOL's complaints about rent calculations. They cited the job-coding practices of the area managers, who administered local programs. Each program bureau paid for the area manager's salary in proportion to time spent by that area manager on the program. However, area managers allegedly allocated much of their time to a catchall "900" job code, which was paid for equally by the programs. Because the area managers actually spent little time on VR service delivery, VR was, according to this argument, paying more than its share. Moreover, VR's management expertise was too often drafted for central administration projects that proved of little value to VR and detracted from VR management services.[26] As evidence of VR's low status, Arizona's VR program had slipped to fifty-second in the federal rankings.

Vocational Rehabilitation was apparently not the only HEW-supported program to resist integration. According to William Soltau, district manager of the Casa Grande services integration project, the

Bureau of Social Services resisted both training its people in other program areas and reliance on the common intake system, preferring to handle both intake and service within the division. Social Services, like VR, elicited the aid of their federal counterparts to make their point, and as a result several compromises in local office cross-training and initial processing were made. Soltau explained:

I ran right up against the wall with HEW and Social Services, [who said that] you cannot take a person who's employed as a Social Services worker and have him function in another capacity part time. . . . I couldn't balance the time only on a monthly basis. But on a quarterly basis I felt that we could balance it out. Social Services just literally said, "No way. This is illegal, you don't do this."

Within six months of his arrival, Huerta returned control over local VR programs to the state VR office. (Later he was to win a battle over whether the director of DES or the head of the state VR program was to appoint the VR program's top staff.) More extensive changes were to come six months later.

When he arrived in July 1975, Huerta had promised one year of study before making major changes. One year to the day later, Huerta released a plan entitled *Management Improvement Goal*. In it he cited the evidence (in a way reminiscent of Charles Morris in Washington) that an extensive study and possible reorganization were warranted.

There has been evidence of a decline in the quality and quantity of services of the programs administered by the agency, as evidenced by Voactional Rehabilitation, Unemployment Insurance and Employment Service dropping considerably in national comparative standards; the agency faces the possibility of fiscal sanctions, as evidenced by the high error rate in the assistance payments area, . . . morale within the agency appears to be at an all time low, as evidenced by unusually high turnover in certain categories and by employee complaints of communication problems and lack of information and/or direction. Work standards are limited, if not absent in certain areas.[27]

The study, he stated, had led him to believe that major changes were needed.

The Director found from this review that the quality of performance in every program was seriously deficient and that programs were not being administered in accordance with uniform statewide standards. He found frequent cases where operational decisions on the basic administration of a program, i.e., the application of federal and state regulations, were inconsistent and/or incorrect across the state. The Director concluded that these deficiencies were in part caused by the organization structure which severely constrained the Department's programmatic specialists from giving clear and uniform direction to employees throughout the state on the proper administration of each program.[28]

The changes he intended to make were to take place in two distinct phases. In Phase I, the area manager and program consultant positions were abolished, and program managers were appointed to take their place in each of the districts. These program managers were to be trained by the district managers and operate under their supervision until the director determined that the programs were ready to assume full responsibility for services delivery. Phase II, which involved the full assumption by program managers of local control, was accomplished in March of 1977, after eight months of training. The difficulty of the transition can be deduced by the incessant activity of the DES management analysis team during the month of March. Acting as the implementation and troubleshooting agent for the department, management analysts were in constant motion from one district office to another, answering questions and settling disputes. While indicating a commitment on the part of the central office to making the management improvement goal work, this activity also suggested that many parts of the department were uncomfortable with the transition. Even the program bureau heads were dissatisfied in some areas. Officials in VR felt there was still too much consolidation of administrative functions. Officials in the Bureau of Social Services felt it should be they, and not the district managers, who ran the master assessment unit in the multiservice centers. Despite completion of the process in March of 1977, much still needed to be "shaken down." In conjunction with the power shift was the re-separation of Unemployment Insurance from the old Bureau of Income Maintenance to form separate bureaus of Unemployment Insurance and Assistance Programs. Functions of the central services bureau of the Field Service Division, such as job banks and research and statistics, were redistributed to the program bureaus.

Representative McConnell, chairman of the House Rules Committee and one of the few legislators who was consistently active in legislative oversight, was disillusioned with the turn DES took after Huerta's arrival. He became one of the major proponents of redividing the department into its two federal program components, on the grounds that the original legislative intent had been frustrated. McConnell's concerns centered on rising administrative and services costs (according to McConnell, a 46 percent increase over four years) unaccompanied by a corresponding improvement in services. He also questioned the usefulness of the Huerta administration's management techniques, stating that 50 percent of the active effort of middle managers was spent on a management-by-objectives program. General legislative interest in DES had waned, however, and McConnell was unsuccessful in promoting hearings about the possible breakup of DES during the 1977 session.[29]

The management-by-objectives system McConnell complained about originated in the DES Division of Planning and Management Analysis, an OMB-type office. Compared to other states, the division's influence within DES appeared to be enormous. Huerta brought one of his former staff members from Washington, D.C., Roger Root, to head the division as an assistant director. Root's first assignment was to institute a management-by-objectives program which DES called an Operational Planning System (OPS).

A great deal of the attention of the first administration had been placed on simply putting all the pieces together, setting up an organizational structure that made sense and getting some continuity to the programs irrespective of their fund structure. One of the pieces that was missing, I felt, was some kind of a uniform management concept that managers throughout the Department could use to interrelate among themselves, horizontally, and to report vertically up and down the line of management; in other words, a management-by-objective type process uniform to the Department. . . . It has long-range, three-to-five-year goal setting; short-range, annual objective setting; and monthly progress assessment conferences occurring throughout the Department where supervisors and subordinates are sitting around the table talking to each other on the basis of commonly agreed upon work plans consisting of objectives.[30]

The Operational Planning System was not well received in Arizona, especially among DES operating agencies and in the legislature. Some DES critics, such as former DES director Mayo, said that management by objectives was suited to organizations capable of producing an easily objectifiable product, and not to human services, the output of which is more amorphous. Resisting OPS training as gibberish from the Phoenix "head shed," local services personnel complained about the amount of time taken away from services delivery and a lack of faith in the effectiveness of operators' contributions to departmental planning. These objections were seen in Phoenix as an unwillingness to have accountability established at the local level.

It is a very conservative department and it's a conservative state. The managers were reluctant to acknowledge any management deficiencies that they had and were threatened by a change, particularly when the change was presented in the context of increased accountability by managers.[31]

Interestingly, Root saw the resistance to OPS as centered in the HEW-type programs, which were less accustomed to dealing with quantified work products than DOL programs. DES Deputy Director Arlyn Larson admitted, "It's still a forced system. . . . [I]f we just walked away from it, it would die in two weeks, maximum. In some areas it wouldn't take that long. It would take a day. It is not philosophically accepted yet." It was argued by the Huerta administration that DES was never effectively integrated, and that the management improvement goal replaced a nonfunctioning system, especially in the administrative area.

Stimulated by these kinds of negative emanations from DES, legislative interest was sufficient to generate talk of commissioning in 1977 a study of DES by the consulting firm of Touche, Ross & Company at an estimated cost of $250,000:

We don't have any idea how many people [DES has], how many are on state payroll, how many are on federal payroll, where they are in any given program. . . . They appropriate the dollars for the state portion of the payroll and they get the money on the federal programs and they throw all that into a revolving fund.[32]

This attitude was viewed with sympathy by Larson, who felt that legislators who tried to "understand this agency, understand its budget, understand what goes on, understand its effectiveness or lack of effectiveness in the delivery of human services" would experience a great deal of difficulty. "It is not — at this point in time — a readily comprehensible agency."

DES director John Huerta was not enthusiastic about legislative involvement in DES activities. Like Mayo, he wanted latitude to run his department.

There's a role for a member of the state legislature on one side of the street and there's a role for an administrator in the executive branch on the other side of the street, and they ought not to mix the two. I'm a professional. They created the legislation and gave me the authority to do whatever is necessary to deliver services — I'm going to do that and they ought to stay on their own side of the street.

However, Huerta recognized that the attempt by McConnell to redivide DES was probably a result of his failure to involve the legislators in the policy process.

Because I did not use McConnell in the same way as my predecessor did, he has indicated we are not conforming with enabling legislation. . . . I was hired to run that Department and make it deliver. In my estimation, we are going in that direction. In the meantime, because of disagreement in the way that I manage the Department, he has attempted to come at the Department and take it apart again.[33]

During the 1977 session, the Legislative Council outlined the scope of the proposed study, designed to cover three areas: effectiveness of human services integration, personnel placement and classification, and management systems — evaluation and design. This third item represented the results of negotiations between DES and the Joint Budget Committee over the development of a new accounting system. The Committee pushed for independent analysis to avoid an agency "cleanup" of the study and successfully argued for such a study with the legislature.[34]

Both the Office of the Governor and DES were involved in determining the specific direction of the study.[35] In line with Arizona's general distrust of consultants, approximately 20 percent of the projected amount was spent to develop an outline of the study's approach and content before the full study was approved. The six-week initial study or "diagnostic survey," which was competitively awarded to Touche, Ross & Company, served the purpose of settling disputes among the factions as to the specific nature of problems within DES, that is, whether DES merely needed a Management Information System or a new identity as separate departments.

The full study was indefinitely postponed when Governor Castro left office to take an ambassadorship offered by President Jimmy Carter. The impulse to do the study, however, was partially symptomatic of reactions occurring elsewhere (but as sharply in Arizona as anywhere), to state-managed, federally funded programs that are suspected to be growing out of control. This appears to be not merely an ideologically motivated suspicion of big government, but a practical concern that federally financed programs could bankrupt the state.

Arizona legislators have looked around the nation to see what happened to Medicaid and what the fiscal ramifications are. They're just unbelievable. In 1967, the State of Montana appropriated $1.6 million from the general fund for Medicaid at the initial start-up of the program. Now they are spending $50 million, which is $25 million of state money. This year it was projected to go to $84 million. Texas has astronomical amounts in this thing. The [Arizona] legislature is afraid of it.[36]

Florida's Model Reorganization

In contrast to Arizona, where the debate over reorganization was a low-key affair with few issues and little controversy, reorganization in Florida involved textbook politics involving the legislature, the governor, human services professionals, and the federal government. The contending parties were relatively well informed, well matched, and equal to the tasks of advocating their views, guarding their interests, and adjusting to changed circumstances.

The Legislature
As the years passed following the creation of the Department of Health and Rehabilitative Services, legislators intent on achieving integrated human services became increasingly irritated. A lightning rod for the legislature's unhappiness with the maintenance of program autonomy within the department was the Comprehensive Services Delivery System (CSDS) Project. In 1969 the U.S. Department of Health, Education and Welfare decided to initiate ten sophisticated pilot projects to develop and demonstrate, within limited geographic areas, computer-based comprehensive social services delivery systems. Florida applied for and secured one such project for Palm Beach County.

The CSDS project was to demonstrate that such chronic administrative problems as duplicative services, uncoordinated case handling, duplication of staff and manpower, and poor access could be overcome. It was to operate as a one-stop, integrated services center that might become the model for all Florida service delivery and the basis for an administrative restructuring of DHRS. All program divisions were to participate. CSDS top staff consisted of a representative of each of the divisions and was headed by a general project manager. However, coordination and cooperation among these representatives were to be voluntary. The project manager was given no clear-cut authority over the semiautonomous units under him.

In the view of many legislators, the CSDS project was a notable failure. Knowledgeable legislators needed only to mention the name CSDS to signal their chief complaint about DHRS: "all-powerful" division directors building up fiefdoms within the department and resisting any effort to cooperate in the delivery of services. One Senate staff member recalls visiting the CSDS project at the height of a controversy with the telephone company, which had refused to bill each service division separately. Because the CSDS staff could not agree on who would pay the bill, the bill had not been paid at all. Even the department's own evaluation of the project concluded that "voluntary cooperation of semiautonomous divisions was inadequate to accomplish the integration of services."

As early as 1972, Representative Richard Hodes, a physician and chairman of the Health and Rehabilitative Services Committee of the Florida house, began thinking of measures that would improve the ability of the secretary of DHRS to manage his department. By 1973 it was evident to others that the performance of the department was not meeting expectations. In Hodes's view, for example, the department could not provide "reasonable answers to reasonable questions," such as how many clients were being served, how much money was being spent, the amount of expenditures for direct services and for administrative costs. Hodes introduced a reorganization bill that would have grouped the program divisions under three deputy secretaries.

Though the governor and the department opposed the proposal, two important changes were made. First, at the urging of the department, the legislature passed a measure that gave the secretary of DHRS authority to appoint program division directors, increasing his control over the department.[37] Second, Governor Reubin Askew appointed O. J. Keller as secretary of HRS, replacing Emmett Roberts, who had agreed with the governor that "a change in leadership is now in order." At the time, this was a popular move with most senators. Louis de la Parte, for example, a long-time supporter of youth programs, an admirer of Keller, and soon to be leader of the legislature's reorganization effort, warmly supported the nomination, and the Senate confirmed Keller unanimously. Representative Hodes was dubious, however. In terms of budget documentation and authentication, he had found Youth Services under Keller an "impossible division" to work with.

Whatever revival of hope for the department occurred in 1973 as a result of these measures was sharply dissipated in 1974. There was no evidence that the department was taking the services integration issue seriously. Many legislators were frustrated by DHRS recalcitrance, and a bill to abolish the department altogether almost passed the House. De la Parte played the key role in the legislature. By then president pro tem of the Florida Senate, de la Parte was widely regarded as the "father of DHRS" for the role he played during the 1969 conference committee that approved a single department of HRS instead of three separate ones. He had been influential in persuading Keller to come to Florida in the first place. He was a good friend and admirer of the governor. Yet he believed the time had come to carry out what he regarded as the original intent of the legislature in creating DHRS. Said de la Parte:

There is very little doubt that the present organizational structure of the department encourages the arbitrary pigeonholing of clients, discourages communication and the pooling of resources among divisions, and creates costly duplication of effort. Further, this "confrontation" of divisions frustrates attempts by the private sector and other state and local governmental entities to acquire knowledge of and tap the comprehensive services available within the department.

Following unsuccessful efforts to persuade Keller that reorganization and further decategorization of service delivery was necessary, on April 22, 1974, de la Parte introduced a bill calling for a thoroughgoing reorganization of the department. In an open break with Keller he proposed the formation of eleven service regions, each headed by a regional director who would have authority over service delivery. The program divisions in Tallahassee, which at the time had the authority over service delivery, would be abolished and replaced by three deputy secretaries: for Administrative Services, for Program Development, and for Regional Services. The regional directors would report to the secretary through the deputy for Regional Services. In addition, de la Parte's proposal called for central intake and case management in each region. Instead of being bounced from place to place, each client would have a single caseworker, total client needs would be monitored and assessed, and regional directors would have the authority to solve service delivery problems.

The bill led to an epic and at times confusing fight in the Florida legislature. The bill passed the Senate but with an amendment, labeled "crippling" by de la Parte and an unfortunate "mistake" by its own sponsor, that allowed implementation to be delayed for a year. In the House, Hodes had reintroduced the bill he had first introduced the previous year. He strongly preferred it to the de la Parte proposal, which, in his mind, would have created regional "fiefdoms" in place of categorical program "fiefdoms." The department supported neither proposal, but with the governor's backing Keller finally agreed to support a compromise that would establish the eleven service regions and the central intake, diagnostic, evaluation, and casework management operations in each region, at the same time leaving the program divisions and their authority largely intact. In the end, the compromise bill was voted down by the House Government Operations Committee, to which it had been referred. Observers offered numerous reasons for the negative vote: too much discretion left to the secretary, poor legislative craftsmanship, insufficient time allowed in the bill for planning prior to implementation, and intense opposition lobbying by the medical, nurses, pediatric, mental health, mental retardation, cerebral palsy, epilepsy, and other associations.

It was to be a brief respite for the department. By the end of 1974, the legislature was determined to reorganize DHRS. Funds had been appropriated to DHRS to be used in developing a reorganization proposal, but nothing satisfactory seemed to be forthcoming. On October 15, 1974, Dempsey Barron, president-designate of the 1975 senate, announced a "massive onslaught" against governmental bureaucracy. Of DHRS, which he described as the "monster of all state bureaucracies," he said, "We're pouring $400 million annually into this bureaucratic haystack and as the money sifts down it is eaten up by government before it reaches the people it is designed to help."

Though de la Parte had decided not to run for relection, help for proponents of de la Parte-style reorganization came from another quarter before the year was out. In August of 1974, the Governor's Management and Efficiency Commission, a blue-ribbon group of Florida businessmen appointed by Governor Askew to advise him on making Florida government more efficient, recommended that DHRS be reorganized along lines similar to those contained in de la Parte's original proposal. Their recommendation, and the prestige behind it, helped build a strong foundation for the legislature's successful 1975 reorganization effort.

The Governor
Florida's recent governors have doubtless been hampered by the fact that Florida's 1968 constitution left the governor relatively weak institutionally. Only about one-third of the heads of state departments are directly responsible to the governor, another one-third are elected, and the remaining one-third report to the governor and the elected cabinet as a collegial body. This situation, among others, limits the governor's ability to carry out his policy agenda and forces him to husband his political resources carefully. Hence, the Governor's Office seems to have been caught between legislatively initiated pressures for services integration on the one hand, and the strong preference for voluntary cooperation and coordination by the service divisions in DHRS on the other. Moreover, the influence of the federal government had been notably inconsistent. While HEW officials such as secretary Elliot Richardson and under secretaries John Veneman and Frank Carlucci had personally supported the efforts by Florida governors toward achieving more responsive and efficient services delivery with less federal red tape, Congress and the federal program offices in D.C. had been largely unsympathetic.

Askew had taken an interest in furthering services integration, and he took steps to enhance his role in human services policymaking as well. Following discussions in 1971 with HEW secretary Richardson, who was seeking to develop national support for services integration, Askew obtained (under the Intergovernmental Personnel Act) the services of David Beecher, acting commissioner of HEW's Community Services Administration in Washington, D.C., to assist Florida in exploring ways to plan more effectively for, manage, and integrate human services programs. It was Askew's contention that the multiplicity of programs in DHRS hindered him in establishing his own priorities and effectively following the progress of the department. Moreover, observers contended that relatively few issues were even reaching him, and that when they did, they often had been filtered through the Department of Administration and arrived with a budget officer's bias.

On behalf of the governor, Beecher helped institute a series of management reforms of the type that Richardson was actively employing as secretary of HEW. One such reform was a management conference system adapted by Beecher from the one used by Richardson (which was the same system adapted by Huerta in Arizona). Askew would meet regularly, perhaps once a month, with his senior advisers on DHRS policies, programs, and budgets. The agenda for these meetings would consist of a limited number of important issues of concern to the governor. Preceding such meetings were meetings of the Clearance Council, whose function was to prepare the agenda for the management conferences. In deciding what should go to the governor, council members, who included key DHRS aides and staff of the governor, were forced to negotiate with one another, and to winnow from the list issues that they could decide themselves or that would prove embarrassing if brought before the governor unresolved. The governor's staff sought to force council members to do adequate staff analysis before proposing an item for the agenda, insuring that the members were prepared for the meetings. Once an agenda was decided on, the governor's aides were responsible for preparing an agenda book containing appropriate backup papers and materials.

From observers' accounts, the process had several results:
1. Before the process was begun, officials in the Budget Division of the Department of Administration, affectionately known as the "fiscal Fascists," held a disproportionate number of high cards vis-à-vis the program people. Once the division saw that they had to account to the governor for their positions, a number of smaller matters began to be ironed out in a mutually satisfactory way.
2. The governor developed a personal agenda of priority items on which he became quite knowledgeable, thus adding to the effectiveness of his leadership.
3. The morale of the program people was lifted by their regular access to decision makers and the improvement in their relative bureaucratic strength.

The governor's interest in services integration, his staff's expertise in management-by-objectives processes, and the department's growing experience with CSDS and computerized case management were pulled together in 1972 into a single effort of planning and analysis: the Comprehensive Services Planning and Management Improvement Project (known as CSP). One outcome of this project, though apparently not a major goal, was to be a departmental reorganization plan. However, this project, the progress of which was being inhibited by the lack of strong interest on the part of the department's leadership, was virtually halted in 1973 following the replacement of Emmett Roberts by O. J. Keller as secretary of DHRS. Keller, with little knowledge of and no commitment to CSP, let it lapse.

The Secretary of DHRS
Nevertheless, Askew believed he had found in Keller the right person to lead the Department of Health and Rehabilitative Services. He considered Keller a genuine servant of the people, dedicated to giving the best services to the whole person and to maintaining high-quality human services. De la Parte describes Keller as totally committed, determined to do good. It turned out, however, that Keller's views about the way the department should be organized differed from those of de la Parte and others in the legislature.

Legislative critics of DHRS had been somewhat mollified in 1973 by promises that the department would submit a reorganization proposal. In 1974, in the absence of a strong departmental directive to produce a carefully crafted plan, departmental staff, realizing the mood of the legislature, put together a reorganization proposal that, by the admission of those involved, was hastily drafted and too steeped in tradition. Nevertheless, it became the departmental plan that was discussed with the legislature. Though legislative leaders were unhappy with it, the principal alternatives — the de la Parte bill and a compromise version of it — could not be enacted in 1974. However, the DHRS appropriation included funds for the department to use in consulting with program officials and service providers throughout the state and coming up with a comprehensive reorganization plan for the 1975 session.

The Askew administration formed an Executive Steering Committee for Reorganization chaired by the deputy secretary of DHRS, E. W. Sandberg, and consisting of the division directors or their representatives. All CSP material was turned over to this committee. The executive committee studied a wide range of reorganization alternatives, from one that retained strong program division control to one patterned after the de la Parte proposal. In the end the committee endorsed a reorganization proposal patterned after the Hodes proposals of 1973 and 1974 that retained the program divisions, grouping them under three substantive deputy secretaries who would exercise strong statewide oversight and review. It also established a system of DHRS area coordinators to oversee services delivery, with certain "pragmatic exceptions" to enable the department to deal with constraints on the use of federal funds, county health issues, and statewide institutions that did not lend themselves to local management integration.

According to DHRS Secretary Keller, the proposal embodied

what I thought made sense, [which was] to have a coordinator in each of the regions with a small staff. That person would be the eyes and ears for the Secretary . . . someone to head off crises, someone who could deal with the judges, someone who could create a stronger link between the state agency and its different divisions and the private agencies . . . someone who could also coordinate services so that you could combine intake services, office space, and transportation facilities — in other words, someone who could make better use of the resources.

Keller's objections to the legislature's proposals had centered around a lack of accountability, confusing lines of authority, and the possible erosion of professional expertise in specialized programs. He contended that the introduction of generalists at the decision-making level would tend to dilute the programs and also weaken the department's attraction for top-quality professionals. Keller used his work in Youth Services to demonstrate his point: "When I came to this state in 1967, it was with the firm understanding that in the youth corrections field, I'd be able to implement my ideas if I could sell them. I did sell them . . . and it worked." If the legislature persisted in separating operational and planning functions, Keller feared that "the top people in those specialty areas will not come to a state where they cannot directly implement the program." Keller also worried that the regional manager, who would be responsible for hiring the specialists, would not be equipped to "get the right people for the right programs," as it takes a certain expertise and familiarity with the program just to evaluate an applicant's suitability.

Integration under a regional system proved to be the most discouraging aspect of legislative reorganization for Keller. Under this arrangement, he argued, program officials would be responsible for planning only, thus eliminating accountability. Keller illustrates the potential problems as follows:

I'm the Secretary and I'm sitting in Tallahassee. Up to this time I have been able to say to my division directors located around this lake, "You're the Mental Health expert . . . it's your program, now what's happening, why is a hospital blowing up in Miami?" The future could be, I bring in my director and he says, "You know, I wrote the plan, I wrote the policies and those damn people down there in Hollywood, South Florida, they don't follow it." So then I call the District Administrator down there and say, "I've been talking to my director and he says he wrote the plan and you people aren't following it down there." "Oh," he says, "those crazy goddamned people in Tallahassee will put anything on paper. They don't have to run the program. I've got to run it." And then he might add, "Look, how many programs have you given me to handle down here, nine? Why pick on me just because they have a problem at the mental hospital? Look at the good job I'm doing for you in Drug Rehab." So you see how it could get to be.

Thus, the program model appeared to Keller to be the only one that guaranteed professional control, from the planning level to the delivery of service. As a professional himself, Keller resented the taint on professionalism that was widespread in the legislature. Said Keller:

Their feeling is that the State divisions are really kind of bad guys, that the division heads are power hungry chiefs of principalities, all of them guarding their own little fiefdoms. . . . I haven't found that to be true, but maybe I am on the whole very cooperative, and if I asked them to do something, they really tried to solve some of the serious problems.

As many observers and officials pointed out, the opportunities for political manipulation and "empire building" might be far greater under the regional system than under the division system; with authority located in the regional offices, there would be nothing to prevent local co-optation of the whole system and inappropriate competition between regions. They maintained that while the divisional organization focused attention on a comprehensive state program plan, the regional structure would shift that focus to the amount of payroll and facilities coming into each district. The regional structure, then, would be antithetical to the original justification for a statewide service organization — that is, to provide a nonparochial authority that would be accountable for all aspects of planning and operation.

Regardless of convictions about the regional system, the Keller administration of DHRS was not able to swing much of the legislature to its view. The DHRS and its provider-group allies seemed to spend virtually all of their political capital opposing significant alterations in the status quo in the 1970–74 period. Had they better appreciated not only the nature of the concerns of key legislators such as de la Parte and Hodes but the political interest of the legislature in keeping the initiative on the reorganization issue, they might have yielded more ground than they did on matters such as achieving better coordination of service delivery in the field and providing information to the legislature. In that way, they might have forestalled the argument that "they will never change on their own; we will have to make them change" and thereby maintained greater power to influence the outcome of the reorganization debate. The "we-versus-they" attitude appears to have been self-defeating for the department and its allies.

The Reorganization

The legislature in general and the Senate in particular had several points of apparent leverage with the governor. The first was an environmental reorganization bill, prepared by Senate president Dempsey Barron's personal staff, which proposed to merge the state's four environmental agencies into one superagency responsible to the governor and the cabinet. This proposal would have weakened Governor Askew's control over Florida's pollution control and land-use programs, and he strongly opposed it. The second was Governor Askew's commitment to the reconfirmation by the Senate (required by law) of O. J. Keller as DHRS secretary. The third was a series of incidents that put DHRS in a bad light with the legislature and the public. One involved an individual acquitted of murder by reason of insanity whose subsequent convalescent release and employment as an armed guard raised an outcry against the "coddling" of criminals. Another involved a lease for additional space for the central office that appeared to many to be both unnecessary and signed according to questionable procedures.

In earlier discussions with his committee on reorganization, Askew had ruled out approaches that he viewed as unresponsive to the legislature's desires for services integration at the local level. He took a personal hand in drafting the final proposal of the steering committee and offered it to the legislature with his endorsement. His objective was to use this proposal as a basis for negotiating a mutually satisfactory arrangement with the legislature in 1975. In December of 1974 he asked the incoming lieutenant governor, James H. Williams, to meet with the legislative leadership and thrash out reorganization issues prior to the start of the 1975 legislative session.

By then, however, it was much too late for patient compromise. The Senate, the House, and their respective DHRS committees had new, aggressive, and, by most observers' accounts, politically ambitious leaders who were in no mood to make deals with the governor prior to introducing their own proposals. Moreover, the Senate and House were far apart in their views on reorganization. When the 1975 session opened, DHRS committee chairmen Jack Gordon in the Senate and Barry Kutun in the House introduced comprehensive HRS reorganization plans.

The Governor's Office analyzed the two bills, and Askew met individually with the committee chairmen to discuss their proposals and his. When it became clear that the Askew administration would be unable to get its own proposal to the floor of the legislature, Askew's aides were assigned the task of working with key legislators of both houses to insure that the reorganization that finally emerged from the conference committee was as close as possible to one that the governor could live with. Moreover, as political temperatures on the issue rose, Askew himself chose not to get into open warfare with the legislature except on a limited number of specific issues about which he felt most strongly. For example, the department and specifically Keller were under intense political fire from the legislature. Askew wanted to be able to support Keller's reconfirmation personally without having the entire reorganization question tangled up in the raw politics of that confrontation.

As the 1975 legislative session approached its end, Askew's office worked with the legislature, helping to engineer the compromises that would produce a workable department. A successful compromise from the governor's perspective was that concerning the treatment of juvenile offenders. On the other hand, a provision backed by the Governor's Office that would have had regional directors appointed upon the recommendation of the state program officer — a feature thought necessary to attract the best people to the state program offices — was excluded from the final bill. Moreover, the Senate would not reconfirm Keller as secretary of the reorganized department. When head of the Division of Youth Services, Keller had refused to cooperate with the CSDS project, and the Senate had become distrustful of his administrative abilities and of his willingness to carry out the intent of the reorganization.

On the whole, the Governor's Office professed considerable satisfaction with the reorganization. Because Askew had three years more to oversee departmental activities, he felt he had the time to get the right people into key positions and make the new organization work. Upon signing the final measure passed by the legislature, Governor Askew said:

People problems will not go away overnight. We should have no illusions that these are perfect pieces of legislation but they are better than what we had before. They will improve our management and consolidate our delivery of social services. They will take the department closer to the people it serves.

Implementation

It was the opinion of many observers that the adversary role that the legislature developed with DHRS during the Keller administration continued after Keller's departure. The next DHRS secretary, William J. "Pete" Page, was strongly committed to the legislative goal of a fully integrated department, and an effective partnership with the legislature might have developed. The legislature, however, was reluctant to relinquish the oversight role it had developed during the reorganization debate. DHRS was given less than one year (until July 1, 1976) to complete the reorganization, and a number of legislative committees geared up their staffs to make sure the job was done as they felt proper. Further, the legislature set up a Joint Oversight Committee on the Reorganization of the Department of Health and Rehabilitative Services to insure continuous monitoring of departmental progress.

The reorganization initiators in the legislature (many of whom later formed part of the Joint Legislative Oversight Committee)[38] were, in fact, pleased with what they perceived as the immediate benefits of

decentralization. Representative Barry Kutun, chairman of the House
DHRS Committee, noted:

It's amazing the pulling together that's going on in the communities.
For the first time there is total contact between HRS and all the other
agencies — United Fund, the Red Cross, etc. The D.A. serves as a
focal point in the community.

Another house member commented, "I am pleased that it's [the District Administrators] down there making the decisions rather than
some directors in Tallahassee." Yet the distrust of DHRS administration that prompted the legislature to take the reorganization initiative
appeared to remain. Legislators still worried that authority would
remain centralized in Tallahassee, that the bureaucracy was growing
rather than diminishing, and the DHRS management problems indicated continuing reluctance on the part of the department's "old
guard" to comply with the intent of reorganization.

Many observers within DHRS believed that the legislature's oversight widened the gap between the legislature and DHRS. In their
view, legislative demands on the agency for increased efficiency,
economy, and information during a period of transition were both
unrealistic and counterproductive.[39] Secretary Page, for example, often
felt harrassed by the Oversight Committee's repeated requests for him
to appear and testify on the progress of reorganization or on problems
that had arisen.

The persistent problem at DHRS remained that of personnel. The
1977 National Academy of Public Administration study *Reorganization in Florida,* which Page requested at the height of his difficulties
with the legislature, stated: "The legislature mandated limits without
knowing the number of staff necessary to do the job."[40] Staffing cuts
(specifically in the central office, where Page had cuts of up to 50
percent), combined with the unsettling effects of personnel reassign-
ments, resignations, and inexperience among new staff members,
helped contribute to a delay in producing a reorganization budget for
the legislature for 1975–76 and again for 1976–77 and gave the
department a reputation with the legislature for "poor management".
The 1976–77 budget was organized along pre-reorganization lines,
did not indicate priorities, and exceeded the previous year's budget
by $223 million. This budgeting increase was the final straw for many
legislators who had seen DHRS as an economy measure. Combined

with this were a DHRS failure to produce the statistics desired by the oversight subcommittees, persistent delays in paying bills, and the drumfire of complaints by committed opponents of reorganization, such as Vocational Rehabilitation, which (as in Washington and Arizona) strongly resisted decentralization and integration.

The legislature held firm on resisting VR pressure to change the structure. The departure or fall from power of such knowledgeable reorganization proponents such as de la Parte, Hodes, Kutun, and Senator Kenneth Meyers did little to strengthen relations between the legislature and DHRS. In addition, Page showed little interest in legislative liaison or in cooperating fully with oversight efforts, and legislators reacted with anger to his attitude toward their role. Deteriorating relations led the National Academy of Public Administration to call for "a more sympathetic and patient understanding by legislative oversight committees of the complexity of the goals which the legislature has mandated."[41]

Perhaps ironicially, however, the efforts by VR to overturn the reorganization promoted solidarity between the legislature and the department concerning the reorganization. VR interests persuaded HEW to disapprove Florida's VR plan, thus blocking VR's integration into the regional system, on the grounds that Florida's new administrative setup violated federal law requiring the states to have a single organization unit to administer VR programs.

VR's argument was that integration would diminish the effectiveness, quality, and level of funding of vocational rehabilitation programs in Florida, turn rehabilitation counselors into generalists, and turn VR as a whole over to the politicians. Therefore, rehabilitation interests insisted that DHRS ought to utilize the "savings clause" in the Florida Reorganization Act that allowed adjustments to conform to federal and state regulations, in order to return direct line supervision between the VR program and the point of service delivery, and grant the state program director final authority over VR personnel and budget decisions. Page was quick to point out that these changes would invert the authority of the secretary and the VR program director, destroy the integrity of the department (that is, create an administrative duality), and violate Florida law.

After a suit by the Florida Rehabilitation Counselors Association failed to halt implementation of the reorganization act, the American

Rehabilitation Association, in an October 1975 "call for action," characterized the changes in Florida as a "national problem" and committed itself to "an organized, strong effort to see that the intent and provisions of the Rehabilitation Act of 1973 are carried out in Florida," that is, "that the State of Florida *not be granted a waiver that would permit reorganization of the Vocational Rehabilitation Agency*" (emphasis in the original). Page responded by traveling to Washington, D.C., to urge radical modification of the Rehabilitation Act of 1973 to give the states greater flexibility in administering VR programs and more oversight of these programs by the state. He urged an end to the "single organizational unit" requirement.[42]

He met with little response in Congress. Few legislators seemed willing to discuss the arguments that Page presented concerning the values of reorganization. Illustrative are remarks made by U.S. Congressman John Brademas, while sitting as chairman of the House Select Subcommittee on Education of the Committee on Education and Labor:

Though we might argue the merits and demerits of such plans as that submitted by Florida and debate various delivery mechanisms, at least it was my own view that if we had learned anything from the period known as Watergate, it is that the law and the intent of Congress must be compiled with and the fact that some persons may disagree with the law is no excuse for ignoring and disobeying it.[43]

When HEW rejected the state plan in May of 1976, DHRS appealed the decision. In November, an administrative law judge found in favor of HEW. Further appeals to the HEW secretary, who had traditionally favored integrative efforts, were unsuccessful. While secretary, Caspar Weinberger had delegated authority in this matter to the commissioner of the U.S. Rehabilitative Services Administration in February of 1975, and subsequent HEW secretaries F. David Mathews and Joseph Califano both asserted that, regardless of their personal sympathies, they had no authority to grant a waiver. Florida then brought suit in federal court opposing the HEW position, but federal courts consistently upheld HEW. Askew was able to persuade HEW secretary Califano to continue federal funding of state VR programs until some settlement could be arranged with the incoming governor, Robert Graham, the Florida legislature, and the new DHRS secretary.

In mid-1979, it looked as if each side might have its way. Despite the failure of its appeals for modifications in or exemptions from federal vocational rehabilitation law, the secretary of DHRS, David Pingree (formerly a legislative aide to Hodes and a DHRS assistant secretary under Page), with the support of the governor and legislative leaders, was negotiating with Congress for amendments to federal laws that would permit VR services to be delivered by nonprofit agencies operating independently of DHRS. In the meantime, the Florida reorganization had remained invulnerable to the VR challenge. Although HEW had announced as early as March of 1976 that over $30 million in federal VR funds to the state were to be cut off, Florida had succeeded in retaining both funds and its innovative structure for over three additional years.

Services Integration

As noted, both Mayo and Page had set out to achieve top-to-bottom integration of services within their departments. The essential difference was that Mayo was attempting it more or less on his own initiative; neither the governor nor the legislature in Arizona fully understood the issues and the implications of services integration. In contrast, all parties in Florida knew exactly what such a reorganization entailed, and Page was carrying out a mandate to do it. This difference goes a long way toward explaining the results in the two states. The goal of services integration, as visualized by the first DES administration at least, was essentially abandoned in Arizona:

A trend was started to [integrate] to the degree it was possible, including the cross-training of employees to become knowledgeable of a variety of programs. Or at least become knowledgeable enough that they could talk to an individual intelligently and get them to the right places to get specific services they needed. That has been turned around. The present administration of DES is taking the attitude that these programs are more separate than that. What we're really ending up with right now is several separate agencies within DES programmatically. The feds want this. . . . It makes it easier for them to see what their programs are doing.[44]

In the opinion of at least one observer, services integration might have worked but Mayo's tenure was "just not enough to get it totally off the ground, and certainly insufficient to evaluate it. It was starting to move; and there was starting to be some acceptance of it." Moreover, it was noted that DES did not promote services integration on the grounds that it would mean cost reductions. "We didn't delude ourselves into thinking we were going to have reduced overhead costs. However, we hoped that we could slow down the growth of overhead costs by consolidation. And I think that occurred."

Services integration gradually acquired a constituency. Although committed to Huerta's MIG program, many of the district and area personnel were still strongly supportive of services integration, which after all gave them a powerful role in human services delivery. The district managers and their staffs were not going to yield easily the power they had gained.

The opposition proved stronger, however. For example, Thomas Tyrell of the Division of Vocational Rehabilitation was unstinting in his support of Huerta's policies. The Arizona VR program released a series of performance data that showed a significant improvement in its "score" following the return of its authority over field operations. Its ranking rose in 1976 from fifty-second to thirty-eighth. The program cited figures of 1789 rehabilitations per year before DES was created in the Fall of 1973, 1181 in the last year under Mayo, and 1667 for FY 1977. (The number rose to 1992 for fiscal year 1979.) Further, both unemployment insurance and job services climbed consistently in national ratings following the change.[45]

When the Arizona multiservice centers began, all intake was done on the same form, so that client problems could be clearly identified. The backup and delay problems during the recession convinced DES administrators that clients who desired a specific service, especially job services or unemployment insurance, should be allowed to bypass the common intake procedure. Studies by DES under Huerta indicated that only 40 percent of all clients needed information and referral services and only 1 percent of all clients required the master assessment or in-depth help for multiple problems. These figures were in sharp contrast with studies done during the Mayo administration indicating that 75 to 85 percent of all clients had some linkages with more than one program. These Huerta findings were used by both sides in the dispute over services integration. Milton Graft, district manager in Tucson, noted that, in light of the size of the one-stop centers, 1 percent of the total case load was not a negligible figure.

"So one percent of the people up there — 180 out of 18,000 — went to master assessment. That makes a pretty good case load for a month of special services." Thus, because of their efforts, though DES planned for partial separation of programs in the new multiservice center in Tucson and opened a few separate job services offices elsewhere, many multiservice centers such as the one in Mesa, a suburb of Phoenix, remained integrated. These centers had their own constituency, mostly composed of center staff, who still argued for common intake procedures and the master assessment concept.

This mixed outcome appeared to perpetuate an internal power struggle involving control over the common intake and master assessment process. In several areas, mainly urban, former area managers became multiservice center heads. Moreover, district managers remained in charge of services coordination, which they interpreted as including overall responsibility for the one-stop centers and thus control over services delivery. This arrangement was constantly being attacked by the programs offices, thus producing an unsettled state of affairs throughout the department.

Services integration in Florida also had a rocky beginning. Unlike Arizona and Georgia, where an election and turnover of power provided an opportunity for opponents after only two years, services integration in Florida had an initial four-year run. In this regard, the circumstances in Florida were similar to those in Washington. The difference between Florida and Washington lay in the department leadership of services integration, which was much weaker in Washington; Page was a tenacious believer, while Smith was hesitant. Moreover, Evans's appointee to replace Smith after two and one half years of turmoil had no particular commitment to a district structure. Morris was like Huerta in believing that doctrinaire adherence to the district system was not in the interests of the department.

Florida opponents of services integration could not demonstrate where decentralization had resulted in the oft-predicted "fiefdoms" and "empire building." Instead they focused on extensive administrative problems that they believed were affecting the quality of services. The transfer or resignation of many experienced personnel and the creation of new positions and procedures at all levels produced massive slowdowns and some foul-ups in benefit payments, vendor reimbursement, and general accounting.

The accounting confusions were particularly troublesome. As late as FY 1977–78, state auditor general Ernest Ellison announced that DHRS was unable to account for $39 million of revenues and expenditures because of poor record keeping. DHRS was banking in part on demonstrable benefits from the services integration initiatives, but as the months passed these benefits proved slow in coming. Collocation was slowed due to problems in obtaining adequate facilities and the reluctance of the Department of General Services to approve new leases. The common intake procedure, christened the Case Assignment and Management System (CAMS), remained at the pilot stage. Victims of personnel restrictions by the Department of Administration and of the failure of a computerized management information system to develop, CAMS workers increased slowly in number and effectiveness. Information system inadequacies, as well as difficulties with federal regulations, contributed to additional problems with the single eligibility system. Without concrete results to show off, DHRS was left in a politically vulnerable position and opponents had the opportunity to foster the impression that DHRS continued to be a problem.

The centerpiece of services integration in Florida was the district system itself. It was the idea of decentralizing services administration to district managers that most appealed to the legislature and, as in Georgia, Washington, and Arizona, decentralization was seen as the backbone of services integration. Resistance to the district system was based on both programmatic considerations — complaints that generalists were incompetent to manage professionals — and administrative problems. In Arizona and Washington, resistance to the district system ultimately brought about its demise after little more than two years. Georgia's district system never really gained a foothold. Only in Florida did it survive a turbulent transition.

When Page, former HEW regional director in Atlanta and associate administrator of HEW's Social and Rehabilitation Services, became DHRS secretary in July of 1975, he immediately set out to decentralize the department, as the legislature insisted. Although committed to decentralization, he also favored a strong central staff to complement the strengthened districts, and in this he encountered resistance. The legislature saw a strong central office as antithetical to decentralization and had limited the program offices to a total of 450 professional staff (later argued by some legislators to mean 450 staff, period, whether professional or not). Page was consistently unable to get even half of the staff requested for his own office (eighty-three positions were requested and thirty-two approved), and he believed this failure reduced his ability to reorganize the central office so that it would support decentralized operations. Lack of staff was seen by Page and many of his aides as contributing to the management oversight and information problems DHRS encountered as reorganization progressed.

In contrast, the district decentralization occurred relatively expeditiously. Page designated 692 positions for district administration, and by October of 1975 he had appointed administrators for all eleven districts. Authority over the statewide institutions was transferred to the districts on February 16, 1976, and authority over programs was transferred on March 1, 1976, with model services networks (the substructure used for actual delivery) to be established in each district by that date. From the outset, districts were allowed a great deal of leeway in how integration was implemented. The Case Assignment and Management System units, for example, were not mandatory; some districts set them up, others adopted less formal arrangements for promoting integration. While this variety was seen as a natural accompaniment of the shift from central to local control, it complicated the process of assembling management information on a statewide basis.

Not all observers felt that decentralization was proceeding on schedule. Some district administrators cited a reluctance on the part of the central office to give up control of various programs and the insufficiency of their own staff to effectively assume control in areas such as budget development. Adding to their problems was the influx of new personnel and the unfamiliarity of the roles that had to be created.

Development of the district's role remained a primary concern of DHRS administrators. Although chosen by Secretary Page according to a uniform standard,[46] district administrators adapted to their roles in widely varying ways. Some were better at it than others. Certain districts became more "integrated" than others, and district-headquarters relations varied among districts. Page himself admitted that he had little time for district liaison because he was given inadequate staff. Each district administrator had to struggle with the problem of relating to his service networks (which by all accounts were staffed with experienced personnel and worked quite efficiently), the private providers who delivered services on contract, and the local governments.

Problems at the district level came to a head with the change in governors and the appointments of Pingree, former assistant secretary for both operations and administration, as Page's successor. Soon after his appointment, Pingree fired two district administrators and shifted several others. His moves were viewed by many as a necessary use of secretarial authority on a recalcitrant department, especially in the face of still another possible reorganization by the legislature, the creation of a separate Department of Health.

Some district officials, however, felt that the central office was to blame for many of the problems they were experiencing. The central office, for example, was seen to have demanded much from the district in terms of information and time without feedback, useful analysis, or promised program manuals and standards. There was a feeling that DHRS goals for computer systems were much too ambitious for the facilities provided the districts. Districts felt that the promised fiscal and personnel autonomy was slow in coming and that a central office arrangement of decision making by three coequal assistant secretaries had proved troublesome. Not only did it often prove impossible to make decisions without consensus or resolution by the secretary, but the three divisions sent different and conflicting signals down to the districts.

The confusion continued concerning the allocation of responsibility between the districts and headquarters and the conflicting desires for local flexibility and uniform standards. Continuing as well was the debate over how the reorganization effort had affected services delivery. In its 1977 study, NAPA noted a distinct division among observers along lines of occupation. They found that professional associations and private providers were usually critical of reorganization, while DHRS generalist staff considered the quality of services as definitely improved.[47] Part of this difference of opinion arose from what NAPA saw as a disagreement over the proper measures for services quality, including accessibility, proximity and convenience; administrative efficiency; professional quality (as measured by professionals); and promptness, attentiveness, courtesy, and responsiveness of service providers.[48] One or more of these standards were used by various observers to draw their own conclusions, but few used all of them, leading to a large divergence of opinion over what exactly was occurring "out in the field." Although the NAPA study concluded that accessibility of services had definitely been improved by integration, it noted that reports on accountability, responsiveness, cost, and efficiency were mixed, depending upon the observer, and that conclusions about quality of services were therefore difficult to reach.

Aftermath

The processes of change were no less turbulent in Arizona and Florida than they were in Georgia and Washington. As in the latter two states, the successors to Castro and Askew had the opportunity to do something about the problems of his state's largest human services department. Again, in neither state did a major shake-up or dismantling of the department occur.

The prospects for further change appeared considerably greater in Arizona than in Florida. In Arizona, the Department of Economic Security appeared to rest on shaky foundations because of unresolved philosophical and bureaucratic conflicts between the welfare-oriented programs sponsored by the U.S. Department of Health, Education and Welfare and the employment-oriented programs sponsored by the U.S. Department of Labor. It is a mix that remains relatively unusual among the states. That this should be so is not self-evident; the association of job-oriented and welfare-oriented programs has more intellectual appeal than the more common associations between health or vocational rehabilitation and welfare. The likely explanation is that the employment-oriented programs have a large, labor-market-oriented constituency that, with strong federal support, has consistently been able to fend off stigmatizing associations with welfare activities. Yet the political force of this constituency is probably weaker in the states than it is in the federal government, and should a state such as Arizona succeed in combining these programs, the idea might become more popular.

The possibility is greater, however, that the legislature or an aspiring governor would see merit in splitting the department and combining the public-assistance and social-services functions with other agencies after the model of Florida. An obstacle to such a move would be Arizona's powerful and conservative counties which, as has been noted, have been singularly successful in blocking implementation of a Medicaid program. Should Arizona health politics shift, the agenda of reorganization possibilities would expand.

Also affecting reorganization possibilities in a state like Arizona is the competence of departmental administration. In a state in which the competence of state government is not taken for granted, the legislature is relatively uncommitted to the status quo, and because intradepartmental organizational arrangements are unstable, DES is particularly vulnerable to mistakes. The change of administrations in 1978 brought a veteran of Georgia's human resources department to the leadership of DES. Such a development hints at the possibility that a national talent pool of combat-toughened human services executives may contribute to future stability, continuity, and competence in departmental administration, especially during times of change and transition.

The prospects in Florida appear substantially different. As in Georgia and Washington, the configuration of DHRS has more elements of stability than does DES in Arizona. Though it is possible to imagine the legislature or the governor moving specific program divisions around, a wholesale dismantling of the department does not appear likely to gain widespread political appeal. The possible exception is health. The Florida Medical Association, other health interests, and county health officials have never been enthusiastic about DHRS, and at times of trouble they advocate separation. In 1977, a constitutional revision commission recommended creation of a separate Department of Health, which would have included the Mental Health Division as well. This proposal failed when all proposed amendments were defeated by Florida voters. Some kind of crisis in the Florida health care system could reignite interest in a separate health department. The prospects for this or any other kind of structural change appear to be closely tied to the success of services integration and the district system.

Services integration may have survived its period of maximum vulnerability. The reasoning of services-integration supporters is often analogous to that of cancer specialists: categorical "cancer" can be assumed to be cured if there is no recurrence of the disease within five years. Florida approached the fifth anniversary of the change with services integration in excellent health. Most administrative problems had been virtually overcome, a period of relative stability in state and departmental leadership had begun, and a considerable degree of satisfaction with the system was expressed by service workers and administrators.

Could anything upset this solidifying status quo? The experience in all four states suggests that it would take more than routine problems to topple the integrated system. A significant reason is that district administrative personnel could be expected to become a constituency for the status quo of growing political importance. Just as the administrators of state institutions once enjoyed influence based on their ties to legislators, district administrators are in a position to exploit the value of the casework they can do for "their" representatives in the legislature. Districts may indeed become political fiefdoms or, short of that, enjoy the support of the legislature because of the specific benefits they can produce. Without question, power had been shifted from the state program offices to the districts.

Would anyone, apart from program people, ever want to alter this new arrangement? The obvious answer is that the governor and his or her top cabinet officials might. Just as state executives have in the past fought for control of state institutions, they may in the future want greater control over districts. Their leverage is already considerable, however, and only an extraordinarily weak governor would fail to use it with at least modest success. The governor retains substantial control over the executive budget and over the appointment of the DHRS secretary, who appoints district administrators. Even when the governor wanted to push power into the districts, the state officials in charge of the budget, the personnel system, and audit were able to slow things down considerably. Nevertheless, the possibility that substantial autonomy could develop at the district level may help explain why full decentralization of services administration has not received the unqualified backing of any governor in this study and why it has had the enthusiastic if somewhat skeptical support of so many legislators.

5
At the Headwaters of Change

Change in the organization of Minnesota's human services has been gradual and modest in scope. Neither the governor nor legislative leaders have made sudden, bold moves to reorganize the services system, and they have been ready to make compromises on the modest measures they have proposed. "Unlike some other places where departments of human resources or something like that have been created almost by fiat," says a former state planner, "we wanted to spend our time building the consensus for change ahead of time." One senses that the approach to reorganization of Jimmy Carter or the Florida legislature would have been politically unthinkable in Minnesota.

Minnesota has an institutionally strong governor, an increasingly professional legislature, and well-organized interest groups. One additional factor affecting organizational change is the strong role of county government and the respect for this role in the Minnesota legislature. "Minnesota's services are state supported and county administered," is a common and approving description of the state's human services system. Moreover, it reflects a guiding political philosophy more than alliances between county commissioners and state legislators. The most successful modifications of the system have been three measures passed by the legislature between 1973 and 1976 that offered Minnesota's counties incentives to improve the coordination of services planning and delivery. Proposals by the governor to reorganize state agencies have had only limited appeal in the legislature and then mainly to the extent that reorganization would aid counties in services administration. Indeed the most far-reaching change in human services administration in the state — its dimensions were similar to the changes at the state level in Georgia and Washington — occurred in and at the initiative of Minnesota's largest county, Hennepin.

The role of county government in Minnesota is unique among the states in many respects. Of general interest, however, are the questions the state's recent experiences raise concerning the virtues of an incremental, consensual approach to reorganization. Even though gradual and well trimmed, recent changes have been regarded by many observers and participants as "too much, too soon." Those who stand to lose through organizational realignments or who dislike any disruption and uncertainty find grounds to object. Forging a consensus to support modest changes may not be appreciably easier politically, all things considered, than overcoming resistance to major changes.

The Human Services Act

It is generally acknowledged that the initiator of interest in human services reform was state representative Howard Knutson. Appointed vice-chairman of the legislature's Health, Welfare and Corrections Committee in 1969, Knutson was charged with deciding what to do about the "welfare mess." Since most welfare functions are heavily financed and completely administered by the counties, Knutson immediately ran into trouble trying to understand the system: "Nobody really knew. The Department of Public Welfare couldn't tell us; they didn't have a handle on it either." Based on the information he gathered in visits around the state, Knutson introduced a bill in 1969 providing for state takeover of the welfare system. At the time Knutson's plan seemed to him to be the only way to reduce the confusion, cost, and lack of equity in services delivery.[1] It failed to pass, however, and though reintroduced in 1971, failed in the Senate.

Knutson persisted. At his instigation, an interim House subcommittee on organization and administration of welfare was then established. The subcommittee's members held hearings throughout the state, talked to welfare commissioners and recipients, solicited complaints and suggestions, and collected documentation on the kinds of services available, expenditures, and the actual workings of the system. The major revelation, Knutson found, was the lack of services integration. "We found that workers in the system couldn't talk to each other and that, for example, seven case workers were handling one family."

Throughout the study period, Knutson was in close contact with the human services people in state government who were also interested in these issues. A coalition formed involving Knutson, Dean Honetschlager, head of the Human Resources Planning Division of the State Planning Agency, and Duane Scribner, staff aide to the governor and head of the Office of Program Development. According to Honetschlager, who accompanied Knutson's subcommittee on its field visits, the study effort corroborated a concern at the local level that was real and documented, but it also started turning the legislative committee away from the "welfare mess" into something that started going toward simplification. It was a switch of interest, of theme, . . . from the amorphous welfare mess to something more specific about the lack of an understandable, accountable system.

Enactment

During this "learning period," Knutson abandoned the state takeover approach. After looking further into the problem, hearing from the Association of Minnesota Counties, and obtaining views from other states that had attempted state-level welfare administration, he concluded that the takeover should not be pursued. Instead, consensus was developing around the idea that the counties' role should be strengthened by using state funds to encourage groups of counties to integrate all human services at the local level. This idea developed into the Human Services Act (HSA), which was passed by the legislature in 1973.[2]

The Human Services Act provided a mechanism to encourage creation by counties of a Human Services Board to manage centrally those human services supported or regulated by the state departments of Corrections, Health, and Public Welfare — court, public health, public assistance, mental retardation, social, and mental health services. The Human Services Board, consisting of at least one county commissioner for each member county and with at least one-third of its membership being private citizens, would be aided in the task of integration by a Human Services Advisory Committee, with a maximum of twenty-five members evenly divided among clients, providers, and private citizens of the counties. This Advisory Committee, with the aid of task forces on particular subjects, would participate in both planning and budget formation by the Human Services Board. Multicounty boards were encouraged by the imposition of a 50,000 population minimum as a condition for receipt of planning funds from the State Planning Agency, which would administer the program. Individual counties were in fact specifically excluded from receiving a planning grant under the act. The organization of services within the Human Services Board's purview was to be entirely at the discretion of the board, with the possibilities ranging from a loose confederation of services to full integration.

While the Human Services Act was identified in many minds with Knutson, the bill appeared to be a result of

a lot of people talking about the problem — or the possibilities — and then somebody solidifying these random discussions into a proposal. . . . For example, Knutson and Honetschlager collaborating on a piece of legislation . . . with state agency people collaborating with them. We tend to have a fairly open process that leads to a consensus or approach that then has the ability to be sold.[3]

This collaboration subsumed some jockeying for position within state government. The State Planning Agency worked closely with Knutson in developing the act. The Governor's Office of Program Development (OPD), specifically its director Duane Scribner, lobbied extensively for the bill. Moreover, the governor insisted that all matters relating to the act be coordinated with OPD, not State Planning. An emerging low-key rivalry between the two offices later developed into an open disagreement over the direction human services reorganization and reform should take in Minnesota.

The governor's role in passage of the HSA was for the most part indirect. When Wendell Anderson was elected governor in 1971, many hoped he would be one of Minnesota's first strong governors. According to Scribner, the governor "wanted to be identified as someone who had a strong commitment and feeling about senior citizens, the handicapped, and people generally who are in need of help." The fact that Anderson "wanted to be serving people in some systematic way" was a consistent theme in his early messages. As with other governors, however, Anderson was not perceived as being personally involved in the day-to-day discussions of human services reform. Rather, the efforts of his staff — in the State Planning Agency and the Office of Program Development — put Minnesota on its present course of human services reorganization within a general policy framework the governor had established, and using the power of the governor's office.

Scribner's views were formed during his own visits around the state with Anderson at the beginning of his term.

There was a general feeling that the system was in a situation where all the new demands of federal programs, state programs and state laws were putting counties and local service organzations that dealt with the state into a very difficult situation. But they had very little in the way of capacity to analyze or even find their way through what some of them call the maze of state government. At the same time, there was a great deal of concern of the same kind in state government about the federal government. We had a whole series of independent federal planning organizations in Health and in Developmental Disabilities and so on. And the pressure was always to fragment and make them individual units that reported to the highest possible level — which was always the Governor's Office — which got in the way of coordination.

The problems became even more evident as Anderson prepared his first budget message. Scribner continued:

It became obvious that one of the areas of rapid expansion — which was very difficult to assess and impossible to control — was the whole array of what we call social funding: Medicare, AFDC, Title XX. When you complicate that by the fact that there were all these actors in it because of all the strong local involvement, you had a situation that had major budget implications as well as good government and organizational implications.

Therefore, the governor decided to make attempts to hold down spiraling costs and establish a reputation for effective management in the human services area.

A direct result of this decision was the establishment of several administrative units. The first was a Human Resources Planning Office created in 1971 within the State Planning Agency and headed by Honetschlager. The second was a Human Services Council (chaired by Lieutenant Governor Rudy Perpich), which from 1972 to 1975 brought the heads of the state's human services agencies together for discussion of policy problems.[4] The third was the Office of Program Development (OPD).[5] Established under an HEW Services Integration Targets of Opportunity grant in 1972, this office was to operate within the Governor's Office, and its director was to be directly responsible to the chief executive. Its purpose was to build a "capacity for change" in Minnesota and to intervene on behalf of the governor in human services issues. Capacity building was defined as "increasing the capacity of state government in influencing information gathering, planning, resource allocation, and delivery process."[6] All state agencies were expected to cooperate with OPD both in and outside of the council setting. The theory behind this office was that the governor — who had statewide visibility, direct responsibility to the electorate, statutory responsibility for program policy, budget responsibility for the state executive decision-making structure, and the political following necessary to influence legislators and decision makers — constituted the single element of state government with the capacity to intervene at all levels of decision making within the state's human services system.

One of the strengths . . . for the location was that it would put services integration kinds of judgments directly into a situation where there would be access to the Governor and the media and the likelihood of impacting on budget decisions.[7]

From the inception of these offices, the State Planning Agency was perceived by outsiders as the most active, although much of the staff work was done by OPD. (The Council accomplished little or nothing.) "A decision was made at one point that the people who would be out front in terms of public visibility, selling the idea and the rest, would be the State Planning Agency, and OPD would fall into the background,"[8] a decision made in part because of the temporary nature of OPD funding. State Planning began to work with the state agencies and specifically with the Department of Public Welfare on reform of human services administration. Reform at the state level was to come later. The State Planning Agency in conjunction with Knutson and others began drafting the legislation that would become the Human Services Act. Although State Planning's Honetschlager recalls that HSA was built on a consensus among the expanding group of interested officials, he felt that it really "belonged to us."

Throughout this period, OPD had been working at various tasks: consulting with local groups, developing a computerized information and referral system, studying a standard client identifier and related privacy issues, and doing public relations work to insure local community support for services integration efforts. The office also encouraged the testing of the Human Services Board concept. Thus OPD as well as State Planning had come to embrace the multicounty emphasis of the Human Services Act. Having consulted with the agency heads and county commissioners, OPD decided that HSA merited the governor's support and accordingly sought the governor's help in getting the bill through. Although originally proposed by Knutson, the "ownership" of HSA in a subtle way changed hands as the governor's influence, OPD's expertise, and State Planning's program goals were brought to bear.

The Governor's Office had a commitment and a developing reputation for being a very strong lobbyist with the legislature itself and believing that the legislature is really the place where policy is set. . . . We had a highly organized legislative lobbying effort; people were assigned to individual legislators and we worked on it. We covered the legislature like a blanket.[9]

Thus, HSA *became* a governor's bill. "We included it on our program," says Scribner, "and that supposedly enhanced its opportunity for passage; and it also made it a part of our lobbying effort."

While the county-oriented HSA approach was being developed, other proposals for reform were surfacing. One of the more interesting was based on a reorganization study by volunteers from the Minnesota business community, designated by the Governor's Loaned Executive Action Program (LEAP). This program was management oriented and designed to bring a "bottom-line" approach to state government. It consisted of sixty full-time management specialists "borrowed" from Minnesota industry, whose salaries continued to be paid by their companies. These specialists were divided into task forces on the major executive departments, and each task force conducted a six-month study leading to recommendations in December of 1972 as to how each department could be more effectively managed. A majority of the recommendations, including those for separate departments of Finance and Personnel, were acted on favorably by the legislature. In addition to management suggestions in the human services area, LEAP proposed a three-phase, state-level reorganization of the Department of Public Welfare. This approach brought it into conflict with the thinking being incorporated into HSA. Said Kevin Kenney of the Minnesota House of Representatives staff:

We called the LEAP representative . . . before they issued their report to tell us what they were going to recommend. They started down this line [state-level reorganization] and Howard Knutson and I finally said, "You've got it all backwards. What we've got to do is let those people out there [in the counties] try to reorganize so that it becomes a sensible system to the people for whom it exists and then . . . let the state department respond to that organization, not the other way around."

When HSA was introduced by Knutson in 1973 it followed precisely this approach and had Governor Anderson's support. During that same session Representative James Rice introduced a bill that would create a Department of Human Resources, but it generated little interest. Rice's bill was held over for discussion, but the Human Services Act was passed without a dissenting vote.

The Human Services Act stirred little controversy. It was seen as part of a continuing and popular trend toward strengthening local control over services administration. Along with a Community Corrections Act passed during the same session, HSA promised to place greater control over resource allocation in the hands of those who were responsible for services delivery. Moreover, the HSA was permissive and involved only minimal appropriations. In assessing the legislature's stake in HSA, Kevin Kenney noted:

The legislature obviously had a strong fiscal incentive in the state income maintenance program. The costs were getting out of control and they had no management of it or very little management of it. Human services and all those other services, they obviously have a strong political stake because it's the local people who elect them. . . . They're constantly hearing gripes that we are not getting this service or that you have to jump so many hoops . . . and clients are caught in the middle. [Legislators] come here every session and pump in all kinds of money for [services] and then they hear the people are not getting it.

One state legislator, Representative Shirley Hokanson, who was later involved in amending the HSA, maintained that "you don't get a vote anyplace in human services," but she observed that the 1973 legislature wanted to "get a handle on the whole thing" and HSA seemed to be an acceptable way to do that.

The Association of Minnesota Counties was a consistent supporter of HSA. There was hesitation, however, which one of its staff explained as follows:

Twenty years ago the state might have been seen as acquiring agency control of functional areas through direct service provision. Now, through rules and regulations, plan approval, and dollar dispensing the state accomplishes the same thing, but cannot be directly attacked, as the service units and professionals are all at the local level.

In some circles of county government, HSA was seen as an attempt at state takeover of services delivery. Worries in this regard were not based on the political appeal of providing human services.[10] Hesitation was based on fears of the increase in state control over county government. Human services have never been a popular concern, especially in rural counties.

There's only really one county, and that's Hennepin County, where the county commissioners are full-time. All the other commissioners (434) are part-time and the majority are farmers and small business-men, with only thirteen women out of that number. Human services is not a popular issue with them from a lot of standards. (1) It is the most complicated issue they deal with; (2) it is an issue that you cannot — with a few exceptions — be politically positive about and expect to stay in office. More typically, people run for county com-missioner with a campaign to clean up welfare fraud and hold dollars down.[11]

Some observers, mainly in state government, saw HSA as purely a public relations measure, put through for effect without much advice from those who would have to live with it. According to one official, "As far as the agencies were concerned it came out of nowhere. We had no role in designing the Human Services Act; it was almost entirely State Planning."

Thus beneath a placid surface lurked diametrically opposed views of what HSA was intended to accomplish. Such latent conflict was not serious at the time, however. Because the bill was permissive, not obligatory, no one felt especially threatened.

Other factors also contributed to the success of the bill, including the timing of its introduction and the reputation of its author. The legislature had recently shifted its political balance. For the first time in Minnesota history, both houses and the governorship were con-trolled by the Democratic-Farmer-Labor party. Although this factor would subsequently reduce Republican Knutson's effectiveness, at that time Knutson's acknowledged integrity and expertise along with support from the Governor's Office made for easy passage of HSA. The legislature and the Governor's Office were working well together. As one observer noted: "It was sort of the Democrat's dream year. . . . The momentum was there for getting good bills passed; and it [HSA] passed very quickly."

In addition to the HSA, the 1973 legislature also passed the Com-munity Corrections Act, founded on similar principles and aimed at strengthening local authority over corrections facilities and programs. The act required the creation of an advisory board for all corrections-related activities, both state and local (excluding state institutions), and provided funds directly to the county for their new role. Concerns were raised as to the benefits of the Community Corrections Act's complex reimbursement formula. Yet, because the act enabled counties to develop alternative administrative approaches and integrate previously fragmented programs, it was relatively well received, and several counties immediately began implementation of a pilot project. Even more successful was the Community Health Services Act, passed in the 1976 session. Like the Community Corrections Act and HSA, it esablished an area board, usually with county commissioner membership, to oversee local programs. The act not only encouraged the integration of local health services, but brought new state money into the counties. The flexibility and financial incentives made the act popular with the counties.

With passage of the Community Corrections Act (and later the Community Health Act), another type of problem was being spawned. Although both the Health and Corrections acts permitted reliance on the HSA-instigated Human Services Boards, such arrangements were seldom established. In fact, the relative success of the three acts is striking. As of 1978, ten counties were participating in HSA, approximately thirty were participating in the Corrections Act, and eighty out of eighty-seven were participating in the Health Act. One reason for the success of the latter two was the initial decision to set the population threshold at 30,000 instead of 50,000, thus allowing more single-county and bicounty arrangements.[12] Another factor was that the program categories were left relatively intact, thus defusing opposition from categorical interests. Whether human services will be easily assimilated into counties already having health and corrections boards remained to be seen. As one county commissioner observed, "The Health and Corrections interests both supported integration in principle, but when it came to detail, they began to balk." While some saw this growth of various possibilities for services delivery as an expansion of local options, others viewed it as brewing disaster and asserted that human services were more complex and fragmented than before the passage of the HSA.

Implementation

Reservations and outright opposition to HSA, largely absent during enactment, were sparked during implementation. The initial consensus proved fragile. The new Act had to be sold to reluctant county commissioners and hesitant professionals. Many commissioners, though receptive to the HSA concept, were wary of being forced to work in new and unfamiliar groupings. This, in fact, was the reason for the permissive rather than mandatory legislation. Moreover, the population base had been reduced from a starting figure of 100,000 to 50,000 in order to make the act more palatable to people opposed to "regional government." Apparently Knutson himself had favored a figure of 75,000; State Planning preferred a still higher figure than the original 100,000 that might promote broader regionalism throughout the state. The counties, on the other hand, constantly sought to reduce the figure to 15,000 or 20,000 because, as one observer put it, "the larger numbers tended to jeopardize a lot of sacred jurisdictions." Although lengthy negotiations ultimately resulted in the 50,000 figure, the issue of the minimum population base would come back to haunt implementation of the Human Services Act.

Minnesota's eighty-seven counties ranged in population from four thousand to one million and ran the gamut in both need for services and outlook. Though counties at opposite ends of the spectrum were actively involved in human services reform, their diversity made the task of HSA implementation complicated.

Responsibility for HSA implementation fell to Richard Broeker, who had been a consultant to the State Planning Agency. As an associate dean of the School of Social Development at the University of Minnesota at Duluth, and as former president of the Minnesota Social Services Association, Broeker was knowledgeable about human services issues in Minnesota. He worked for Planning on a "special project basis" and also kept close contact with the legislature. Since Broeker got along well with Knutson, there was little confusion between them over priorities or methods in implementing HSA.

Broeker immediately undertook a statewide tour to "peddle" HSA to the counties. On the face of it, he could argue that HSA would be a useful tool for county commissioners. By establishing a Human Services Board, the commissioners could enhance their control over county human services departments and coordinate the planning, budgeting, and programming of county services. The hodgepodge of boards and planning and budgeting requirements would be simplified and authority could be concentrated in a Human Services director responsible to the Human Services Board. Nevertheless, the minimum-population-base requirement dictated that groups of counties would have to join together to form a board, meaning that commissioners from neighboring counties would share control as well as authority over their collective Health, Welfare, and Corrections programs. This was a problem since, as one observer put it, "They didn't like to talk to the guy next door, much less work with him." The elected commissioners were not the only problem. For professional health, welfare, and corrections workers, HSA's reorganization contained the threat of constant "political" interference with the delivery system. Moreover, local agency heads saw the act's governing mechanisms as reducing their status. As county welfare directors were relatively powerful at the local level, Broeker tried to "sell" HSA as "the great equalizer," a measure that would increase other departments' roles in human services decision making. Nevertheless, Knutson recalled, most professionals sought to keep their programs outside of the HSA arrangement.

The process of lining up the counties — of persuading the various sets of actors that they would benefit from HSA — proceeded with difficulty throughout 1974, but there was interest. Said Broeker:

I worked very hard for the county boards and used my relationships with the state organizations. . . . There were two groups of counties — seven counties in the northeastern part of the state and nine counties in south central Minnesota. By the end of the first year those sixteen counties plus a fairly large number of other counties all had active interest in going ahead.

These county groupings followed the lines of previously existing Minnesota Development Regions. Products of a 1969 state Regional Development Act (amended in 1971 to allow broader participation), many of the thirteen local planning regions were in fact just coming into full operation in 1973. Fifty-three counties expressed interest in a feasibility study under HSA auspices. Two groups of counties were chosen as the two pilot projects allowed for under the Human Services Act.

The contrast in approach between the two regions, Planning Regions III and IX, appears to explain their relative success. Region III consisted of seven counties of unequal size and population centered in the northeastern mining region around Duluth.[13] Design of the pilot project created one Human Services Board through the mechanism of the Region III Development Commission (RDC). This arrangement incited several power struggles involving the county welfare departments, mental health boards, and other operating agencies over whether the RDC or the counties would exercise the greater authority. These struggles were based in part on the counties' fears of being "swallowed up" by the aggressive regional commission and in part on fears that the smaller counties would be dominated by the largest one, St. Louis. Moreover, in attempting to convince the counties of the benefits of services integration, regional officials appeared to place too much emphasis on the technical aspects of the program. According to Broeker:

They flooded the place with data — more and more data — where as in Region IX they took a much more political, organizing approach. I felt that Region III wouldn't go because they were making it so complex the county commissioners couldn't deal with it.

Eventually Region III, unable to resolve either political differences between the participants or problems with the act itself, decided not to participate in the program. Broeker saw this withdrawal as resulting in part from overcommitment to democratic processes characteristic of Minnesota.

The good government movement can be used to hamstring you, by making you involve everybody and putting everything to a vote, so you lose the whole sense of what you are trying to do with the obsession of the process. That's what happened in Region III.

The other pilot, Region IX, was a group of nine counties of approximately equal size located in the south central agricultural district.[14] Originally, the HSA structure had made provisions for only two pilot projects, but the nine counties in Region IX concluded from their feasibility study (done by the RDC) that the best approach would be to create three Human Services boards of three counties each. The counties successfully petitioned the state legislature for a special exemption to permit this.[15] The manageable size of its boards was believed to have had a good deal to do with the region's relative success in implementing HSA.

Success in Region IX was also consistent with Broeker's assumption that "integration is largely a political issue. It's not a technical issue." Broeker found:

The clients in general could care less. The only thing that upsets a client is a disruption of service, particularly when it's a check. . . . The staff were really not concerned one way or another. They saw their lot as remaining the same. . . . The key was getting to the county commissioners. If the county commissioners would support it, anything would go.

But the county commissioners had not previously been primary actors in county services delivery.

The county commissioners were extremely dependent on their welfare directors. The welfare director in the rural counties in Minnesota is the most skilled administrator in the county. He knows how to deal with federal forms. For a rural county commissioner, who does not do a lot of writing, a farmer, you become very dependent on these people. So you can get the county welfare director to go with you or he can by default cause the county commissioner to veto the project by indicating he is not going to support the county commissioner.

One county observer noted:

For most counties over the years human services has primarily meant welfare. So the county commissioners have had to rely on the welfare director to interpret regulations, give direction, etc., and their relationship with the welfare director has shaped a lot of their thinking in the whole human services area.

The final report prepared by OPD at the conclusion of its grant tended to support Broeker's view of integration as a political, nontechnical issue:

Perhaps the most important lesson learned was that an important organizational change or technical innovation in which local decision makers have a significant stake must be preceded by a skillful and thorough community organization effort if it is to stand a chance of success over time. . . . In integration efforts sponsored by OPD the opinion of an influential decisionmaker was a greater factor in the final decision than the empirical data describing problems and solutions.[16]

Between the period that Broeker began his efforts at "community organizing" to promote human services boards and before the pilot projects were ready to become operational, several problems developed. According to Scribner, "There were a number of professionals out there who fought — and I think some are still fighting — the concept." The major thrust of HSA was the transfer of services management from the agency-oriented program directors to a committee of generalists — and often to a single generalist administrator responsible to that committee — and often (although not always) from a single county to multicounty or regional body. The agencies predictably saw HSA as a serious turf infringement.

An agency looks at it and says, "I won't be as independent and as autonomous. . . . Instead of being out there with visibility, we will be part of a bigger thing; we will have to work with those other people who are trying to control us and take us over."

An overwhelming challenge was getting the counties to work together:

It really took leadership on the part of the county commissioners to say, "I'm willing to give this up," because what they had to do was enter into a joint agreement that turned over a portion of their funds to the Board. And they would lose control of them essentially, except for the fact that they might have two out of the six county commissioners on the Human Services Board.

Thus implementation problems multiplied.

There were some complaints from the counties about Broeker himself. While he was by all accounts the most knowledgeable and enthusiastic HSA proponent, his youthful, energetic, and sometimes aggressive style did not always succeed with rural county commissioners. As one county staff member noted, "You admire the technique, you knew he was a good salesman, but then the product becomes suspect." Some county commissioners were aggrieved by what they believed was the failure on the part of HSA's sponsors to involve them more in the planning stages. Then they felt that during the initial months after passage, too much was made of the benefits to be had from HSA and too little of the practical problems that would be encountered and how they were to be dealt with.

Finally, as the initial pilot projects were about to go operational, the counties complained that the state agencies were not being helpful. "[The counties] were saying, 'This is great but you must get the state departments squared away.'" The problem was that the state agencies were just not designed to handle requests and questions from the multidisciplined Human Services boards. This problem was not unexpected, and many HSA supporters viewed it as a positive side effect of HSA.

We knew state-level reorganization would not be popular, neither in the legislature nor the agencies, as it is very hard to find a constituency for reorganization at the state or federal level. There was an awareness that by starting at the local level, it could conceivably generate the pressures that would help accomplish the state-level reorganization.[17]

These expectations were to be realized.

Amendment

The perception of the need for change at the state level, acknowledged both in the legislature and in the Governor's Office, led to the introduction of two bills in the 1975 session of the legislature: one to create an office responsible for developing a state-level reorganization plan, and another containing several amendments to the Human Services Act. By this time, however, the political climate had shifted, and the bills very nearly died. Their close call reflected enlivened controversy over the Human Services Act itself, as well as ill feeling between the Governor's Office and the Senate.

The amendments to HSA were introduced in the House by Representative Shirley Hokanson. Although Knutson, now a senator, coauthored the bill in the Senate, partisan feeling had grown to the point that, as a Republican, he was no longer effective as a sponsor. Some observers considered the amendments to be "technical, not too controversial"; others maintained they raised important issues about HSA. Concerning the rise of controversy over HSA, Hokanson commented, "It's the old story. Everybody agrees with something conceptually, and in 1973, it was conceptual, permissive legislation for the counties; you can do it if you want. Then, once Dick and the outfit got going on this in 1974, then you got some reaction."

One amendment called for permissive language concerning the numbers of lay people to be included on the human services boards; the commissioners apparently did not want to get "bogged down" with uninformed private citizens, and the legislature was in a mood to compromise. A second issue concerned the 50,000 population floor. Several smaller counties, such as Scott County, wanted to establish Human Services boards of their own. While this ran contrary to the legislature's hopes for "economies of scale," it was finally decided to include some exceptions for individual counties if the State Planning Agency approved. The third major issue concerned alternatives to the Human Services Board format. One county had been operating under a "professional planning council" and sought approval for this model. Hokanson recalled:

One region came in and [lobbied] to have something called a joint planning council. "Let's go back to a loose configuration and we'll all get along together. . . ." It was very hard to say, "That isn't what [HSA] is about. You don't need legislation to get together. This is an economy — or management — thing."

Apparently professionals who sought this model were successful in putting some pressure on the legislature, as language was eventually tagged on referring to "other possibilities" with regard to the Human Services Act. A counterproposal from Broeker would have required Human Services boards by 1978. It was his belief that the political costs of opting for a Human Services Board at the county level could be minimized by eliminating any choice in the matter. "We could have had Human Services Boards wall to wall in this state," Broeker said, "but when professionals came in and lobbied against it, everybody chickened out."

The office to develop a state-level reorganization plan was designed by OPD and State Planning. As they saw it, the Office of Human Services would continue OPD's function as a temporary change agent in state government. The Office of Human Services would be charged with keeping reorganization alive and preventing the state bureaucracy from obliterating what thus far remained an incomplete reform movement by converting the concept to an operationally complete system.

As such, the Office of Human Services became a relatively controversial proposal in 1975, and it was only with great difficulty that the office was finally approved. In particular, apprehension concerning the bill persisted within the Senate. According to Scribner, who was again responsible for lobbying:

The Governor's Office fought tooth and nail, all the way from committee, to subcommittee to committee, on the floor and in the conferences, to get that Office of Human Services. That became the key piece . . . to get it all together in one place, the whole reorganization.

While the difficulty was due in part to "temperamental personalities" as well as to increasing hostility between the Senate and the Governor's Office, a major factor was the upcoming 1976 election in which a large percentage of senators would be running.

Several professional associations had become apprehensive of the direction the state was taking. Vocational Rehabilitation, as noted in the previous chapter, had mounted a national campaign against this very sort of thing. VR had a reputation for being a powerful agency in Minnesota and was capable of generating heavy pressure on legislators. Thus, despite legislative opposition, VR had enough political clout to get a bill through the 1976 session which separated it from the Department of Education and left it a freestanding agency.

More opposition came from the state agencies. Scribner attributed this to:

administrative and professional concern in the state agencies over the Office of Human Services bill; because the bill proposed studying all eleven separate agencies — some of them small and some of them big — with an idea to creating maybe only one department.

And so the opposition at the state level surfaced and made it much more difficult. In fact, I don't think we ever did get enthusiastic commitment from the agencies to the Office of Human Services. They kinda said, "Well, we'll go along with this because you want it." But we always had the feeling that there were folks in there that were doing what they could against it.

As it happened, the bill creating the Office of Human Services and the HSA amendments only survived as a rider to the 1975 Health and Welfare appropriations, and Governor Anderson had to supplement the availability of funds with an executive order establishing OHS.

Change of Direction

The creation of OHS altered the processes of change in a number of respects. First, the legislature essentially dropped out of the human services picture for the next two years while the state-level reorganization plan was being developed. Second, enthusiasm for the HSA pilot projects ebbed, and it was noted that OHS did not show full support for the HSA pilot projects. The Human Services boards were an unproven approach, and insufficient data were available to justify their full support. Indeed, after the Office of Human Services was established, many felt that the county-oriented approach to human services reform was abandoned, with attention shifting almost exclusively to reform of the state agencies. A third development was the selection of a director for OHS. In the view of a number of legislators, Broeker, who knew the people and the politics of human services, would have been a logical choice to head the new agency, but because of remembered political disagreements with the governor he was never a candidate. Governor Anderson instead appointed William Quirin, a former legislator and highway department lobbyist, to the position. "With that," says Knutson, "a good thing went down the drain." The choice was especially unfortunate from Knutson's point of view because Quirin was too exclusively a "governor's man." With Quirin, "they got control of the project," and communications with interested legislators broke down. Hokanson noted that "the subcommittee on Governmental Operations had to beg to get information from OHS."

Under Quirin, the process of developing a state-level reorganization plan began with his borrowing one full-time staff member from each of the operating agencies. These individuals served as liaison to his office and reported back weekly to their agencies. Next, meetings were convened of all the departmental commissioners at which they were asked to identify the major obstacles to effective human services delivery. According to the OHS *Final Report*:

The major focus was to be on management reforms rather than services integration. But within the management reform, OHS was seeking policy integration for the major human service policy areas, such as income, job training and placement, health, social services, and corrections. The mechanism for policy integration was to be a single accountable organization and policy focus for similar programs.[18]

OHS studied six alternative organizational structures. The umbrella over the existing agencies (their example was Massachusetts) was rejected because "a council or secretariat has limited authority over the agencies, and it is difficult to initiate coordination because each agency retains its own planning and budgeting responsibilities, management support functions, special interest group connections, and client focus." A structure oriented around target groups — children, the aging, the handicapped, the unemployed, and poor — was not considered further because it would perpetuate fragmentation of service delivery to clients with more than one problem. In addition, there would be problems in relating to federal revenue sources, which were program oriented. An option whereby all existing planning agencies, commissions, and the like related to the four basic program categories of health, welfare, corrections, and employment would be consolidated into four departments was dismissed as insufficient to achieve policy integration. Abandoned as well was a "superagency" option, which would have incorporated ten agencies into one department.[19] OHS felt that, in Minnesota, program visibility was as important a consideration as centralization of administrative functions and that the two objectives should be balanced. In addition, the OHS report suggested that such an agency would be too big and complex to manage.[20]

The structure ultimately recommended resulted from identifying programs with a common purpose or mission, and programs having similar work activities and common personnel systems (programs having state employees, those having local employees, and those having both). On the basis of this analysis, two clusters of programs were created: employment security and health and social services. These clusters were converted into reorganization proposals by aligning proposed state statutory activity with federal statutes and regulations in terms of organizational requirements, powers and duties of the agency head, required programs and services, linkages with other agencies and programs, personnel requirements, and advisory committees. Drawing on the experience of Arizona,[21] this process avoided some of the pitfalls encountered by the Arizona Department of Economic Security. Because there had been little prior analysis, Arizona's DES (like Washington's DSHS) had to define itself after its creation. For this reason, a great many implementation problems had not been anticipated. OHS planners wanted to avoid similar turbulence in Minnesota.

In December of 1976 OHS recommended to the legislature that two new departments be created: the Department of Economic Security (DES, comprising Comprehensive Employment and Training Act [CETA] and Work Incentives [WIN] programs, Unemployment Insurance, Employment Services, VR, and Income Maintenance) and the Department of Health and Social Services (DHSS, comprising Corrections, Social Services, and Health). The Economic Security cluster would include all programs for which the client outcomes were direct benefit payments and job training and placement, while the Health and Social Services cluster would include programs focused on residential care and treatment, regulation of public and private service providers, and financial assistance and planning for community programs.

The OHS planners argued that state-level reorganization was necessary to achieving human services reform at the local level. They stated in their December 1976 publication, *Economic Security and Health and Social Services: A Strategy for Change in State Government*:

Minnesota cannot expect continued change in the local delivery of human services without first making significant changes at the state level. There is a recognized need to reorder state functions and activities in order to allow for more effective management of state delivered services and to continue the momentum of county change efforts by more effectively supporting locally managed systems.

Regardless of OHS hopes for the effort, critics argued that concentration on state-level management changes had not produced all the results predicted, as even OHS came to admit. As noted in the OHS *Final Report,* prepared after legislative debates over reorganization had occurred:

There were several problems with the management change focus. The legislative focus is at the target group level, since this is the level of concern for lobby and vested interest groups. Furthermore, it is difficult to make the case that a reorganization which focuses primarily on management changes will, in fact, result in better services to clients, or that better services will develop rapidly. Rather, the management focus tended to raise concerns of big government, additional layers of government, lowered program visibility, and a lack of management capability to manage a large department that has many separate programs.[22]

The location of OHS in the Governor's Office had been hoped by staff to remove them from "day-to-day operations of any of the agencies that were to be studied and potentially included in the reorganization plan. It also gave the office a degree of objectivity whereby it could assess the overall human services system in Minnesota." Such placement also caused problems:

The placement in the Governor's Office did cause some vagueness, however, relative to who the client was that OHS was serving. The Governor's Office was obviously a client, but so was the Department of Administration, which has state reorganization responsibilities. The legislature was also viewed as a client, since it had directed OHS to submit a reorganization report to the 1977 legislative session. Finally, the delivery agencies saw themselves as clients of OHS, in terms of the reorganization proposals that OHS was developing, and in terms of the technical assistance that OHS was offering existing Human

Services Boards at the county level. This variety of potential clients did in fact cause OHS some problems with respect to how the various reports should be written, *i.e.*, what audience should the recommendations be addressed to, and who should screen the recommendations.[23]

Governor Anderson had indicated that all involved departments should offer complete cooperation in the reorganization effort. Nevertheless, when the OHS proposal was presented in 1977, the agencies were far from supportive. When Anderson left that year to fill Vice-president Walter Mondale's vacated Senate seat and Lieutenant Governor Rudy Perpich moved into the Governor's Office, "The agency people thought they were released." As it took some time for the new governor to take "ownership" of the reorganization proposals, some of the momentum behind them was lost. Coupled with a change in reporting status for OHS from the Governor's Office to the Department of Administration nine months into its operation, these events generated doubt about the support of the Governor's Office for the OHS proposal.

The OHS proposal was firmly supported by a majority of influential and knowledgeable legislators, including House Speaker Martin Sabo and representatives Rice and Hokanson. Almost immediately, however, the Department of Health and Social Services bill was held over for study. One explanation for this development is that Governor Perpich did not have enough political leverage to overcome opposition to both DHSS and DES, nor did the legislature care to adopt both proposals as its own. DHSS was seen as more controversial and unlikely to get the necessary support at that time. Both the state Health and Corrections departments initially expressed animosity toward a DHSS. (Some of the pressure for creating DHSS was defused by the success of a contemporaneous bill that altered the powerful state Board of Health from Administrative to advisory status. Subsequently, the Health Department shifted its position on DHSS and supported it.)

Ultimately composed of four divisions — Management Support, Employment and Training, Unemployment Insurance, and Vocational Rehabilitation — and a strong Commissioner's Office, the Department of Economic Security was "pushed through" the legislature. According to Representative John Brandl, many legislators were for it because it would "bring together the worlds of work and welfare, change the public conception, the stigma, and make work more accessible while minimizing the number of organization units." However, aggressive "arm twisting," as one observer put it, on the part of the governor also influenced the outcome.

Categorical Controversies

The two main controversies surrounding the DES proposal were the transfer of DPW's Income Maintenance Program to the new department and the inclusion of Vocational Rehabilitation.

The somewhat ambivalent stance of DPW occasioned by the projected loss of a significant program on the one hand, the governor's mandate to support the DES proposal on the other, is evident in the testimony of then DPW commissioner Vera Likins before the Senate Committee on Operations:

I should like to preface anything I have to say on the proposal to create a Department of Economic Security with the statement that in my belief almost any organizational structure can be made to work — with significant support and control from the chief executive and sufficient financial support and policy direction from the Legislature. This applies to the present organizational structure as well as to the proposal. In this sense, there are no insurmountable problems that would be occasioned by the passage of S.F. 202.

After this seemingly supportive beginning, Commissioner Likins proceeded to list the "surmountable" problems surrounding the creation of the department. In addition to noting that collection of services would cost a good deal more than the $150,000 allocated for management start-up costs, Likins stated that she could not see any appreciable improvement in (or, for that matter, detriment to) quality of services, cost effectiveness, or efficiency engendered by a new department. Ultimately, Commissioner Likins's testimony emerged as a model of political balancing. Although taking a formal stance of bureaucratic neutrality, Likins tied high projected costs and effort to low anticipated gains. While noting in conclusion that it made sense to establish one department where all income needs could be met, the sum total of her testimony remained negative in tone.

Within Minnesota government as a whole, the most vocal opponent to the integration effort was the Division of Vocational Rehabilitation, which up until 1977 was a part of the Department of Education. VR lobbied aggressively, but unsuccessfully, to stay out of the Department of Economic Security and to retain the independent status it had won from the 1976 legislature. The story is worth telling for what it reveals of the inner dynamics of organizational change.

According to August Gehrke, then acting commissioner for Vocational Rehabilitation in Minnesota, VR has been historically associated with education. Nevertheless, as part of Minnesota's Department of Education, VR considered itself misunderstood — as well as mistreated:

In 1957 when I became Assistant Commissioner for Vocational Rehabilitation and Special Education, I administered both programs. But conceptually Education and Vocational Rehabilitation are miles apart, as Education is a flow-through activity that has a centralized unit all done out in the field, i.e., the school, while VR is a direct operation, our counselors in the field do the work.

They just did not understand that concept. . . . Every now and then a legislator or governor would say, "Hey, commissioner, you got to get a handle on those guys." So they tried to get a handle on it. . . . They took advantage of the opportunity and integrated about twenty-six or twenty-seven of our staff through the indirect cost method. They took over one million dollars of our money away from the handicapped and they took those people. So we lost control of accounting; we lost control of personnel; we lost control of public information, our data processing, our library, our training.

This series of incidents, coupled with VR's self-perceived lack of political visibility, led the division to fight for separate agency status. According to Gehrke, the Minnesota Rehabilitation Association (MRA) went to the legislature "and showed them where over one million dollars of Rehabilitation money was taken away from the handicapped, and control of twenty-six positions that formerly did Rehab work. It was being integrated, and it was not going to the handicapped."

Convincing the legislature was difficult, especially as human services integration was a popular topic of discussion in the legislature and in the Governor's Office. Yet MRA was able to line up several supportive legislators and managed to get the Republicans "fairly well solidified behind us." Despite a mandatory delay on actually achieving independent status that was put into the bill by amendment, VR was at last free of the Department of Education, at least in principle.

The Office of Human Services, however, was moving in a different direction. Along with other human services agencies, VR officials were obliged to participate in a reorganization exercise that they knew was likely to jeopardize its hard-won independence. VR did attempt to explain its position to OHS:

There was no consensus; we met with [OHS] on a regular basis. Bill Quirin went before the Council for the Handicapped and the Handicapped asked him what input did we have? What input do the consumers have? "We told you when the meetings were. You could have come and participated." Now is that input? That is no input.

Gehrke believed that VR was ignored by OHS, and at the same time Governor Perpich's attitude was changing. "Prior to his becoming Governor, he gave little evidence of interest in OHS legislation. But as he became Governor, it became obvious he was supporting it." In fact, shortly after assuming the office, Perpich called a meeting of all the commissioners and announced that he had decided to go ahead with DES.

When the DES bill reached the legislature, it was heavily lobbied by the Minnesota Rehabilitation Association, the American Federation of State, County and Municipal Employees Council, and a number of client groups. Said Gehrke, "MRA showed them about twenty organizations who were opposed to it including almost every consumer. . . . We had people who went to Arizona and came back frustrated; they wanted no part of it. We showed them evidence again and again."

The division became a separate department on July 1, 1977, following the delay required in the 1976 law creating it. As OHS reorganization studies proceeded, possible incorporation into DES raised a number of concerns in VR. Legal questions were raised about the fact that not all of the state's VR legislation was incorporated into the DES bill. The issues were similar to those debated in Florida, and, in fact, Gehrke was among the witnesses who testified against Florida's 1978 reorganization:

I testified August 2, 1976. I was then President of the National Rehabilitation Association, and this, of course, was when HEW said Florida was no longer in compliance. The National Rehabilitation Association then joined as a friend of the court with HEW and I was one of the witnesses in that area.

Very specifically [the law] says that in order to obtain money from the federal government, you must have a state administrator and there has to be that unit — the organized structure — identified as VR, and not integrated into the rest of the programs. My testimony was to the fact that Florida did not comply with the law.

While the Florida issue was on its surface "legalistic," Gehrke considered the rationale behind those legal requirements to be the heart of the matter: preserving the quality and expertise of the VR system.

For instance, in Florida, the trained rehab counsellors are now doing social work; they're doing everything. . . . [The handicapped] should be able to go to a person who has specific training in that area and who is prepared to deal with the issue. If I have a very bad tooth to be pulled, where do I go? I go to a specialist.

The "generalist" emphasis of the services integration movement, then, was seen as a major threat to VR's expertise. Although former OHS employees assert that DES avoided both program homogenization and the generalist approach, VR's fears were not assuaged. Moreover, VR was not convinced that integration actually benefits the client. Gehrke recalled the "one-stop boondoggle" in Arizona,

where people were forced to go through every single avenue of human service intake when they only came in there to pick up an unemployment compensation check. The only problem was that they were unemployed. They had to go through a comprehensive review system, which was absolutely unnecessary.

Integrated service centers, Gehrke argued, force the clients to respond to the center's needs rather than the other way around.

At the state level, VR felt the human services reorganization movement did not serve its interests because the trend toward multidiscipline agencies jeopardized accountability and control of funds as well as visibility for the handicapped's special needs. Although the implementation of the new Minnesota Department of Economic Security proceeded on schedule and all divisional support systems (including VRs) were integrated on January 1, 1979, some observers expressed the belief that it would be some time, if ever, before VR considered itself part of a "group effort."

The Legislature Decides
In the Minnesota House, the rationale behind VR's inclusion in DES was that it belonged with other state-employment-related services. In addition, by the time the bill passed, many legislators were so tired of VR's "overkill" lobbying that the ultimate response was negative, not positive.

In the Senate, Knutson was interested in seeing VR retain its independent status. More important, Senator John Chenoweth, a long-time "friend of VR" and the chairman of the Governmental Operations Committee, wanted it out of the reorganization. The battle between Senate forces favoring exclusion of Vocational Rehabilitation from DES and House forces favoring inclusion was protracted. An amendment to remove VR was added to the original reorganization proposal by Senator Chenoweth's committee. The House then reamended the bill to include VR again. The Senate bill's co-authors split. Senator Moe's motion to concur in the House amendment carried 31-28, while a Chenoweth countermotion lost 27-34, making the final vote 36-23 to include VR in DES somewhat anticlimatic.

In general, the strongest forces to be arrayed against DES appeared in the hearings before Chenoweth's committee. Set against professional rehabilitation, client, and local interests were both the Human Services Boards and the Association of Minnesota Counties, which strongly supported VR's inclusion. Federal representatives of HEW's Rehabilitation Services Administration and DOL's Employment and Training Administration from the Chicago regional headquarters appeared at the request of local officials to testify as to what the consequences of reorganization would be for federal approval of grants-in-aid to the state. One observer remembers these representatives warning the legislature that the state might have to write new plans and get them approved. "None of these things were hurdles, all could be done, but they kept raising them as if they might be grave problems."

Although federal opposition to DES was relatively slight, the presence of these two federal agencies during a state debate over human services organization was strongly reminiscent of the Arizona experience, and not coincidentally. The history of the Arizona Department of Economic Security had been an object of intense interest to Minnesota since the early planning stages of its own DES. The Office of Human Services had invited John Huerta, the director of the Arizona agency at the time, and Deputy Director Arlyn Larson to Minnesota for a series of conferences on the Arizona experience. Subsequently, a delegation of Minnesota legislators visited Arizona to discuss the

Arizona agency in detail. The conclusions derived from information gained during these visits were mixed. Many representatives found positive elements in Arizona's DES; yet senators such as John Chenoweth were strongly influenced by its negative aspects (and by the antiagency arguments of Arizona representative Sam McConnell). Therefore, the history of Arizona's DES played a significant role in the hearings before the Minnesota Governmental Operations Committee, as did that of Florida's Department of Health and Rehabilitative Services. Chenoweth's apparently persuasive argument against DES was that Arizona had experienced a two-to-three year period of reduced services quality, during which time the department directed a good deal of money and effort to internal reorganization. Why, he argued, should Minnesota sacrifice its premier position as a state with already high-quality services if improved communications and collocation of services could be obtained by means other than reorganization?

In the end, Income Maintenance was not included in DES. Though this exclusion undercut the original "workfare" rationale for creating a new department, it also assured that the bureaucratic infighting that had occurred in Arizona would be avoided.

Not all of the administrative reform efforts of the legislature in the 1977 session were concerned with DES. House Speaker Martin Sabo,[24] who had been a strong supporter of the Human Services Act, introduced a bill to award state social services money to counties in the form of block grants. According to Kevin Kenney, the proposal was born out of Speaker Sabo's frustration with the constant battle for funds by the categorical program agencies. He saw block grants as a way of refocusing the concerns of state agencies and further decentralizing decision making to the counties.

Other Reform Efforts
Sabo's proposal also represented an effort to correct the perceived imbalance between rural and urban counties in the allocation of budgetary resources, especially Title XX funds. The urban counties, with large planning staffs and sophisticated grantsmanship, had consistently been able to garner more money per client in the human services area than the smaller counties. The gap was as much as $4.00

versus $16.00 per capita, and Sabo's bill included a complicated redistribution formula to narrow the gap. The bill passed in the House, but bogged down in the Senate because of resistance from program interests who feared that county commissioners might not be as liberal as state administrators in allocating funds to human services, state personnel who felt they would lose the power of the purse, and larger counties, such as Hennepin and Ramsey, which got disproportionately large shares of the funds. Proponents saw this bill as a companion to the state-level reorganization bills. Opponents saw it as an attempt to get interest groups off legislative backs and to put a lid on the total amount of money spent on social services.

At the end of the 1977 session the future of Sabo's effort, like the proposal for a Department of Health and Social Services, was in doubt. It had been heavily amended, and neither Governor Rudy Perpich nor his brother George Perpich, chairman of the Senate Health and Welfare Committee and initial Senate proponent of the bill, supported its passage. Some observers saw this backing off as a response to the growth of organized opposition, focused on the complexities and contradictions within the bill and on the possible disruption of Community Health Services Act structure. Health interests, including the Department of Health itself, charged poor drafting and failure on the part of proponents to take into account the strength of existing mechanisms. These interests were given primary credit for the successful blocking of the bill during that Session. However, a modified form of the proposal passed the legislature two years later.

Established with a two-year sunset clause, OHS went out of existence in 1977, its recommendations only partially implemented. In a candid analysis of its accomplishments, authors of the OHS *Final Report* acknowledged a series of missteps. For example, they had underestimated the lack of consensus in both the legislature and the executive branch on the need for change at the state level. The technical aspects of the reorganization were not sufficiently well developed. OHS did not spend enough time explaining and advocating their proposal. During the study period, the few existing county Human Services boards could have been supported to a greater degree and further boards established, thus generating greater local support for services reform.[25]

Hennepin County

As instructive as changes made at the state level were changes occurring in many of the counties, especially Hennepin County. Centered in Minneapolis, it is Minnesota's most densely populated county
and often sets the pace for state government rather than vice versa. In
the field of human services, Hennepin has all the problems of a large
urban area and a sizable staff to address them. A product of these two
factors is Hennepin County's 1977 reorganization plan, which was
designed to "combine and coordinate human services to assure better
service delivery to clients within a rational and efficient administrative
structure." Oriented toward the client, reorganization was intended
to integrate services in the technical sense. As in all such efforts, there
were additional stakes of a political nature involved, and not all
participants had the same goals.

The reorganization plan was the work of the Office of Planning and
Development (OPD),[26] established in 1973. According to Jean Marie
Burhardt, then its director, OPD grew out of Hennepin's efforts to
rationalize and coordinate its delivery system during the early 1970s.
OPD was established four months before the state legislature enacted
the Human Services Act, and in fact was involved in developing it.
Regardless of this initial participation, Hennepin County chose not to
enroll in the Human Services Act after ratification. This was not only
because its own reorganization efforts were already under way, but
out of a conviction that the problems of Hennepin County were
unique within the state and required an approach tailored to them.

Prior to reorganization, welfare and social services were provided
by seven independent departments reporting to two separate jurisdictions, the County Board of Commissioners and the District Court
Bench. In 1972, the county board established a Coordinating Committee composed of the heads of the human services departments:
Welfare, Mental Health, Mental Retardation, the Hospital Community
Health Plan Program, and Veterans' Services. The main goal of the
committee was to address duplication, overlap, lack of coordination,
and waste in the county delivery system, and to get better control of
the cross-departmental effects of federally funded social services. The
Coordinating Committee was to develop a long-range plan for the

delivery of human services while serving as a coordinating unit for day-to-day operations.

To staff the planning functions, people were drawn from the operating departments. This should have increased communication between agencies as well as assured each agency of involvement in the reorganization plan. But some observers felt this did not always occur. Because of a tendency for the departments to assign policy people instead of program people to the committee, the effort at times lacked the program expertise needed to address integration problems at the services delivery level. Furthermore, the borrowed staff often had divided loyalties as well as other work to do. Thus, the project produced an awareness among the committee members — the department heads themselves — that the committee needed a human-services-oriented staff with its own identity.

Accordingly, the position of "associate county administrator" was created with responsibilities encompassing all health and social services, and OPD and its staff was to report to this official. The office was designed to stimulate cooperation and joint planning without becoming a central planning office in the sense that all planning and program development emanated from it.

Along with providing technical assistance to the research and planning activities of the Department of Welfare, OPD was to coordinate the development of comprehensive information support services throughout the county. In addition, it was to take the planning lead in any areas that were considered interdepartmental. Most important was OPD's function of budget review, which became the office's "life blood" and source of internal power. Some time ago, Hennepin County had centralized personnel, information systems, and accounting functions. The centralized accounting system had then been operating nearly six years, and OPD was able to use it effectively. As staff to the county board, OPD assisted in determining priorities for the use of the county's resources. Since this included everything from midyear contracts to the annual operating budgets, OPD held a strong position vis-à-vis the agencies. Backed by the county's consolidated accounting system, OPD had access to all fiscal information. With such information, OPD could point out areas where fiscal inefficiency existed. Though this kind of power worried officials in the services departments, they appeared to accept OPD as an "unfortunate fact of life" rather than as an opponent they could realistically defeat.

In December of 1975, in response to a variety of service problems, the County Board of Commissioners ordered a comprehensive study of human services delivery in Hennepin County. OPD was assigned responsibility for the study and commissioned to prepare a reorganization proposal for 1976. The study process began with the formation of eighteen employee groups. Although members of each group were randomly selected, the groups were carefully composed so as to include, for example, the appropriate percentage of unionized employees. The perception of OPD was that, whatever the final proposal, they would eventually find themselves in a "bargaining kind of arena." OPD wanted to make sure that the union, for example, could not later claim, "We haven't been consulted."

Each employee group was led by an OPD staff member and was given a set of questions to answer concerning various aspects of the service delivery system, including problem areas. This information was then condensed into a preliminary report that identified service delivery problems and advanced tentative recommendations. The reorganization proposal, which was designed on the basis of this staff work, consolidated the county's human services into three new departments: Physical Health, Community Services, and Economic Assistance. Following review by the employee groups, a report was prepared, public hearings were held, and a final version of the proposal was submitted to the board of commissioners. The plan was approved by the old county board in December of 1976, after county elections had been held, and was reaffirmed by the new board in early 1977.

Among those who opposed the plan were physicians associated with the Hennepin County Medical Center (HCMC) and the county judges, whose control over court-related human services was threatened. The judges were able to forestall changes within their spheres of influence, but the medical center ultimately lost outpatient mental health services through reorganization.* The doctors remained un-

* Originally all out-patient services were to go to community services, but as a compromise the center kept crisis intervention and the psychiatric element of Children and Adolescent Services.

convinced of the reorganization's value and for a time actively sought to reverse the changes it brought about, but with only partial success. Two issues were at stake: administrative control of county health programs and location of county mental health services.

The Hennepin County Medical Center originally controlled the administration of all county health programs. Seven years previously, the county commissioners had established the position of director of health and hospitals, to whom programs outside the jurisdiction of the hospital (alcohol programs, the pilot City Health Center, and contractual services such as Community Mental Health), as well as the hospital's director, were to report. Then the commissioners decided to reorganize by combining health programs and social services under one official. The office of Health and Hospitals was abolished and the health and welfare programs were consolidated under a director of health and social services. Commenting on this change, Dr. Richard Raile, HCMC chief of pediatrics and medical staff director, said, "What this has basically done is put in a layer of administration — new layers of administration — between the operating agencies and the policymakers." In other words, the hospital administrator no longer related directly to the county board but rather to the associate administrator who reports to the board. The result was:

We see a considerable decrease in [the board's] understanding of the problems of Health delivery. And it is primarily because if they have a question about health they don't bring it to the health administrator — the one that's directly responsible for delivering the services. They ask someone in the county building for answers, and he doesn't understand often much better than they exactly what the implications are for delivery.[27]

The 1976 OPD reorganization proposal brought this issue to the fore by recommending that a single Physical Health Department be established, consisting of the HCMC, the medical examiner, emergency medical systems, and a new Community Health Division, all under a county administrator for health. Medical interests insisted that the administrator's office be physically based in the medical center itself. According to William Kreykes, then hospital administrator:

Without that the county will experience what they've done the two previous times — setting up the top administrative person with no support from the Medical Center. Frankly, if the county is going to do anything in health it has to emanate out of here, because this is where the key staff are.

Although the new health administrator did not necessarily have to be an M.D., medical interests asked that a health professional serve as the hospital's advocate with the county board. It became clear that the matter of *who* filled the slot was as important as the issue of how the new office fit into the overall organizational design.

The second reorganization issue concerned the transfer of the hospital's out-patient mental health program to the new Department of Community Services. While OPD strongly supported this move, and mental health professionals themselves sought to escape the hospital's "medical model," HCMC's physicians saw the change as a threat to the hospital's ability to provide continuity of care. Raile explained:

They [OPD] have determined that out-patient mental health is a social service, not a health service. And so when we have a patient in psychiatry in the in-patient unit, and that patient is going to leave, we have to transfer him to a different unit of government. . . . They won't even have a common record except as we dictate things, and send them summaries, and vice versa. I think it's a mistake.

The problem Raile saw was that hospital would have to build a new capacity in order to follow up clients leaving the in-patient facility:

The main reason we're going to have to duplicate is because we cannot set their priorities for them. We cannot say, "We have got here thirty new patients that you must take because we are sending them over to you" . . . we could if they were under our administration . . . but as they are in a different segment of the county, we have to convince the county administrator or the County Board that it's necessary and that's too many layers to go through to get it done.

Nothing in reorganization was so unacceptable, from the hospital's viewpoint, as to spark a major confrontation. However, reorganization did not seem to promise better services either; the whole thing appeared to the hospital to be a case of change for change's sake. A partial compromise was finally reached, where two mental health programs remained entirely or in part with the medical center. Community Services contracted out Crisis Intervention to the hospital and split Children and Adolescent Services, with the psychiatric elements remaining at the medical center while the social work elements were placed under Community Services.

Both Raile and Kreykes held limited hope for reorganization in Hennepin County. In political terms, reorganization was seen as an attempt on the part of the board to reduce the hospital's independence. Since only 7 percent of the hospital's budget came from county property taxes, the commissioners had relatively little control over it. Raile sensed some frustration with and mistrust of the hospital because of its relative independence. Thus, by making the top health administrator "someone who was their man," the board seemed to be aiming at making the hospital politically more responsive. Raile explained:

The Medical Center is somewhat of a threat to the county — to politicians — because we are not very political as a group. . . . Most of us are here as faculty of the university. We're not really interested in the whims of what's good politics or not. We're interested in meeting patient needs, and the education of health manpower.

And when someone feels that something would be nice in his district, we're not very responsive to him politically. So there has been a sense that they would like to get a better handle on us as an organization.

Political considerations aside, the aspect of reorganization that troubled Raile most was its irrelevance to the hospital's work — delivering quality health care. While coordination and integration may sound good, Raile said,

I am not sure that it's worth the investment of people's time and money, particularly if you're more interested in delivering the service to the individual. You can put it down on a nice piece of paper as to what a wonderful thing health coordination is, but when it gets right down to the recipient of the resources, I don't know that they benefit a great deal by this coordination.

In stating their case, Dr. Raile and other medical spokesmen were in effect providing evidence of the kind of resistance to change that motivated county officials to proceed with their reorganization.

Scott County

Located just outside the Twin Cities, semi-rural Scott County is another instructive example of county reform efforts beyond the framework of the Human Services Act. It sought and was granted an exception to the 50,000 population minimum in order that it could proceed on its own. Since the turn of the century, the county has evolved from being an "incidental" provider of welfare services, such as a county poorhouse and the post-Depression social security programs, to its present position as a prime provider of services. Human services now make up better than half of the county's budget and involve nearly half of its employees. Nevertheless, the county has always played what is called a "residual role" in human services — the county did what town, private, and voluntary agencies could not do. Thus, as the townships relinquished welfare and other service responsibilities, Scott County gradually assumed them and made a concerted effort toward active leadership in county services provision. Increased control for the county board (consisting of five county commissioners elected by district and sitting as the Human Services Board), centralized accounting, and a management information system are all aspects of Scott County's attempt to rationalize human services planning and delivery.

In Scott County, as elsewhere, delivery systems developed along concurrent, categorical lines. Programs in Mental Health, Mental Retardation, Welfare, and Corrections were formed in response to federal or state incentives. Meanwhile, the county was expected to finance its part of these service activities with almost no influence over their cost, effectiveness, or relevance to local needs. Aggravated by the tremendous growth of programs during the 1960s, the fiscal issue became increasingly important to county residents. Program budgets went up, but the commissioners were reluctant to raise taxes. Moreover, state-level funding of programs seemed to follow an erratic path. As interest groups pressured the legislature, whichever discipline was in the ascendancy would get the largest chunk of new funds, and then, after a "romance period" of perhaps five years, fall back into the categorical pack. Or at least so it seemed to county officials. This ripple effect made planning difficult. In addition, the commissioners discovered that clients' problems required a more sophisticated approach than they had previously been able to offer. Realizing that continual care, case monitoring, and other complex systems were now necessary, the commissioners became receptive to state-level initiatives in human services reform.[28]

The growing official awareness of lack of accountability, good management, and planning in Scott County coincided with state-level attempts to rationalize Minnesota's human services system. Thus, the Human Services Act of 1973 seemed to provide a handle with which the commissioners of Scott County could modernize their system. Initially ineligible for HSA because it did not meet the required 50,000 population base, Scott County obtained an exemption in 1974. This exemption, in the form of special legislation, was seen at the time as having been gained through a combination of the intensive lobbying of the Scott County Human Services director and the legislature's desire to get HSA in operation as soon as possible. Subsequent efforts by other counties to obtain waivers or exemptions were less successful.

In March of 1974, an interim planning committee submitted to the state and received approval for the consolidation of Health, Welfare, and Corrections functions under a Human Services board composed of the five county commissioners and three citizen members.[29] Subsequently the reorganization effort was planned and executed by Thomas Lindquist, the county's first Human Services director. The fact that Lindquist had previously been the county welfare director proved a boon, at least in one way, in the early stages of implementation, and potential resistance to loss of "turf" by the Welfare Department was thereby avoided.

Although little opposition to reorganization was present at first, controversy soon began to embroil the director's office. Lindquist's promotion from his previous position led other county human services officials to view reorganization as a "welfare takeover." Within two years, Lindquist was being attacked by the Minnesota Nursing Association, the Association for Retarded Children, the Day Activities Center Association, and parts of the school system. The conflict was intense and resulted in a large staff turnover. Lindquist saw this opposition as reflecting apprehension concerning reorganization more than specific grievances, "because we have sought to define our responsibilities and relationships. It's all of a preliminary nature."

This view was a matter of opinion. When the Scott County public health staff (three nurses and one secretary) quit en masse, they asserted that reorganization itself was conceptually acceptable. They were leaving, they said, because communication lines with the county administration were down. Moreover, they said the county was out of compliance with Medicare and Medicaid regulations because health programs were being run by a nonmedical administrator.

Lindquist's strategy — at the heart of the controversy — was designed to change the role of the professional, to make professionals accountable to the Human Services Office. This goal was chosen as the central focus of his initial integration effort in conscious preference to the utilization of colocation and one-stop service approaches. Lindquist's goals — to identify a job and do it effectively at the most reasonable cost — were best achieved, he believed, through the development of a comprehensive information system, which he designed with the aid of Touche, Ross & Company. Comprehensive information, Lindquist felt, strengthens services, brings credibility, and results in more support for services. He explained:

When I develop a computerized management information system that gives me a running inventory day by day, week by week, of every piece of activity in the system, I know when somebody makes only two home calls as opposed to six. . . . Now that puts me in a position to ask questions about work planning, all kinds of things which are a threat to them.

Lindquist, whose background was in business administration, saw this management information system as the most sensible approach. Most of the new people hired in Scott County after the high turnover in 1976, as staff who opposed Lindquist's approach left, had previous experience with the sort of system he was developing. At the same time, the new system was apparently proving itself with regard to cost:

[While] our costs have increased in residential care about 290% since 1974 when we started keeping our data, and our direct service costs have increased about 183% since 1974, the county levy has remained the same. The fact is that we have been able to mix and match monies much more effectively. We have increased our budget by several millions of dollars each year and it does not cost the county one dime.

Having demonstrated the savings inherent in reorganization, Lindquist's office aimed for fully operational information and accounting systems by the end of 1977. Lindquist felt that many professionals remained apprehensive.

As we move into the system, people that were previously autonomous under the old system, had their own agency, [now] have to conform to certain structures and systems that they previously did not have to conform to. . . . Under this system, MBO [management-by-objectives, which he was instituting] requires that you plan in advance for expenditures. . . . If you didn't plan for that, the answer is, when you come for the money, it's not there. There are lots of people who didn't like that, so they repudiated the system.

The center where these changes were to be generated was the Special Projects Office. This office was to study the various county programs with a view toward improving their effectiveness and efficiency, and generate alternative proposals for service delivery. For example, Scott County's infant stimulation program had already been studied. It was found that the real merits of the program lay in a parent's sense of accomplishment in obtaining immediate, visible results by working with the retarded child, rather than in permanent improvement in the child. Previously, infant stimulation had been offered by the county on a case-by-case basis. Lindquist decided the program could clearly be operationalized by having one therapist train parents in groups. "What looked like it was going to cost anywhere from a quarter of a million dollars or up [was] suddenly going to be operationalized at a cost of less than $50,000."

This sort of change, according to Lindquist, was seen as a threat by staff, as what were once "professional judgments" were in the hands of administrators whose priorities were not those of the categorical service provider. Morever, the Special Projects Office would subject the programs to continuous evaluation. Nevertheless, Lindquist and the county board believed that the professionals and their programs must be made more accountable and that services must be planned and delivered on a cost-effectiveness basis. Although measurement of the quality of services was an admitted impossibility, county commissioners hoped to be able to pin down the amount of money spent for each specific job, including both direct and indirect costs. In this way they could identify the actual cost of administration or dollars spent per hour or per client. Although the MIS was not computerized until the end of 1978 and the real benefits of computerization and full input would not be evident for another six months to a year, county commissioners were convinced that already integration had allowed them to spend less money as a whole but more money on specific services.

In addition to staff resignations, elements opposed to reorganization applied pressure on the county commissioners to oust Lindquist. These elements included not only professionals but also middle management at the state agencies who disliked disruption of traditional communications with the local services system. The county board was supportive and Lindquist remained confident that reorganization would proceed:

The County Board is supportive because they can't go back to the old financing system without raising taxes 20 to 30 million dollars. They have to maintain the Management Information System and accounting in order to get the mix-match funding privilege. Because of privacy laws, re-establishment of the old agencies is impossible. You can't go back; the issue is to have options about how you go forward.

In contrast, the highly charged political atmosphere served as a frustrating but unavoidable constraint on human services reorganization.

I cannot go any faster than the commissioners will allow me to go. If I were in private industry, I would have accomplished twice as much in half the time that I can accomplish in government, for the simple fact that the technology is not the problem. It is not that we don't know how to do it; the problem is the fact that you have the will to do it. And that's what politics means. That's where if you lose the will, then you have lost the ability.

In January of 1978 Lindquist resigned his position, largely because he was exhausted. At the time of his departure, he had successfully completed implementation of his proposed common budget and management information system, and these systems remained operational. His Special Projects Office was slow to assume the program analysis and delivery innovation role that Lindquist had envisioned for it, if only because its director, Susan Smith, took the place of Lindquist upon his departure, and there was some delay in hiring her replacement. Scott County commissioners had shown a definite commitment to the Human Services Board approach right up to Lindquist's resignation, and there was little doubt that the programs Lindquist began would be carried on by his successor, chosen in December 1978. During the hiatus between permanent directors, the county commissioners themselves moved to insure the effectiveness of the new management information system, requiring information input and cooperation as a condition for continued employment by the county.

Aftermath

Faith in voluntary and gradual changes — in contrast to the "top-down," formula approaches (Florida, Georgia, and Arizona) — remained strong among those who had been involved in the design of Minnesota's human services reforms. Advocates of past proposals were most frequently criticized for their failure to build enough political support, spend enough time with interest groups, and "sell" their concepts. Future change would depend, in this view, on successful "bottom-up" creation of consensus, which would mean cultivation of county commissioners, service workers, and interest groups.

The correctness of this view is not self-evident. Proponents of DES concede that controversies associated with its creation were minimized by the failure to adopt its most controversial feature: the integration of welfare and employment programs. Controversies associated with HSA implementation were reduced not only by keeping the reforms voluntary but by later amendments and exceptions that represented a considerable retreat from the intent of its designers. The apparent success of the Corrections and Community Health acts was based in part on the absence of a threat to obviously powerful categorical program interests. One way to reduce the costs of change is to reduce the extent of change, and Minnesota change agents appear to have chosen that strategy.

One explanation for the popularity of this approach among human services reformers in Minnesota is their emphasis on improvements in services delivery. Advocates for services integration with a delivery system perspective are apt to recognize that service worker behavior and reforms in the techniques of field administration will not change simply because change is required by law or regulations. They are also more likely to realize that reform of services delivery does not have wide political appeal, and it is difficult to mobilize support for it. The patient building of acceptance is necessary for change to occur.

Experiences in Florida, Georgia, and elsewhere suggest, in contrast, that when services integration is viewed as an economy measure or as a means of achieving greater control over categorical program interests, advocates are more likely to adopt bolder strategies, to see boldness in the interests of economy as a means of building a broader and more committed constituency, and to accept compromises more grudgingly. Depending on their competence, they may also be more successful in promoting the kinds of structural changes that will alter the incentives motivating planning, resource allocation, and the assessment of performance within state human service organizations.

To a significant extent, the experiences in Hennepin and Scott counties comport with the latter perspective on the change process. The county commissioners, acting from both political and budgetary motives, were apparently determined to achieve substantial reforms involving services integration. They were evidently less concerned with building consensus within the services system than with achieving changes in the status quo, and they appear to have promoted more extensive changes in the status quo in their counties than were achieved on a statewide scale.

This approach to change has its problems. Though significant changes in the status quo have occurred in Florida, Georgia, and even in Washington and Arizona, there is simply no firm evidence that economies, cost containment, or more effective services have been the result. Gradual change built on consensus may be, in the end, the only kind of change that can bring about genuine and verifiable improvements in services delivery.

Whatever the approach, the agenda of change possibilities remained relatively broad in Minnesota. It is hard to imagine successful proposals that do not incorporate the counties into the delivery system. Subject to that constraint, advocates for change might find any of a number of ideas attractive, including the original Department of Health and Social Services and Department of Economic Security proposals, Department of Human Resources concepts, and measures for integrating services in the field. It seems unlikely that opposition from categorical program interests will govern the pace of reform. It is more likely that change in the future, beyond that which is occurring, especially in the counties, awaits an advocate, a governor or legislative leader, who has a strong personal interest and who casts the issue in management or efficiency terms, thus appealing to a broad constituency.

6
A Case of Inertia

Advocates for change in human services administration have made limited headway in Pennyslvania. Even the consolidation that occurred when Pennsylvania's Department of Public Welfare (DPW) was formed in 1957 did little more than create a loose confederation of largely autonomous agencies.[1] Despite the examples of two successful and well-publicized local services integration projects (one under DPW auspices), severe budgetary problems, and an unwieldy state administrative structure, neither the governor nor the legislature in the 1970s showed any sustained interest in building a constituency for reorganization or administrative reforms.

A proponent for change of even the modest proportions attempted in Minnesota would immediately encounter numbing inertia in Pennsylvania. The legislature, especially the House, is large, disorganized, and relatively uninterested in human services policy and organization. Program interests have little inclination to work together. The counties, which administer most programs, are diverse, and reluctant to surrender any more of their limited autonomy to central authorities. To observers in the state, the prospects for change have seemed poor.

Yet it was not long ago that similar statements could have been made about most of the states in this study, certainly, for example, about Georgia before the election of Jimmy Carter. The case for governmental reorganization is as strong in Pennsylvania as it has been anywhere. The efforts needed to achieve it would have to be at least as great as elsewhere, however. The magnitude of the effort required, rather than any unique or peculiar feature of Pennsylvania politics, appears to have inhibited the governor and legislative leaders from taking up the issue.

Past Reorganizations

A brief look at earlier political interest in executive reorganization suggests that the issue is dormant, rather than nonexistent.

The first extensive modern attempt to reorganize Pennsylvania state government was that of George Leader, governor from 1955 to 1959. Contemporaries viewed Leader as a charismatic individual endowed with a willingness to confront the legislature on critical issues. His initial effort, culminating in the Reorganization Act of 1955, resulted in several departmental transfers of function, though not nearly the number Leader had aimed for. A transfer of the State Planning Board from the Department of Commerce to the Governor's Office underlined Leader's conviction that the Office of the Governor lacked power and staff. Subsequently, following recommendations by the Pennsylvania Economy League to the previous governor, John S. Fine, Leader expanded his own personal staff under a secretary to the governor (largely in the legislative and public relations areas) and added bureaus for program evaluation, budget, management methods, personnel, and accounts, all under a secretary of administration.[2] Since its creation, the Office of the Secretary of Administration has continued to grow in size and influence. Initially, the new Office of Adminstration was perceived as a professional rather than a political staff. As such, it provoked resistance from program officials and legislators who resented the intrusion of "eggheads" and "P.A. boys" into previously sacrosanct territory.[3] Leader interpreted this resentment as legislative resistance to badly needed reform in the executive capacity of the state.

In dealing with what he considered the biggest roadblock to change in Pennsylvania, political patronage, Leader attempted to enlarge the coverage of the merit system (in 1955 14,000 state jobs were under the merit system and 51,000 under political patronage) in the hope of ending the long-term and somewhat infamous role of politics in appointments to Pennsylvania state jobs.[4] Though Leader fell short of his goal, major expansion of the merit system occurred under William Scranton, who was governor from 1963 to 1967, when 13,000 DPW employees were put under the state merit system. By that time, both state and federal programs encouraged the institution of full merit systems, and eventually this result was largely achieved. State mental health and mental retardation staff who delivered services at the county level were converted to civil service in 1976, and the staff of each county's area aging agency were converted to state civil service as of 1977. In combination with the efforts of public employee unions, particularly the American Federation of State County and Municipal Employees (AFSCME), the ratio of political to nonpolitical jobs has been reversed.

Leader also moved to consolidate human service programs. In conjunction with the Pennsylvania legislature, Leader sponsored a Merger Committee, which recommended combining the departments of Wel-

/

fare and Public Assistance to form the present Department of Public Welfare. In all, five coequal program bureaus were incorporated into DPW, including the bureaus of Mental Health, Aging, Children and Youth, Public Assistance, and the Blind. According to some observers, this reorganization had more than administrative implications. Harold Shapiro, Leader's welfare secretary, had been replacing political appointees in critical state mental hospital posts with qualified professionals. His actions generated resistance among the powerful boards at these institutions, many of which had members who were legislators. Some legislators advocated the merger of the departments of Public Assistance and Welfare, in the hope of ousting Shapiro. However, Leader was able to forestall this move and appoint Shapiro as head of the new Department of Public Welfare. Leader's unusual personal energy and charisma explain his relatively substantial accomplishments in the face of inertia and active opposition.

A more recent effort at reorganization initiated by Governor Raymond Shafer (1968–72) also met with only partial success.[5] In 1969, the Bureau of Systems Analysis in the Governor's Office of Administration updated an earlier study recommending a thoroughgoing executive reorganization. The focus of the study was economy and efficiency in state government, and much attention was paid to the nationwide movement toward increasing the planning and management capabilities of state government. The forward to the study catalogued the reform efforts of some two dozen states and quoted governor of Massachusetts John Volpe: "(I)f our States *fail* to economize, if they *fail* to become more efficient, if they *fail* to streamline their administration and their operations, then even all the gold in Fort Knox won't be enough to support our archaic forms of State government from coast to coast."

The study's release was timed to allow implementation within the transition period between governors. Although the study recommended the reorganization of fifty-two government units into twenty, only two departments were ever created: a Department of Natural Resources and a Department of Transportation. Even the proposed Department of Natural Resources did not remain unscathed. It became a Department of Environmental Resources after sportsmen's groups succeeded in detaching the Fish and Game Commission. Health interests, which feared a lessening of their role in controlling health programs in the state, resisted the proposed Department of Human Services (DHS). This department — which would have combined the Department of Public Welfare and Department of Health plus the Bureau of Vocational Rehabilitation, Veterans' Assistance, and Government Donated Food — was never authorized. The Department of Human Services was offered to legislators as an administrative improvement with no program rationale that might have attracted some interest. Further, there had been no joint executive-legislative group, such as Governor Leader's Merger Committee, to involve the legislature in the planning process. Therefore, when doubts arose, proponents of a Department of Human Services could generate little support.

Shortly after releasing the proposal, Governor Shafer tried an unusual maneuver. He appointed the secretary of Health, Dr. Thomas Georges, to a second post as acting secretary of Public Welfare.[6] The move was intended to show that a consolidation, such as that reflected in the DHS proposal, could work, but it had the opposite effect. Both Health and Public Welfare saw the move as contrary to their interests. Each department soon charged that Dr. Georges was ignoring it for the sake of the other. The legislature, which was debating the issue of DHS at that time, saw the move as an attempt to act without legislative authority. With Georges's eventual resignation (for a variety of reasons, including legislative hearings formally exploring DPW regionalization but widely perceived as aimed at Georges), the dual-secretary role ended.

Since that time little or no support has existed in Pennsylvania for consolidation of governmental units, and some seventy-odd agencies still report directly to the governor. Not only that, but approximately 2600 municipal units of government have jurisdiction over services delivery. Thus, power and responsibility for human services are diffuse, and defining the purposes, nature, and support necessary to achieve changes requires painstaking effort.

The Shapp Administration

The failure of Governor Milton Shapp's administration to effect change cannot be attributed to an absence of effort. During his eight years as governor, from 1971 to 1979, Shapp's office initiated several proposals to improve the consistency of regional planning and to promote services integration. Their common shortcoming seemed to be inadequate effort to build a constituency for change among legislators, local officials, state agencies, and the public. There appeared to be neither executive leadership, an active use of the power of the office to win support (in the manner of Jimmy Carter or Dan Evans), nor the patient construction of informal networks of change agents (as occurred in Minnesota). Even a well-conceived reorganization strategy might not have succeeded during this period; a poorly designed one was bound to fail.

The initial effort of the Shapp administration in the human services area was singularly unsuccessful. Early in his tenure, Shapp issued an executive order requiring all state agencies and boards to conduct their planning in terms of ten uniform regions. At the time, more than sixty different regional schemes were being used by state and federal programs. Through the Governor's Office of State Planning and Development and the Pennsylvania Program for Balanced Growth, the governor hoped not only to coordinate state planning but to insure that the "geographic aspects of all State and Federal programs should be eventually consistent with the uniform regions."[7] Resistance from the agencies and boards as well as failure on the governor's part to follow through brought an end to this effort. As a result, not one change in any Pennsylvania regional structure occurred from the 1972 mandate.[8] Even when agency heads strongly supported regionalism and the uniform regions, which was the case with DPW secretary Helene Wohlgemuth, change was nearly nonexistent.

Following Shapp's decision in 1974 not to reappoint Helene Wohlgemuth to a second term as DPW secretary, he convened a Governor's Commission on Human Services with Wohlgemuth as its head. The primary recommendation of this commission was an initiative entitled the Governor's Regional Improvement Program (GRIP). Again, the objective was to strengthen regional decision making by decentralizing and realigning authority over program administration in terms of the ten uniform regions. Each region would be headed by a management team, which would coordinate all services and programs within the region and settle disputes at the regional level. For a variety of reasons, the idea was abandoned at the final planning stages by the Governor's Office. Supporters of GRIP argued that the governor's

staff and the agency heads feared that their role in services coordination and planning would be greatly reduced and they therefore
vetoed it. Doubts were expressed concerning the merits of the idea:
Would strong regions really mean better services? Finally, some involved in the effort objected to the likely appointment of Helene
Wohlgemuth as the director of GRIP. Certain objections could be
countered. GRIP supporters charged, for example, that cabinet offices
confused delegation of authority with relinquishment of authority. The
objection to Wohlgemuth was a basic roadblock, however. During
her tenure as secretary of DPW, from 1970 to 1974, she had alienated
a number of state officials. The fact that her appointment as head of
GRIP was viewed as consolation for Shapp's not reappointing her as
DPW secretary meant that Wohlegemuth opponents had to oppose
GRIP.

Prior to this time, the governor's staff had taken over functions,
mostly of a policymaking nature, in Developmental Disabilities[9] and
drug and alcohol programs previously carried out in the Department
of Public Welfare. The governor's inclusion of the Developmental
Disabilities Planning Council in his own office was intended to enforce
coordination from the top, following unsuccessful attempts to get the
agencies to coordinate their activities voluntarily. Many observers feel
that this maneuver accomplished little more than the nourishment of
separatist ambitions by other categorical programs. Drug and alcohol
programs were in fact added to the Governor's Office by the legislature
for the same reasons that Developmental Disabilities had been placed
there. These programs have since effectively increased their visibility
and political appeal, with the budget rising to $16 million and a staff
three times the size of the DPW Mental Health Division, in which
they were formerly located. Yet services administration was still the
responsibility of mental health–mental retardation officials in thirty-
seven of forty-one drug and alcohol county units. Thus, these coordination functions of the Governor's Office were often seen as dupli-
cating those of DPW, especially within DPW:

The reality was that the [Developmental Disabilities] Council hasn't
been effective at all, so the MR has remained just as potent in making
its decisions about mental retardation as it always was. The DD
Council, in effect, became another layer of bureaucracy to deal with.[10]

According to another official,

A great many excellent program developments arose in the Shapp administration. But little was done about real services integration. The Governor's Office was interested. But its activity seems to be devoted to trying to achieve coordinated human services delivery by its own staff activities. A better way would have been to give leadership to the Department of Public Welfare, the legislature and citizen groups. . . . The Governor's staff interest in the subject projected them into a peer relationship with DPW. You can't coordinate your peers.[11]

Shapp's next move was to create, by executive order, a Human Services Management Council to further integration efforts. The Executive Order mentions interagency coordination and promotion of the uniform substate regions, but participants did not see the council as especially effective. Agency heads met together to discuss human services policy only during the monthly meetings of the council, and these meetings were chaired not by the governor but by the governor's special assistant for human services, Milton Berkes.[12] Such arrangements had the paradoxical effect of fostering the view that the governor was insulating himself from the agency heads.

Professional staff for the Human Services Management Council came from the Governor's Office of Human Resources (OHR). In conjunction with the Office of Intergovernmental Affairs in the HEW regional office and the Pennsylvania Intergovernmental Council (PIC) Task Force on Human Resources, this council's primary role was to oversee five grants designed to promote services integration at the county level. Using a human services coordinating board for the first year, counties chosen for the demonstration selected the programs, but they were required to include the basic county programs covered by Title XX of the Social Security Act. Eventually, the demonstration projects were designed to cover all state and federal human services programs. The goal was the development of a viable model for a countywide human services system that could be utilized in any county in the state.

The approach closely resembles that involved in Minnesota's 1973 Human Services Act, and not accidentally. Gary Rossman of the Pennsylvania State Association of Counties indicated that he had conferred at length with the Minnesota Association of Counties concerning HSA, its successes and failures, and had incorporated much of the Minnesota experience in the pilot program.

Detractors of the effort point to its shaky premises — that adequate financing would be available, that counties could utilize the Human Services board effectively, and that an integrated approach would be viable in other than the more rural counties. At least one observor, Norman Lourie of DPW, questioned whether this sort of pilot project could be effectively led by the Governor's Office alone without a legislative commitment:

The Governor's Office ought to be bringing these departments and programs together, working with the cabinet officers towards broadening local service integration. Doing the Department's job out of the Governor's Office won't change the Department's behavior. The next Governor can drop the effort. There is no legislative base or motivation to change, and legislative change is essential.

Lourie continued: "They may improve what goes on day-to-day, but they cannot change the inconsistencies and barriers of the legislative base." Other DPW officials candidly admitted that they did not place great faith in the Governor's Office to achieve services integration in Pennsylvania. One noted, "My impression of the Governor's Office of Human Resources is that . . . it's been more of a holding company than an innovator."

Officials associated with the county projects see the problem somewhat differently. While not meeting with overt opposition from DPW, they have universally encountered a lack of support, especially during the critical start-up period. Moreover, the majority do not share the DPW view of the Governor's Office. They see the Office of Human Services and the Human Services Management Council as effective human service innovators in Pennsylvania government. Since the original demonstration projects began in 1974, DPW support for county initiatives has increased. Yet no project staff or participants were confident that such support would survive the 1979 change of governors.

The Legislature

In 1977 the Commonwealth of Pennsylvania was without a budget for nearly six weeks before it was finally approved by the legislature. The primary issue in the budget deadlock was a proposed $300 million in new taxes (the proposed state budget totaled $5.4 billion).

The tax issue in Pennsylvania loomed large for several reasons. Taxes had not been raised since 1971, and were actually lowered in 1974 during Governor Shapp's re-election campaign. The tax increase was connected to increases in the budget for social services, which triggered revival of a long-standing conflict between Philadelphia and Pittsburgh urban interests and the state's rural counties. During the crisis, five to seven hundred welfare recipients, primarily from Philadelphia and Pittsburgh, appeared in Harrisburg to protest the state's failure to issue welfare checks until the budget was approved.

After forty-two days without a state budget, the Senate compromised between raising income taxes by 2.3 percent to raise the $300 million and holding the line on the social services budget by taking the $300 million for social services from the state college and university budget. The delay in approving the $5.1 billion budget left the state schools without funds until September, or whenever the legislature would again take up the tax question.

This sort of paralysis, not at all unprecedented in state government, is the result of a number of problems, some acute, others chronic, that affected the manner in which the legislature approached both long-standing issues and possible reform. For example, Speaker of the House Fineman, once regarded as the state's most powerful Democrat, resigned May 21, 1977, in an influence-peddling scandal, leaving the House without a leader to push through the budget. The House minority leader, Robert J. Butera, a gubernatorial candidate, took the opportunity to announce: "The people of Pennsylvania do not want to put one more single tax dollar into a state government corrupted by a leaderless administration."[13] Such infighting, coupled with the unusual size of the House (203 members), is symptomatic of a long-standing problem in the Pennsylvania House of Representatives. One study notes: "Anyone who has attended a session of the House must sympathize with the problems of its members in trying to find out what is going on and with the problems of leaders in maintaining decorum and organizing a majority for the movement of legislation."[14]

Despite some effort to reduce the number of committees from 32 to 23 in the House and 21 to 19 in the Senate, many observers believe there are still too many for effective performance. These committees are staffed in an eclectic manner, with the House Democratic side staffed in teams by committee, the House Republican side centrally staffed, and the Senate staffed on a primarily personal basis.[15]

It is in part, then, basically legislative disorganization that has led to the less-than-effective role the legislature has historically taken in Pennsylvania human services issues. An additional factor, again not at all unique to Pennsylvania, is the relative lack of interest in human services issues among legislators. As one former legislator explained:

Human services integration has not caught on with legislators. . . . [Legislators don't] take on a major interest in human services because of their own personal interest, or because it is good for them politically, because it's not. There are no votes in that. Poor people don't vote, mentally ill people don't vote.[16]

Rather than having a professional background in the area, those legislators who do become involved in human services questions often are doing so out of personal concern (e.g., a retarded child, a major human services facility in their home district). Moreover, general legislative interest in services delivery seems to arise only in the event of a major services breakdown or public outcry about a specific issue. Even then, the response is to revise the budget, as opposed to analyzing the delivery systems and diagnosing their problems. One observer noted, "The systemic problems are much harder to solve. When a constituent comes in and says, 'Why can't I get some out-patient services for my mentally retarded child?' the reaction is to go try and get that service for that particular child." And, as noted by Eva Kepp, executive director for the House Health and Welfare Committee, so long as the legislative role remains ad hoc problem solving, staffing will remain inadequate to undertake serious long-term decision making. The counterpart of Minnesota's Howard Knutson and Florida's Louis de la Parte has not yet emerged in the Pennsylvania Legislature.

Budgetary dilemmas may alter this picture. Legislators were becoming more interested in programs, that is, in *how* the state funds were spent. For example, the shift of drug and alcohol program oversight to the Governor's Office was a legislative initiative aimed at providing greater program oversight. In addition, there have been moves toward sunset laws and full legislative review of new agency regulations and appropriations. In 1976 the legislature began to review state agency use of the federal funds flowing into the state. This process slowed down federal program approvals and resulted in complaints from agency workers in DPW local offices whose jobs are affected by the slowness of the central office to sign contracts.[17] One consequence of the new process was the failure to pay Medicaid and Aid to Dependent Children funds to 815,000 welfare recipients while budget issues were being resolved. A consumer suit resulted in a federal court ruling that the legislature had no power to block distribution of federal funds earmarked for state welfare programs.[18]

Growing concern of legislators over program matters has gradually extended into the area of program policy development. The 1976 Mental Health Procedures Act, written by a consortium of the Mental Health and Welfare Committee and the Department of Public Welfare, is representative. The act makes it more difficult to commit a person and, once committed, to keep him or her in a mental hospital without cause for an extended period. (Similar acts have been adopted in many states.) This act was not uncontroversial. Besides the possible reduction in hospital population (adding to the effects of a controversial deinstitutionalization effort), the adversary nature of hearings required and the increased burden of proof placed on the hospitals caused such an outcry from the mental health community that the bill was threatened (unsuccessfully as it turned out) with revision and canceled appropriations.

Politically conservative legislators also began to take more interest in human services, introducing DPW dismantlement bills in every session during the Shapp administration. The critical committees — Public Health and Welfare in the Senate, headed by Louis Coopersmith, and Health and Welfare in the House of Representatives, headed by Anita Kelly — were consistently skeptical of the curative value of agency subdivision.[19] This view was balanced by the appearance in 1977 of an Aging and Youth Committee in the Senate, headed by Michael O'Pake, which pushed for separate departments and was seen as a prime element behind authorization of a new Department of Aging, created by the consolidation of all aging-related programs, a number of which were previously in the Department of Public Welfare.

While it was not possible to see a consistent policy direction in relation to human services within the Pennsylvania legislature, all the signs indicated that the legislature would be much more involved in human services issues in the future.

Department of Public Welfare

In the absence of consistent and effective leadership by the governor, Pennsylvania's welfare department played a relatively conventional bureaucratic role in issues involving organizational reform. Helene Wohlgemuth, the controversial secretary of DPW during Shapp's first term, was a strong supporter of services integration. Her successor seemed indifferent to the issue. In the aggregate, however, the department was rather more consistent than its leadership during this period. It was not about to be found in the vanguard of change.

The alliance of Public Assistance and Social Services programs of the former Department of Welfare has always been somewhat uneasy. One reason is that the Department of Public Assistance was incorporated into the Department of Public Welfare with little change and remained a largely independent entity within the confederation. Under the jurisdiction of the counties when first created, public-assistance services were soon designated a state responsibility on the grounds that they were too complex to administer effectively at the county level. In contrast to the other programs within DPW, which were still administered by the counties, all public-assistance decisions are handled at the state level and implemented through a system of approximately ninety district offices. With this centralized system and its associated political connections, Public Assistance has not always been a willing partner in DPW, at times exerting its influence in a manner that some considered to be detrimental to other elements in the department. Former secretary Wohlgemuth, for example, found the State Advisory Board of Public Welfare too parochial and uninterested in other programs that affected the well-being of welfare recipients. Norman Lourie, an executive deputy secretary for DPW, asserted, however, that this attitude was natural, as Public Assistance[20] dwarfed its confederates in size of budget.

A private vendor who had dealt with DPW on a long-term basis remarked, "The Department of Public Welfare in Pennsylvania is a mixture of programs — there's no linkages between them. Even though there's a Secretary responsible for the whole thing, it's almost unmanageable."[21] Lourie contended that public assistance was being increasingly involved with other DPW programs through the growing ties — promoted, among other ways, by Title XX — among all human services programs. He acknowledged that for several years DPW programs had all operated in relative isolation; DPW had remained an "umbrella agency" since its creation. The 1974 Council of State Government's study, *Human Services Integration,* found that although DPW contained all the elements necessary to meet the strict definition of a CHRA, "the Project never noted the feeling in the State that the Department of Public Welfare was considered a CHRA."[22]

Not surprisingly, change has been incremental at best, especially with respect to services integration. "We've been [decentralizing services] for six years and it hasn't gotten any better. . . . We are a long way from services integration."[23] Others noted a marked lack of, or even indifference to, statewide planning within the central offices of DPW.[24] Efforts by DPW Secretary Frank S. Beal, Helene Wohlgemuth's successor, to create a planning office remained a project "in the works." A DPW priority to deinstitutionalize the state's mental hospitals, for example, resulted in backlash at the local level, with charges of poorly coordinated or nonexistent community services and understaffed hospitals. Problems in deinstitutionalization and in Public Assistance programs brought assertions of "squeaky wheel" administration, that is, that DPW policymaking consisted primarily of firefighting with little long-range planning.

Citizen and interest-group planning boards, of which Pennsylvania has many, were thought to lack definite policies in their approach to services integration, and were viewed by many decision makers as mere "escape valves" created out of political necessity. While many felt these boards had possibilities as management tools, for both citizens and agencies, they were seldom fully utilized. Edward Carskadon, executive assistant to DPW secretary Beal, noted that the Board of Public Welfare, the citizen advisory board for the department, "pretty much find their own way in terms of what they do." The result was that they did not have an "appreciable impact on policy" and were unable to "affect the direction of the Department a great deal."

A high-profile example of these specialized program advisory boards was the Comprehensive Mental Health Planning Committee, a product of the moves by DPW to deinstitutionalize state institutions. This committee was established to review the Pennsylvania mental health system. The deinstitutionalization movement had greatly affected Pennsylvania's nineteen state mental hospitals, several of them over a century old. Hospital closings and personnel dismissals brought organized resistance from employee unions, in particular the American Federation of State, County and Municipal Employees (AFSCME). Unions represented 85 percent of hospital employees, resulting in what one mental health administrator called the "double whammy of union and civil service."

The problem was not simply a question of loss of jobs. The unions argued that the deinstitutionalization processes should have been used to move the hospitals toward the recommended federal standards concerning patient-client ratios, and thus no job losses would have occurred.[25] In addition, union officials argued that deinstitutionalization itself was a fraudulent doctrine.[26] One problem with deinstitutionalization from the union standpoint was that if an institution was completely shut down, the state mental health worker had no place to go, since community services were run either by the county MH/MR program under an entirely separate personnel and pension plan or under contract with private vendors. Even if the county system would accept state workers, it was unlikely that the state worker would be willing to transfer, as county salaries were generally lower. This inequality of salary long had been a roadblock to state and county services integration efforts.

These problems, in the view of the Pennsylvania Comprehensive Mental Health Planning Committee, were the result of limited coordination between actors in Pennsylvania state government.

When the Federal Mental Health Center legislation was passed in 1963 it focused on community services, and, in fact, it served to set up competitive relationships with the existing institutional network. Further, the Mental Health and Mental Retardation Act of 1966 in Pennsylvania could not focus on the integration of community and institutional services since at the time of its passage the institutional system was by far the dominant and primary resource for public mental health services delivery.[27]

DPW viewed the committee as being at least partially successful in reducing rancor. The unions, in contrast (specifically AFSCME), considered the committee a fraudulent rubber stamp to authorize a pilot decentralization project, and they finally withdrew from participation.

As in most states, the DPW secretary was torn between demands from the Governor's Office and demands from within the department. Interpersonal dynamics could also play a large role. Among other

DPW officials, Helene Wohlgemuth left Pennsylvania government under circumstances thought to have been generated by personality and style conflicts. Yet regardless of how observers characterize these conflicts, they were invariably correlated with group interests, especially the interests of the social workers within the department, the Governor's Office, and the legislature.

Responding to resistance to policy and program changes from the agency bureaucracy, Wohlgemuth attempted to break up what she saw as a social-work clique by appointing people who were not social workers to top posts — for example, by hiring a lawyer as her administrative assistant — and by generating requirements for new positions.

Wohlgemuth's stance resembled that taken previously by Dr. Thomas Georges, also a controversial secretary. Both Wohlgemuth and Georges expressed dissatisfaction with the power of the "social worker" in DPW and the social workers' "bureaucratic" unwillingness to accept the priorities that these two reform-oriented secretaries perceived as essential to solving the client's problems. According to Wohlgemuth, "The bureaucrats have tolerated the worst conditions in order to control the system." From their side, the professional personnel in the agency complained about Wohlgemuth's lack of management skills and expertise. "I was trying to revive some feeling of what the Department was all about. They all seem to wind up tending the organization," Wohlgemuth asserted. She unquestionably motivated people, either positively or negatively. Even Wohlgemuth, however, recognized the limitations of the personal approach. "People have to be treated like people. But have you ever tried to talk to forty-two thousand people who don't know you?"[28] Although able to steer Pennsylvania through such crises as the 1972 Wilkes-Barre flood, Wohlgemuth inspired as much resistance as dedication. She herself expressed awareness of these political realities, but gave them low priority. "If you are never criticized and never cause a commotion, you aren't doing your job. If services are bad, you can't worry about the political spot the Secretary of DPW will be in."

Both Georges and Wohlgemuth were succeeded as DPW secretary by low-profile administrators with business backgrounds (Georges by Stanley Miller; Wohlgemuth by Frank Beal), apparently chosen to calm the stormy seas blown up by their predecessors. The appointment of Beal as DPW secretary during Shapp's second term was greeted with relief by many legislators, who saw him as bringing "business sense" to the office. Under Beal, the secretary's office reoriented its effort away from reform toward husbandry. Some observers saw this shift as a political and fiscal necessity if DPW programs were to survive intact.

Services Integration

Considering the absence of demands for services integration as an economy measure or as a means of increasing executive control, it is not surprising that there is relatively little grass-roots interest in services integration as a means of improving service delivery. Indeed, what seems surprising, given the inertia affecting all levels of government, is that there are any signs of reform in the state. In fact, there are two, both products of fortuitous circumstances and neither likely to infect other parts of the state except in a narrow, technical sense.

The United Service Agency

In 1972, heavy flooding in northeastern Pennsylvania made a multi-county area eligible for federal disaster assistance. Because the county's services had been totally disrupted, the state negotiated a seven-year agreement whereby it would assume responsibility for services and create an integrated delivery system. Katherine McKenna, DPW deputy secretary for northeastern Pennsylvania, became in addition project director for what was christened the United Services Agency (USA). Thus USA was, in effect, a DPW regional organization.

That arrangement might sound hopeful to proponents of change. In fact, it survived, even flourished, in part because it was viewed throughout the state as sui generis. The perception in the state capital was that USA represented a unique contract relationship between the state and the counties, and therefore it was "not replicable." That it could exist at all reflects the character of DPW administration. According to Norman Lourie,

The DPW regional office has enormous power. It is, in fact, a mini-department. . . . [It] operates a series of categorical programs tied together by management strings. With the exception of moving certain monies [i.e., Title XX] among programs, each DPW program could easily be separated into a separate cabinet department without much effect on other programs. There is *no* operational integration philosophy underlying headquarters or region.[29]

In the late 1960s, a DPW model region was created in Philadelphia. Many innovations in program administration of national significance were created, but it might have occurred in Minnesota's Hennepin County for the effect it had on the rest of the state. An unusual project such as USA could survive because the DPW regions were subject to few, if any, homogenizing influences.

These influences were not totally absent, however, and McKenna earned a reputation for being pressure resistant in warding off administrative blows aimed at the project by state officials. For example, the state auditor's office disapproved of USA expenditures without a rigorous, centralized authorization process. "We take strong exception," said one report, "to the approximate expenditure of $1,000,000 for works of consultants that resulted in relatively little benefit."[30] While recognizing that "federal authorities required evaluations of the demonstration project," the auditor questioned the use of consultants in contrast to project personnel. "When spending taxpayers' monies, there should be no luxury items."[31]

This was in fact a challenge to McKenna's philosophy concerning the project. The United Services Agency was concerned with objectively documenting and communicating its accomplishments, and conducted an intensive internal evaluation program since its creation. The evaluation effort was launched in the belief that understanding of integrated systems up to 1972 was theoretical, and no one really knew how integrated systems worked. Therefore, a major goal of USA was to put an integrated system into practice and find out how much of it was "bunk." Outside consultants were needed for this effort. McKenna contrasted this approach to that of the Governor's Office, whose attitude she saw as a merchandizing one with the emphasis on the good points of the project and a tendency to ignore the bad ones.

Another point of disagreement involved computerized accounting. For six years USA had been hand accounting, so that the system could be easily modified as problems became evident. The auditor's office stated that a computer management data system should have been worked out and initiated before the program began. The special audit team objected that "emphasis seems to have been placed disproportionately in favor of program implementation over responsibilities for prudent action and decision making." While McKenna agreed with the factual basis of their observation and pledged that USA facilities would alleviate the situation with a standardized fiscal system, a computerized management information system, and a centralized contracting procedure, she questioned the wisdom of their initial high priority.

It is always easy to second-guess management decision from the vantage point of elapsed time. The Auditor General's staff has access to information which was not available when management decisions had to be made. Consequently, the Auditor General's staff lost sight of the original goals and objectives of the USA Project and presented an anachronistic analysis of the reasons for taking certain actions.[32]

Even the auditor general's report noted, "Despite our difference of opinion in many areas, we respect the abilities of USA management. We found management to be perceptive and extremely devoted to fulfilling the needs of welfare customers."[33] Katherine McKenna had clearly built up an important project. Its success failed to resonate elsewhere in the state, however. With the Shapp administration approaching the end of an eight-year term, the governor was in no position to become a change agent, and there were no other candidates on the scene.

Mon Valley
The Mon Valley Project began in 1971 as a federally funded Experimental Health Services Delivery System Project. Later it was supported by a Services Integration Target of Opportunity Grant and a Partnership Grant from HEW. The Mon Valley Health and Welfare Council, Inc., is a voluntary nonprofit corporation serving the Monongahela River Valley in rural western Pennsylvania and represents a collection of public and private agencies providing health and welfare services. The basic thrust of the Mon Valley project was availability of services and efficiency in their provision. Availability was enhanced through construction of the Mon Valley Community Health Center in 1971, and efficiency was improved through the use of computer systems. Despite some success in marketing computer technology to client service agencies, including a few outside the council itself — the state area aging agencies, for example — the computer approach was not as well received as had been anticipated. While the integrative elements of the Mon Valley effort were effective, the relationships be-

tween the project and the nonintegrated state government constituted a problem.

The Mon Valley project maintained its independence through its federal funding, but this independence also isolated it from the rest of the state service system, except as it became a marketer of computer capabilities and a member of a consortium of service delivery projects that met regularly in Wilkes-Barre, the headquarters of USA. This consortium also contained several county programs, specifically in Lehigh, Lancaster, and Dauphin counties, which were interested in transplanting as much of the technical aspects of Mon Valley and USA as possible. Having voted to begin a new form of government at the county level with "home rule," Lehigh and Northampton counties were presented with a great deal of flexibility on how to organize their new departments of human resources within their counties. Originally, the two counties asked USA to help design those projected departments, but later county officials decided on modified versions of their own design.[34]

Conclusions

As a large, diverse state with a largely unreformed state government, Pennsylvania did not appear to be poised on the brink of innovation in human services organization and administration. Demands for change had not coalesced or become focused in a politically attractive way. Political leaders who were disposed to use reorganization, management improvement, or services integration as central elements in their programs had not emerged. What seeds had been sown in past years had apparently fallen on rocky ground.

Whether and when the commonwealth would approach a state of readiness for chance was impossible to say on the basis of the situation in the late 1970s. A question of some interest is what kind of a change strategy might succeed in a state like Pennsylvania. A gradual, consensual approach would have to be well organized, determined, and firmly rooted in the state's power structures. A major reorganization, even if successful, would incur a high cost in disruption of existing services and hardening of opposition. No effort would be likely to succeed unless groundwork were laid, perhaps in the form of "blue-ribbon" study efforts involving businessmen and academics of the type who contributed to the processes of change in Florida and Washington. What has clearly been missing, perhaps since the administration of George Leader, is not studies or strategies but simply sustained, articulate, clearly motivated interest by a major political actor such as the governor. Only effective advocacy that can command a following is likely to alter things in Pennsylvania.

Whose Needs Will Be Met?

In important respects, every state is a special case. Change, or the absence of it, in a state's human service organizations is shaped by factors and circumstances that are found nowhere else. The personality and program of Jimmy Carter, the consistency and competence of Florida's legislature, and official deference to county government in Minnesota are not interchangeable, reproducible elements in state politics. The rationale for administrative linkages among particular agencies varies from state to state depending on historical factors, accidents of personality, the dialects of local politics, and other idiosyncracies. Changes in the status quo are initiated in a wide variety of ways, at different times and for different reasons, and with varying amounts of forethought.

Examination of these six cases provides a clue that state experiences with organizational change have common elements. Officials in different states are learning from one another. Florida legislators sought advice from their counterparts in Washington concerning the problems of services integration. Minnesota officials studied the experiences of Arizona and Florida while designing their own proposals. Officials in Pennsylvania looked to Minnesota for approaches to the promotion of change in county services administration. While it is going much too far to claim convergence in the understanding of organizational change among the states, recognition among state officials that certain types of experience are generalizable is plainly evident.

An analysis of the cases leads to the conclusion that general propositions or a general perspective about both the processes and the character of organizational change in the states are indeed possible. Though admittedly impressionistic, these propositions can serve as useful guides to analyzing the experiences of other states and to formulating contingent predictions about their prospects for change. These propositions suggest that removal of federal restrictions on state actions would weaken the power of categorical interests in resource allocation and services administration and would promote the application of fiscal and efficiency criteria in human services policymaking.

The Processes of Change

The prime movers in reorganization, administrative reform, and improvements in services included governors, legislators, county commissioners, and appointed officials acting alone and in diverse alliances. There were no consistent patterns in their motives. They acted on the basis of personal and political goals, out of concern for taxpayers and service recipients, and in pursuit of control, economy, and improvements in services delivery. Their choices of purpose and timing do not seem at all inevitable. Carter need not have gambled so heavily on reorganization. Shapp might well have done so. Askew could have made services integration his own issue instead of conceding it to the legislature.

Though no consistency emerged in the initiation of organizational change, clearly change proposals need a powerful and durable constituency. The need to overcome inertia is one reason. A more important reason is that no matter how or why change is initiated, those who believe or suspect they have something to lose will actively resist it. Carter's bold challenge, the coalition promoting county-oriented incrementalism in Minnesota, and the Shapp administration's sporadic and piecemeal experiments all aroused opponents to strong words and deeds aimed at blocking action they saw as threatening. The prospect of organizational change will trigger political conflict, and proponents must be able to muster enough support to resolve it in their favor.

What *is* inevitable, then, is that no matter what impels them, advocates for change will be drawn into political conflicts. They must be able to manage and control conflict situations, or gain the support of those who can, if they are to be successful. As secretary of DHRS in Florida and both advocate and agent for services integration "Pete" Page had enough support from the governor and the legislature to weather threats to the internal reorganization he was attempting to carry out. As director of DES in Arizona Bill Mayo lacked such support and was ultimately defeated in his efforts at a similar reorganization. In like manner, Helene Wohlgemuth was defeated in Pennsylvania.

Though such perceptions may seem obvious to students of politics, they are not always so obvious to those involved in organizational reform in the states. The latter often see reorganization and administrative reform as essentially technical issues. They are apt to view politicians as sleeping lions who are not to be awakened if life and limb are to be preserved. They pay scant attention to the need to identify and mobilize a supportive and powerful constituency. The point here is that organizational change is essentially a political issue and must be analyzed in those terms.

Whether involved in the initiation of change or not, the governor will play a decisive role, perhaps *the* decisive role, in organizational change. If not the initiator, as Carter was, the governor has the opportunity to decide whether to become an active and supportive agent, as Askew finally chose to do in Florida, or to oppose the changes. This is a political choice.

The governors in the study had varying degrees of institutional authority — control over personnel, budgets, organizational structure, and program policy and design — and thus political power. Such authority and power are not fixed quantities, however. Apart from the power conferred on them by state constitutions, legislatures can and often do augment or reduce a governor's powers of office. A governor's power is a scarce resource to be husbanded and used purposefully. Within these constraints, the governor is potentially a commanding presence, a hammer to the legislature's anvil. The governor can propose, mediate, deploy bureaucratic resources, withhold support, and use other measures to influence action. The governor is in an excellent position, in other words, to manage and control the conflict associated with change, whether or not he or she is the initiator.

The cases suggest the extent to which the pace, character, and success of organizational change are colored by the governor's performance. Without passing judgment on the details of their performance, Carter, Busbee, Askew (after 1975), and Evans all played the role of the strong governor, attempting with at least some success to retain control over the change process. Anderson allowed his office to be used for purposeful effect, though he was more in the background than the others. Shapp and Arizona's Williams and Castro appeared to exert little or no personal influence as proponents, agents, or opponents of organizational change, behavior that seemed to be reflected in the disorderly, uncertain character of decision making on organization issues.

The legislature, too, is powerful, but its power is exercised in different ways. It has the strengths and weaknesses of a collective body. Occasionally a legislator — a speaker, president pro tem, majority leader, or appropriations committee chairperson — will achieve dominant influence by virtue of his or her power to control committee leadership and membership, the disposition of legislation, or budgetary allocations. On rare occasions, influence will be based on expertise or reputation. For the most part, individual legislators become influential to the extent that they are able to articulate the demands of powerful constituencies, define and focus the attitudes and desires of other legislators, discover bases for compromise and collective action, or take the lead in creating legislative opportunities by exploiting problem situations or the vulnerabilities of political opponents. Because its membership is continually flushed by electoral tides, sustained and continuous legislative leadership and consistency in legislative preferences are problematic. The study revealed how often the collective behavior of legislators shifts as a result of elections or shifts in the political fortunes of individual members.

A legislature's agenda and preferences are typically defined when reacting to executive actions or when prodding the executive to act. Legislative behavior in these regards often seems over time to be quixotic, inconsistent, opportunistic, self-serving, and unpredictable. Thus, legislative activity can prove intensely frustrating to the executive branch. This characterization of the legislature's role and behavior underscores the importance of the governor on an issue like reorganization. The governor, not exclusively but much more than any other executive branch official, can determine the effectiveness of the legislature by how he or she interacts with it. A governor or a cabinet official who actively seeks to manage and control interactions with the legislature — to define issues, put forth alternatives, mobilize support, suggest compromises, and, in general, show regard for the legislature's role — will enhance the effectiveness of both. This is especially necessary on organizational issues. Executives are tempted to make arbitrary assertions of their prerogatives on such matters. Unless the governor clearly has the upper hand, this will usually be a mistake. A legislature sensing a need and opportunity to establish its own prerogatives is likely to react by dictating the form of reorganization, imposing staffing and budget cuts, engaging in close and continuous monitoring of executive actions, and standing ready to pounce on mistakes.

Florida provides a good example of effective executive-legislative interactions on organizational issues. Governor Reubin Askew appeared temporarily and unnecessarily to lose control of reorganization, which went beyond what he wanted and might well have gotten. The Florida legislature had been prodding him to act, and only when convinced he would not did the legislature seize full control of the reorganization issue. Askew recovered by effectively bargaining for the more satisfactory version of the bill, and from then on he appeared to maintain the initiative on implementation, avoiding an unmanageable buildup of stress with the legislature and leaving it with a sense of ownership of the issue. Washington's Daniel Evans and Georgia's Jimmy Carter appeared less successful in quelling legislative unhappiness, with Carter's reorganization being salvaged by Governor George Busbee's greater skill in this regard. Legislatures elsewhere appeared to take the initiative or to prod the governor into action, but in the absence of effective action by the governor, a well-organized change process did not get started.

In contrast to elected officials and to career employees, the appointed heads of state executive organizations appear to be in a relatively weak position. Unlike federal cabinet and independent agency executives, these officials possess little unreviewable discretion or independence, and their actions are subject to close scrutiny by the other participants in state government. The close quarters in which they operate may well be a reflection of scale; though state human services organizations seem large to state legislators, they are small relative to federal bureaucracies. Because of this, government at the state level seems inherently more penetrable — though not, of course, always penetrated — by elected officials. Except where governors and legislatures are ineffective, or where an agency facility such as a state hospital plays a large role in a legislative district, "iron triangles" (unbreakable alliances among agency officials, interest groups, and key legislators) are less common in state government, at least in human services.

The most convincing evidence for this proposition is the sharp contrast between the influence vocational rehabilitation programs have in Congress and their influence with elected state officials. Because VR programs are relatively well funded and their counselors are well trained and effective, state officials often attempt to leaven human service organizations with VR resources. (This is also the case with employment, public health, and medical programs.) Without question,

VR programs are "saved" — and usually only partially — by the protection they get from Congress, which has steadfastly refused to modify the so-called "single organizational unit" requirement of federal rehabilitation law.

The impression is inescapable that state officials would mix and match human services resources in different ways if not for federal categorical restraints. Professional human service agencies, and their associated interest groups, in general, do not have the same standing with governors, legislators, and county commissioners as they do in Congress.

Most state legislators, for example, are political amateurs who are overworked and underpaid. In dealing with a flood of unfamiliar legislation, they are apt to pay closest attention to representatives of interests that can affect their political careers or are of central interest to voters in their districts. In the absence of pressure, they will respond to legislative leaders, often along party lines. Human service interests, such as associations representing the mentally retarded or the physically handicapped, may sway legislators by well-organized appeals to conscience, particularly if what they are seeking does not appear to cost a great deal and will play well with voters. For the most part, however, business interests and such special interests as liquor, highways, racetracks, teachers, and others with a strong local power base will attract the greatest legislative attention.

Especially vulnerable are welfare agencies. Scorned by many elected officials because of their politically unpopular clientele, shunned by human service agencies whose programs are not closely targeted on the low-income population, welfare agencies are pariahs in state government. Many reorganization initiatives seem aimed at curbing the costs of these agencies and at improving their capacity to make welfare recipients self-supporting (by, for example, combining them with VR or Employment Service programs, with better reputations for restoring their clients to self-support.)

This situation, too, underscores the importance of the governor's role. A governor's human services appointees find themselves caught in the middle in conflicts between the administration and the legislature. Indeed, these appointees often become lightning rods for legislative dissatisfaction with the administration in power. Because they have little inherent power, human services officials must have access to the governor's power if they are to be sustained in their roles. Of course, if they draw too heavily or too frequently on that power and threaten to use it up (many observers felt that was the case with "Pete" Page in Florida), they may be left to their own devices or even fired. Conversely, governors who do not use their power effectively to sustain or control reorganization may put their appointees and perhaps even themselves in a politically untenable position.

The Character of Change

Among the strongest impressions yielded by the case studies is that elected state officials have on the whole a greater sense of responsibility toward economy and efficiency in governmental operations than they do toward the effectiveness or coverage of human services. A composite view is: "Human services have no constituency. Their clients do not vote, at least not in large enough numbers to make a difference to the average legislator. The average voter is concerned about his or her taxes and wants assurances that revenues are not wasted." Even governors who had reputations as being "for" human services, such as Askew and Evans, could not ignore the economy issue, nor could the heads of their human service organizations.

In short, fiscal discipline must be a primary objective of governors and legislatures. They are continuously vulnerable to the charge that government operations are wasteful and inefficient. The passage of Proposition 13 in California and other tax-limiting legislation elsewhere only accentuates what has been generally true: economy and efficiency are salient issues in the states, and nothing is likely to alter that picture.

The significance of this issue helps explain the attractiveness of human services reorganization and services integration. Wherever undertaken on any scale, these measures were viewed as ways to save money by a significant proportion of their constituency. (It should not be forgotten that even the authors of the *Federalist* felt compelled to argue, in paper no. 13, that the Union would save money.) Put another way, such measures seldom gained widespread support unless sold as economy measures or, at the least, as measures that, by enhancing political control over programs, would constrain budget growth. This is not to say that getting better services to more people — a common rationale for services integration — has no appeal. Rather, it is not an appeal that appears by itself to command majority support. Reorganizations of this kind must also appeal to those who believe that there are enough services already, but they are too costly, or that the way to increase services is to make existing services delivery more efficient.

Putative economies are not the only reason for the attractiveness of comprehensive human services reorganization. A theme sustaining these efforts was the need for control and accountability by elected officials. In part, the popularity of this theme reflects widespread concern that categorical program growth threatens fiscal stability in the states. Federal matching grants have indeed stimulated greater spending by the states, and many state officials are evidently concerned lest they be unable to restrain state budget growth. The theme is also one that has been popular since the 1860s and the first appearance of state boards of charities. Since then the trend, though halting and uneven, has been toward centralization and integration as means of attaining control and accountability. The trend has, by and large, been opposed by human services professionals, who preferred old-style board and commissioner arrangements under which they enjoyed more autonomy. In the states more than at the federal level, tensions between professional autonomy in services delivery and political accountability in services administration is likely to be resolved in favor of generalist administrators whose actions are reviewable by elected officials.

Could anything attenuate or deflect this trend? One development that might do it would be the spreading conviction that "it," meaning integrated organizations overseeing decentralized operations, does not work, that budgets grow and services decline in quality and availability, that these kinds of organizations are politically unstable and liable to spontaneous combustion. Anecdotal evidence that combining welfare and employment assistance programs in Arizona did not work has no doubt affected the popularity of that particular kind of reorganization. For the most part evidence as to what works and what does not has been singularly lacking, though, as noted at the start of this chapter, states are increasingly canvassing each other's experiences for it. In this regard, the experience in Florida may prove decisive. Florida's reorganization survived its rocky transition remarkably intact. There will be continuing interest in whether or not it's "working." Evidence of various kinds that it is, indeed, working might stimulate interest in the Florida model elsewhere and accelerate the pace of change in that direction. The theoretical appeal of this arrangement appears much greater to state officials than the maintenance of categorical distinctions, program autonomy, and control by professionals.

This proposition begs the question of what precisely it means to say that one administrative arrangement works better than another. (In the end, of course, the impression created by the Florida experience will matter far more than whether or not evaluators have formulated precise criteria to assess it.) This may be an unresolvable issue on analytic grounds. If generalists rather than program specialists are making administrative decisions, is that proof that it is working or that it is not? What if waiting times are going up and unit costs are coming down? What if a rehabilitation counselor spends 5 percent less time working with handicapped people and 5 percent more helping social workers with welfare administration? An acceptable basis for evaluation will probably be one that encompasses a wide variety of quantitative and qualitative measures and leaves observers free to draw their own conclusions based on their own sense of what is relevant.

Evidence on what works and the preference of governors and legislators are not the only factors determining the pace and character of change. Reorganization and change place heavy demands on the time and political resources of the officials involved in it. In virtually no case of change where some parties feared they had something to lose was the process anything but turbulent and time consuming. The costliness of change appears higher where power and responsibility are fragmented, decentralized, and diffuse, that is, where there are more discrete elements to be changed and where they are hard to get at. If the governor's prestige was committed, heavy demands to iron out differences, resolve problems, and provide explanations were placed on him or her in order to stay on top of the process. If such efforts were not made, the governor was vulnerable to the charge of weak leadership. Awareness of the costs of change is no doubt a deterrent to many would-be reorganizers and an explanation for why others abandon or water down the cause. It is often a sensible decision. The physical and political resources of public executives are limited and must be husbanded. Shaking up or remodeling the system may or may not be worth it.

Governors may have less stamina in effecting change than collective entities such as legislatures and program agencies. So may the appointed heads of human service organizations involved in extensive change. In general, and all other things being equal, time is on the side of the office with more people, either staff or allies, who can share the effort and who are in a strong defensive position. In organizational change, as in battle, the "offense" must be able to overmatch the "defense," the more so as the latter is well protected. A Florida official told of spending fully one-third of his time on "the VR issue," much of it in Washington, D.C., trying to penetrate VR's congressional perimeter. The long-running governors, Askew, Evans, and Shapp, were frequently described as having been worn down by protracted conflict. The heads of human service organizations — Mayo of Arizona, Smith of Washington, Lindquist of Scott County, Page of Florida, Wohlgemuth of Pennsylvania — were bloodied if not bowed in their roles as spearheads of change.

Change, of course, is not only a matter of resources and stamina. It requires specific skills and techniques. These range from a sense of timing and tone in dealing with legislators and an ability to select capable subordinates to an ability to set up expenditure control, personnel, and management information systems. The more extensive and controversial the change, the greater its vulnerability to administrative mistakes. Such problems were the Achilles' heel of the Florida reorganization and a definite factor in the rest. Success may depend on the ability of an agency head tangled up in personnel problems to stay cool when a part-time legislator observes that running an agency isn't so hard if you know how.

Thus, organizational change requires extraordinary political and managerial resources and skills, especially during transition. The study suggests that the magnitude of the effort is often underestimated and that the necessary skills are in short supply. Because officials are seldom elected, or even appointed, on the basis of evidence concerning their skills as public managers, much less their ability to manage a reorganization, the coming together of the necessary ingredients for successful reorganization may be fortuitous.

Policy Implications

This study of organizational change in the states has produced a plausible though general view of what would happen if states were given greater discretion over the allocation of federal grants for human services. Resource allocation in the states would shift in directions favored by the constitutencies of the governor and legislative leaders. On the whole, categorical human services interests are probably less influential at the state level than general taxpayer and business interests and the interests of locally powerful groups such as public employee unions, at least when sizable budget allocations are at stake. For the foreseeable future, the growth of services in many program areas might well be slowed in comparison to what it would be under the incentives in present grant-in-aid statutes. In short, it they had their way the states would probably economize more on human services and allocate resources more in accordance with the wishes of majority interests and the kinds of special interests that are strong at the local level. Control over expenditure allocations would tend to gravitate toward politically accountable generalists. The pace and character of change would vary widely from state to state, leading to greater interstate diversity in patterns of human services spending. Moreover, allocations over time would tend to be more responsive to the shifting political fortunes of individuals and parties.

Whether this would be a good or a bad result depends, of course, on one's objectives. Proponents of maintenance or growth in spending for social welfare, and of spending for special constituencies such as the handicapped, the retarded, and the poor, especially the urban poor, are justified in being reluctant to dismantle the federal categorical grant system. Proponents of resource allocations that conform more to the wishes of state and local electorates, and those who favor the growth of accountability in state government, especially among governors, are justified in favoring decentralization.

A separate but related issue is the extent to which the federal government can affect human services organization and administration as opposed to resource allocation. Would it be possible, for example, without major changes in the categorical grant system, to effectively promote services integration in accordance with, say, the Florida model? One plausible view is that it might be better to let well enough alone. The range of reforms attempted by the states in this study suggests that much can be accomplished even with present federal law; the most serious obstacles to such changes may be state capacities to conceive and execute them. In this light, changes of this kind may well be occurring about as fast as they ought to given these limited capacities and the absence of knowledge about how such changes affect service delivery in the long run. The natural process of change now occurring may be a healthy one.

A different but not incompatible view is that a valuable federal role is in obtaining and disseminating information concerning services integration technology and methods for evaluating various approaches to organizing services delivery. In most of the states in this study, services integration targets of opportunity and partnership grants produced useful if inconclusive information for officials contemplating reorganization. State officials in both executive and legislative branches need and want this kind of assistance, yet they are not in a good position to mount the necessary research effort. Federal investments of this kind, which appear to have declined, might usefully be stepped up.

Beyond these observations bearing on federal policy, a number of conclusions can be drawn that are relevant to decisions by state officials concerning whether and how to reorganize state agencies and services.

Perhaps the most important is that reorganization, especially if it is to be extensive, is a fundamentally political act. It must be conceived, designed, and executed as such. In many states, governors have commissioned studies of state government that have simply ignored the political character of organizational issues, viewing them instead in terms of management systems orthodoxy. These studies have often been submitted to the legislature or to agency review without revision. Relatively minor management changes are the usual results of such efforts, and the opportunity to achieve more significant changes is often wasted.

This observation should not be interpreted to mean that cautious incrementalism that minimizes political conflict is always to be preferred. It is certainly to be preferred if officials sponsoring the change are unwilling to commit much to the effort. A comprehensive reorganization can be a sound political strategy, however, to an administration willing to expend the resources to achieve it. The point is that such judgments should be based on an explicit and realistic balancing of the political benefits and costs.

A second conclusion is that among the key decisions concerning reorganization are the appointments of people who are to carry it out. A governor is especially vulnerable to poor personnel choices. One common mistake, akin to the kind of mistake mentioned above with respect to studies, is to select "management types" who are unable to deal with legislators or who tend to view organizational problems solely in technical, systems-oriented terms. A similar mistake is to appoint someone who will be well liked and have good rapport with affected parties but who has no ability to bring about change, to be tough and decisive when necessary. Appointees of both types will increase the costs of change borne by their elected sponsors.

A final conclusion, relevant to both executive and legislative decisions, is that within the general configuration of a reorganization, certain types of problems can be avoided without much sacrifice of fundamental objectives. Program divisions that are likely to prove especially troublesome might well be left out at the start. Forethought in this regard can be rewarding. As another example, it may be unwise and unnecessary to change all management systems at once, especially if the technology is not in hand or if officials are unfamiliar with these kinds of management reforms. Choices of this nature, while not especially consequential to the aims of the reorganization, can make the difference between a successful and an unsuccessful reorganization.

Success in the initiation and management of change is one of the most grueling tests of an administration's competence. Especially heavy responsibilities fall on governors who, by choice or otherwise, become involved in reorganizations. Their strategic and tactical choices are often decisive in shaping the pace, character, and costs of change. These results, in turn, have a major impact on the beneficiaries of human services. The general competence in such matters of the group of states in this study appeared to be growing, though obviously more in some than in others. At the same time, the direction of change appears to be in favor of general-purpose administration of specialized services, with consequences for services delivery that are as yet largely unknown. Clearly a high priority for state government in the future is to achieve increased competence in managing the process of change. It is both good politics and good policy to do so.

Notes

Chapter 1

1

This number includes programs in the following federal budget subfunctions: elementary, secondary, and vocational education; higher education; training and employment; social services; health care services; health research; education and training of health care work force; public assistance and other income supplements; hospital and medical care for veterans; criminal justice assistance. *A Catalog of Federal Grant-in-Aid Programs to State and Local Governments: Grants Funded: FY 1978,* Advisory Commission on Intergovernmental Relations (Washington, D.C.: February 1979).

2

James Q. Wilson, "The Rise of the Bureaucratic State," *The Public Interest* 41 (Fall 1975): 92.

3

The Intergovernmental Grant System: An Assessment and Proposed Policies, Advisory Commission on Intergovernmental Relations (Washington, D.C.: 1978), p. 12.

4

The Intergovernmental Grant System: An Assessment and Proposed Policies, Advisory Commission on Intergovernmental Relations (Washington, D.C.: 1978), p. 12. For a specific example see *Federally Assisted Employment and Training: A Myriad of Programs Should Be Simplified* (U.S. General Accounting Office, May 8, 1979).

5

Frank Levy, "Observations of a Participant," *Policy Analysis* 1:2 (Spring 1975): 443.

6

Neal R. Peirce, "Power and (Dis)Trust," *Public Welfare* 36:3 (Summer 1978): 16.

7

Elliot Richardson, *The Creative Balance* (New York: Holt, Rinehart and Winston, 1976), pp. 183, 198.

8

Ibid., pp. 197, 204.

9

The questions might have been studied in relation to other issues, such as the definition of the rights and entitlements of service beneficiaries, the allocation of budgetary resources, the adoption and dissemination of innovations in treatment and service, and the processes by which a particular policy issue is defined and included on or excluded from state policy agendas. While important in their own right, these issues are less useful as a basis for studying fundamental political relationships.

10
National Academy of Public Administration, *Reorganization in Florida* (Washington, D.C.: September 1977), p. 91.

11
An account of developments in state approaches to human services organization and management can be found in Kathleen G. Heintz, "State Organizations for Human Services," *Evaluation* 3:1-2 (1976), pp. 106-10, and Harold Hagen and John E. Hansen, "How the States Put the Programs Together," *Public Welfare* 36:3 (Summer 1978), pp. 43-47.

12
See particularly Yeheskel Hasenfeld and Richard A. English, eds., *Human Service Organizations* (Ann Arbor: University of Michigan Press, 1974).

13
Useful surveys of the literature on organizations are in Chris Argyris and Donald A. Schön, *Organizational Learning: A Theory of Action Perspective* (Addison-Wesley, 1978), pp. 319-29; and Robert L. Peabody and Francis E. Rourke, *Public Bureaucracies*, in James G. March, ed., *Handbook of Organizations* (Rand McNally and Company, 1965), pp. 802-37. See also Michael E. Cohen, James G. March, and Johan P. Olsen, "A Garbage Can Model of Organizational Choice," *Administrative Science Quarterly*, 17:1 (March 1972), p. 1.

14
See, for example, Alfred D. Chandler, Jr., *Strategy and Structure* (Cambridge, Mass.: The M.I.T. Press, 1962); Meyer N. Zald, "Political Economy: A Framework for Comparative Analysis," in Meyer N. Zald, ed., *Power in Organizations* (Nashville, Tenn.: Vanderbilt University Press, 1970), pp. 221-61; and Paul R. Lawrence and Jay W. Lorsch, *Organization and Environment* (Cambridge, Mass.: Harvard University Press, 1967), esp. pp. 156-58 and chap. 8.

Chapter 2

1
Further discussion of these issues can be found in Mayer N. Zald, "The Structure of Society and Social Service Integration," *Social Service Quarterly* 50:3 (December 1969), pp. 557-567; and R. Clyde White, *Administration of Public Welfare* (New York: American Book Company, 1940), especially chapters 2 and 4.

2
This section draws heavily on John Mabry Matthews, *Principles of American State Administration* (New York: D. Appleton and Company, 1939); David Rothman, *The Discovery of the Asylum* (Boston: Little, Brown and Company, 1971); and White, *Administration of Public Welfare*.

3
Rothman, *The Discovery of the Asylum*, p. xix.

4

Blanche D. Coll, *Perspectives on Welfare, A History* (Washington, D.C.: U.S. Government Printing Office, 1969), pp. 22–23.

5

Other than a federal role in public health (the Marine Hospital Service was created in 1798), the main exception to state and private dominance of human services prior to the formation of the Children's Bureau in 1912 was the U.S. Bureau of Refugees, Freedmen, and Abandoned Lands. Created as part of the War Department by Congress in 1865, the Bureau provided relief, assistance in employment and settlement, and health, education, and legal services to veterans and freed slaves and their families and to others made temporarily destitute by the Civil War. The Bureau lapsed in 1872.

6

Rothman, *The Discovery of the Asylum,* p. 239.

7

Modern counterparts to this association are the National Association of State Mental Health Program Directors and the National Council of Community Mental Health Centers.

8

White, *Administration of Public Welfare,* p. 47.

9

The first modern federal-state grant program to survive was authorized by the Vocational Rehabilitation Act of 1920 to provide training, guidance, and placement services for civilians disabled while working in war industries. The federal role was intended to be temporary until the states assumed full control. However, Congress has never permitted the federal program to die. Indeed it has been steadily expanded and, as subsequent chapters indicate, steadily protected by Congress against state encroachments on its independence.

10

Even after the war and during the relatively quiescent Eisenhower years, significant changes occurred, including creation of programs for the disabled, revisions in public assistance matching provisions whereby low income states would be favored, along with steady increases in federal matching rates, subsidies for elderly housing, federal contributions to the medical care costs of the poor and elderly. The National Institute of Mental Health had its beginnings in the National Mental Health Act of 1946.

11

Wayne Vasey, *Government and Social Welfare* (New York: Henry Holt and Company, 1958), p. 379.

12

Ibid., p. 378.

13

Herbert Emmerich, *Federal Organization and Administrative Management* (University: University of Alabama Press, 1971), p. 52.

14

Ibid., p. 59.

15

Vasey, *Government and Social Welfare*, p. 264.

16

See Susan Salasin, "Two Views on Services Integration: Bertram S. Brown and Reubin Askew," *Evaluation* 3:1–2 (1976), pp. 15–16.

17

Early in 1969, President Nixon initiated the Federal Assistance Review program in the Office of Management and Budget. Its accomplishments included establishment of ten standard federal regions, each with a designated administrative center, a Federal Regional Council in each center with the principal grant-in-aid agencies serving as members, and issuance of Circular A-95, which establishes procedures for obtaining review and comments by state and local authorities on federally sponsored projects.

Chapter 3

1

Atlanta Constitution, July 19, 1971, p. 4-A.

2

Atlanta Constitution, January 15, 1971, p. 1-Af.

3

Task Force on Executive Organization: State of Washington, *Report to Governor Daniel J. Evans* (dated November 29, 1968), p. 3.

4

Over 75 percent were physicians, and the rest representatives of nursing, pharmacy, and related professions.

5

Interview with Eugene W. Owen, Office of Special Administrative Services, DHR.

6

Interview with C. D. Warren, director of Mental Health, Fulton County Department of Health.

7

Atlanta Constitution, December 21, 1971, p. 18-A.

8

Interview with William Roper, head of Management Review, OPB.

9

Interview with William Nixon, state auditor. This failure later became a major focus of controversy within Georgia.

10

Interview with James Parham. Parham indicated he tried previously to have the proposal incorporated as part of the reorganization package but was unsuccessful.

11

Letter from William Wright, dated July 31, 1978.

12

Interview with William Jamieson, assistant to the commissioner and board, DHR.

13

Interview with Eugene W. Owen.

14

As well, the executive gained appointment powers over agency division heads, who were previously in the merit system. Act No. 1489, Section 2501 (1972).

15

Atlanta Constitution, September 16, 1973, pp. mag. 8f.

16

Interview with James Parham.

17

Interview with Richard Harden.

18

Atlanta Constitution, September 16, 1973, pp. mag. 8f.

19

Even members of the supposed triumvirate acknowledge some truth in that characterization. Interview with Richard Harden.

20

Parham attributes much of this animosity to an incident in the legislature during the debates over DHR structure with Board of Health chairman Beverly Forrester, in which Parham asserted: "Health is too important to be left to the physicians." This incident also worsened the already poor relations between DHR and health professionals.

21

While Parham was still acting commissioner, Busbee informally put forth the name of William J. ("Pete") Page, Jr. as a possible candidate for the position. The reaction against Page was reportedly quite negative, probably because he had been the head of HEW Region IV (with offices in Atlanta), where he was associated with HEW civil rights policies. Page was to become secretary of Florida's reorganized Department of Health and Rehabilitative Services (see chapter 4).

22

Letter from Charles R. Morris, dated August 19, 1977.

23

Interview with Daniel J. Evans. Though rural, conservative, antiservices legislators were not necessarily a majority, the possibility of a majority to oppose Evans on specific issues was increasing.

24

Seattle Times, October 15, 1972, p. A-26.

25

According to Richard Hemstad, then legal counsel to Governor Evans, this lack of structure requirements would allow the new secretary to shape the department with a free hand during its first year.

26

There was also complaints about the salaries, which were claimed to be at least $5,000 lower in Washington than comparable positions in other states.

27

Interview with Dr. Robert Shearer.

28

Interview with Dr. Robert Shearer.

29

Interview with Senator William S. Day, chairman, Senate Social and Health Services Committee.

30

Seattle Post Intelligencer, July 1, 1960, p. A-10.

31

Letter from Charles R. Morris, dated August 19, 1977.

32

Letter from Charles R. Morris, dated August 19, 1977.

33

R. R. Rathfelder, *A History of the Organizational Structure of the Department of Social and Health Services* (February 1977), pp. 10, 13.

34

Letter from Charles Morris, dated August 19, 1977.

35

Letter from Charles Morris, dated August 19, 1977. According to Morris, in relation to the vendor and assistance payments oversight, when he arrived over two-thirds of the DSHS budget was being paid out to recipients and vendors outside the agency, with only the most limited capacity to monitor or control that spending.

36
Interview with R. R. Rathfelder.

37
Letter from Marilyn Ward, dated July 21, 1977.

38
Interview with Dr. John Beare, director, DSHS Division of Health.

39
Interview with Marilyn Ward, DSHS Office of Citizen Participation.

40
Interview with Dr. Muriel Taylor, Bureau of Mental Health, DSHS.

41
Paper delivered to the Washington Association of Social Workers 1975 Conference by Charles Morris (unpublished).

42
This may be a relative loss of power, that is, in comparison to Dan Evans's strong position and dynamic stands during his first term. In the opinion of Wallace G. Miller, formerly on Evans's staff, the office of governor in Washington State has traditionally been weak.

43
Interview with Daniel J. Evans.

44
Interview with state senator Al Henry. Republican senator Joel Pritchard noted that Evans was just as willing to confront members of his own party on policy issues as he was Democrats.

45
The legislature ultimately allowed the new department $11,368,000.

46
Interview with state senator Al Henry.

47
Interview with state senator William Day.

48
Letter from Marilyn Ward, dated July 21, 1977.

49
Interview with Robert Doble, Planning, DSHS. Doble retains, however, a positive overall impression of the Evans years. "His image grew both in the state and nationally during the first two terms. The last term may not have had the impact of the previous two, but I believe that he is still regarded in political circles, particularly among other governors, as having been a forward-looking and able administrator." Letter dated July 24, 1977.

50

Even among Evans's supporters, eight years was generally accepted as the functional limit for an effective governorship.

51

Interview with Daniel J. Evans.

52

Atlanta Constitution, November 20, 1973, p. 17-B.

53

Interview with Dr. James Craig.

54

One former division head quotes Harden as privately admitting that some AND appointments were made because of relationships with state senators and representatives in the Maddox camp, but this is denied by both Harden and Parham.

55

Atlanta Constitution, November 29, 1973, p. 17-B.

56

Memorandum to Governor Carter from Barbara S. Bent, dated February 20, 1973.

57

Interview with Richard Harden.

58

Letter from Dr. Donald G. Miles, Georgia Mental Health Institute, dated May 24, 1978.

59

Interview with Ace Hagenback, area network director.

60

Interview with Eugene W. Owen.

61

Interview with Richard Harden.

62

Memorandum to Governor Carter from Barbara S. Bent, dated February 20, 1973.

63

Atlanta Constitution, July 18, 1973, p. 12-A. A figure of $800,000 is quoted for thirty-five positions; i.e., $23,000 per position.

64

Interview with James Parham.

65

Atlanta Constitution, May 9, 1975, p. 6-R.

66

Health Resources Association, *An Analysis of the Effects of State Departments of Human Resources on Selected Health Resources Administration/National Institute of Mental Health Programs: Georgia Case Study* (1976), p. 63.

67

Interview with Ace Hagenback.

68

One district health director, Dr. Marjorie Lyncott, was reportedly fired because of her resistance to the area network director in her district, but was reportedly rehired at the insistance of Al Burris, then House Speaker pro tem.

69

Atlanta Constitution, April 28, 1974, p. 2-A.

70

Interview with Ace Hagenback.

71

Health Resources Administration, *An Analysis of the Effect of State Department of Human Resources on Selected Health Resources Administration/National Institute of Mental Health Programs: Georgia Case Study* (1976), p. 87.

72

Interview with David Nelson, DSHS Office of Operations Review.

73

Connection: The Journal of the Western Federation of Human Services (June 1977): 2.

74

R. R. Rathfelder, *A History of the Organizational Structure of the Department of Social and Health Services* (1977), p. 10.

75

Even support services integration was short-lived, and was cited in November 1976 as a problem area by Neil Peterson, head of Community Services in DSHS.

76

Interview with Daniel J. Evans.

77

Atlanta Constitution, February 15, 1974, p. 1-A.

78

Atlanta Constitution, October 13, 1976, p. 3-A. The deal, of course, would be that Busbee would wait on reorganization of Carter's administrative set-piece until after the November 2nd elections. November 2, 1976, was also the date of Busbee's successful constitutional amendment to allow his own re-election. All of Busbee's changes occurred in December 1976. It has been speculated that Busbee's original conviction that DHR should be dismantled was modified by his discovery that the governor had sufficient tools to reform the agency without dismantlement.

79
Interview with Eugene W. Owen.

80
In contrast, an executive official referred to Veterans Services as a classic example of old-school bureaucratic nonmanagement.

81
Interview with representative Sidney Marcus.

82
Interview with William Roper, OPB.

83
Interview with representative Ronald Hanna, chairman, House Institutions Committee.

Chapter 4

1
An early version of the material on Florida in this chapter appeared in *Evaluation*, 3:1-2 (1976), pp. 59-78.

2
Guy D. Spiesman, Gary Dean Hulshoff, and Sam A. McConnell, *Legislative Staff: The Equalizer in State Government*/Final Report of the Human Resources Services Staffing Demonstration (HRSS) of the Arizona State legislature (Phoenix: Goodwill Industries, 1976), p. ii.

3
House Government Operations Committee, *Governmental Reorganization: A Report to the 31st Legislature,* State of Arizona (1973), p. 13.

4
Interview with Gary Hulshoff, Division of Medical Assistance, DES.

5
Spiesman, Hulshoff, and McConnell, *Legislative Staff,* p. 95.

6
Interview with Robert Mienart, DOL Region IX, Employment and Training Administration.

7
Interview with Irwin Hoff, HEW Region IX.

8
Interview with Timothy Barrow, former Speaker of the House.

9
This outcome, a compromise between the Florida house and senate, settled two intensely contested issues. The first was over whether the governor or the

elected cabinet should have primary executive control over health and rehabilitative services administration. The "strong governor" model favored by
the house was adopted. The second was over whether human services should
be incorporated into a single department or into three separate departments
dealing with health, social and rehabilitative services, and youth and adult
correctional services. The single comprehensive department favored by the
senate was finally adopted.

10
Interview with Hal Brown, former deputy director of DES under Mayo.

11
Interview with Charles Smale, acting assistant director for administrative services.

12
Interview with William Mayo.

13
Council of State Governments, *Human Services Integration* (1974), p. 73.

14
Interview with Robert Mienart.

15
Interview with William Mayo.

16
Mayo also privately charged that the staff of the new governor resented him
because he refused to fire all the bureau chiefs and put the governor's appointees in. While there were relatively few major personnel changes outside
of the director's office in DES after Mayo left, only six positions in DES are
exempt: the director, his deputy, and the four assistant directors — of administrative services, program services, field services, and resources planning.

17
Spiesman, Hulshoff, and McConnell, *Legislative Staff,* p. 11.

18
Interview with Charles Smale. Smale noted that when John Huerta and Arlyn
Larson went to Minnesota to advise the task force contemplating a similar
agency in June of 1976, the biggest single message was to take plenty of time.

19
Interview with Henry Diaz.

20
Interview with John Huerta. One of the results of this lack of uniformity, in
Huerta's opinion, was an error rate of 48 percent by AFDC workers, at that
time the highest in the country.

21
Interview with Dr. Arlyn Larson.

22
Louis Quihuis, *Space Utilization Report of U.S. Department of Labor Funded Buildings in Arizona,* Human Resources Committee, Arizona House of Representatives, June 1976.

23
Interview with Robert Mienart.

24
Letter from William J. Haltigan, DOL Region IX, to John Huerta, dated October 24, 1975.

25
Interview with Robert Mienart.

26
Interview with Thomas Tyrell, VR bureau chief. According to Arlyn Larson, use of 900 codes began to be sharply restricted.

27
Management Improvement Goal, dated July 1, 1976, p. 4.

28
DES memo on "The Role of the District Manager," dated November 29, 1976. One of the biggest federal regulations problems was a 50 percent error rate in AFDC, over which HEW was threatening a major audit exception. As Roger Root, Huerta's assistant director for planning and management analysis, noted: "I think that a [fully integrated] structural model was premature given the federal programs did not change."

29
When Huerta's 1976 Management Improvement Goal proposal was being drafted, DES could not get sufficient interest from the legislature to involve them in the process. Interview with John Huerta.

30
Interview with Roger Root.

31
Interview with John Huerta.

32
Interview with Sam A. McConnell.

33
Interview with John Huerta.

34
Interview with R. F. Morris, Joint Legislative Budget Committee.

35
Minutes, Arizona Legislative Council, April 22, 1977.

36
Interview with R. F. Morris.

37
Neither Emmett Roberts, secretary of the department when the measure was passed, nor Keller, his successor, ever used this authority to remove and replace a division head. Whether their power to do so nevertheless enhanced their control over their organization is unclear.

38
The committee continued until March of 1978, when oversight was returned to house and senate DHRS committees.

39
National Academy of Public Administration, *Reorganization in Florida* (Washington, D.C.: 1977), p. 38.

40
Ibid., p. 54.

41
Ibid., p. 40.

42
Testimony before the Senate Subcommittee on the Handicapped of the Committee on Labor and Public Welfare, February 24, 1976.

43
Joint Session with Senate Subcommittee on the Handicapped of the Committee on Labor and Public Welfare, December 10, 1975.

44
Interview with William Soltau.

45
Interview with John Nimsky, member of the DES planning staff responsible for implementation of Huerta's Operational Planning System.

46
Page applied six criteria to his choices for field leadership: prior high achievement, experience and performance in large complex organizations, high tolerance for risk and uncertainty, a good conceptual ability, an ability to articulate, and a personal dedication to the task. Interview with William J. Page, Jr.

47
NAPA, *Reorganization in Florida,* 69.

48
Ibid., p. 76.

Chapter 5

1

According to Duane Scribner, who later worked with Knutson out of the Governor's Office, this problem of equity largely shaped Knutson's approach: "In a county system we have considerable variation in what's offered. There is a lot of local autonomy there, and a lot of difference in the attitudes of county commissioners. You get into a conservative county and they basically think that the poor are undeserving poor, etc."

2

Minnesota Laws, 1973, Chapter 716.

3

Interview with Gary Dodge, State Planning Agency.

4

This council, created under Executive Order No. 45, October 6, 1972, served as a source of task forces for the Governor's Office of Program Development (described below) and did not survive it.

5

Created by Executive Order No. 33, June 29, 1972.

6

William A. Fleischmann and Duane C. Scribner, "Minnesota: Sensitivity to the Intervention Process in State and Local Reform Efforts," in Coping with the Demands for Change within Human Services Administration, edited by Robert Agranoff (Washington, D.C.: American Society for Public Administration, 1977), p. 23.

7

Interview with Duane Scribner.

8

Interview with John Redmond, formerly of the Governor's Office of Planning and Development. Later, rivalry did develop between State Planning and both OPD and its successor, the Office of Human Services (OHS), especially when OHS took the lead in human service development in 1975-77.

9

Interview with Duane Scribner.

10

Interview with Lawrence Granger, Association of Minnesota Counties.

11

Interview with Robert Hiller, assistant commissioner, Minnesota Department of Health.

12

Only nine of Minnesota's eighty-seven counties had more than 50,000 population. Some observed that 30,000 was not any better received, and that the Health Act's financial incentives proved to be the most powerful reason for its popularity.

13
The counties were Koochiching, Itasca, Aikin, Carlton, Lake, Cook, and St. Louis. Of the 330,000 people in the region, one-third were in Duluth, two-thirds in St. Louis County as a whole.

14
The difference in geographic size between the two regions should be noted. St. Louis County in Region III is larger than all of Region IX.

15
Interview with Pamela Schmidt, Region IX staff.

16
Human Services Reform: A Model for Chief Executive Intervention, Duane C. Scribner, director (August 1975): p. 37.

17
Interview with John Redmond, formerly of the Governor's Office of Program Development.

18
Office of Human Services: Final Report (Office of Human Services, Department of Administration, June 1977), 14.

19
The agencies were the Department of Corrections, Department of Employment Services, Department of Health, Department of Public Welfare, Governor's Citizens Council on Aging, State Health Planning and Development Agency, Governor's Planning Council on Developmental Disabilities, Division of Vocational Rehabilitation, Governor's Commission on Crime Prevention and Control, Governor's Manpower Office.

20
OHS, *A Strategy for Change in State Government,* p. 31.

21
Ibid., p. 34.

22
Ibid., p. 14.

23
Office of Human Services: Final Report (Office of Human Services, Department of Administration, June 1977).

24
Sabo was also mentioned by many observers as a major legislative force behind the Human Services Act. His departure from the legislature in 1979 to take a congressional seat was felt to be a major blow to the multicounty board forces. As one agency staff member lamented, "At present, no one at the state level is arguing for regionalism."

25

OHS, *Final Report*. The 1979 legislature repealed the 50,000 minimum population for Human Service Boards, which is likely to stimulate their proliferation.

26

This office should not be confused with the State Office of Program Development, which has the same initials.

27

Interview with Dr. Richard Raile.

28

Interview with Thomas Lindquist, Scott County Human Services director.

29

In 1977, Scott County exercised an option to lower citizen participation on the board to zero.

Chapter 6

1

The Department of Public Welfare comprises public assistance, social services, mental health, mental retardation, and a miscellany of allied programs.

2

Reed Smith, *State Government in Transition: Reforms of the Leader Administration* (1955-59), (Philadelphia: University of Pennsylvania Press, 1963), p. 42.

3

Ibid., p. 134. This perception of intrusion was enhanced by Leader's contemporaneous creation of a Governor's Advisory Committee, largely drawn from the faculty of the three state universities, which conducted management studies of all the executive departments.

4

Interview with Governor George Leader.

5

Smith, *State Government in Transition,* p. 263.

6

Prior to becoming secretary of health, Dr. Georges had been assistant for health affairs to the secretary of DPW.

7

Regionalism: A Progress Report, Office of State Planning and Development, dated October 23, 1974.

8
Interview with Donald Goss, Pennsylvania Department of Administration.

9
Executive Order 1973-10, dated May 7, 1974.

10
Interview with Robert Haigh, deputy commissioner for mental health, DPW. According to some observers, Developmental Disability councils have not been functional wherever they have been established. Created under the DD Act of 1971, the highly varied mix of consumers, citizens, and bureaucrats resulted in an unstructured group which did not function effectively.

11
Interview with Norman Lourie, executive deputy secretary for DPW.

12
No formal cabinet meetings are held because of strict Pennsylvania sunshine laws that the governor feels undermine ability to negotiate in confidence. Interview with Milton Berkes, special assistant to the governor for human resources.

13
Washington Post, August 8, 1977, p. A-1. While the Democrats held a majority in both houses as well as the governorship, their majority was small (116 of 203 in the House; 30 of 50 in the Senate).

14
Citizens Conference on State Legislatures, *The Sometimes Governments: A Critical Study of the 50 American Legislatures* (Kansas City, Mo.: 1973), p. 290.

15
Staffing deficiencies were among the major criticisms of Pennsylvania made by the Citizens Conference on State Legislatures (now Legis 50) in *The Sometimes Governments.*

16
Interview with Milton Berkes.

17
Interview with Eva Kepp, House Health and Welfare Committee.

18
Harrisburg Evening News, August 11, 1977, p. 6.

19
Interview with Eva Kepp.

20
All DPW personnel interviewed did, however, allude to rivalries between professional staff and the politically appointed secretary.

21
Interview with Wendell Raimey, head of Mon Valley Health and Welfare Council, Inc.

22
A CHRA is made up of four major human services programs, one of which is Public Assistance/Social Services.

23
Interview with Jerry Radke, DPW deputy secretary for social services.

24
This is not confined to DPW alone. Former governor Leader expressed dissatisfaction with the state planning unit he had pulled into his office and asserted that the large number of actors in Pennsylvania government made consensus planning impossible.

25
While the number of patients in the nineteen state hospitals at year's end declined from 35,514 in FY 1965 to 14,279 in FY 1975, the number of staff increased from 12,803 in 1965 to 14,733 in 1975.

26
Interview with James McEntee, AFSCME. See also Henry San Tiesteuvan, *Deinstitutionalization: Out of Their Beds and into the Streets,* AFSCME (Washington, D.C.: 1975). The objectivity of this report is at times questioned within DPW.

27
Comprehensive Mental Health Planning Committee, *Final Report: Toward Complete System Integration* (dated September 14, 1976), p. iii. As opposed to 23,000 contacts in 1965, Pennsylvania Community Mental Health Services handled 175,000 contacts in 1975 under basically the same system.

28
Interview with Helene Wohlgemuth.

29
Letter from Norman Lourie dated July 26, 1977.

30
Auditor general, United Services Agency Central, Wilkes Barre, Pa., *Audit Report for the Year Ended June 30, 1975* (1976), p. 30.

31
Ibid., p. 30.

32
Letter to Frank Beal, DPW secretary, concerning the Special Audit from USA director Katherine McKenna and DPW comptroller Hubert Simpson, dated March 7, 1977.

33
Auditor general, *Audit Report . . . 1975.*

34
For example, Allegheny County, citing the additional hierarchical level, abolished an integrated Department of Human Resources that had been created by the previous county administration, and returned to categorical programs. Recognizing the need for improved management and accountability, but not necessarily the establishment of a human services department, the new county commissioners began seeking human services management expertise from the Mon Valley Project.

Selected Bibliography

General

American Public Welfare Association, *Integrated Social Services* APWA (1976)

American Society for Public Administration, *Human Services Integration* (1974)

Center for Human Services Development, *The Integration of Services as a Process, Not a Product,* San Jose State University

Center for State Legislative Research, *Politicians and Professionals: Interaction Between Committee and Staff in State Legislatures,* Eagleton Institute for Politics (1977)

Council of State Governments, *Human Services Integration,* Lexington, Kentucky (1974)

U.S. Department of Health, Education and Welfare (Region X), *People or Paper* (1977)

U.S. Department of Health, Education and Welfare (Region X), *Ties That Bind . . .* (1976)

U.S. Department of Health, Education and Welfare, *Toward Integrated Human Services: Proceedings of the Services Integration Capacity Building Conference* (1974)

Douglas Henton, *The Feasibility of Services Integration,* Graduate School of Public Policy, University of California at Berkeley (1975)

The Human Ecology Institute, *The Design of Human Services Systems* (1974)

The Human Ecology Institute, *Twenty-two Allied Services (SITO) Projects Described as Human Services Systems* (1974)

Paul Mott, *Meeting Human Needs: The Social and Political History of Title XX,* National Conference on Social Welfare (1976)

Henry San Tiesteuvan, *Deinstitutionalization: Out of the Beds and into the Streets,* American Federation of State, County & Municipal Employees (1975)

Project SHARE, *Evaluation of Services Integration Demonstration Projects* (HS Bibliography Series), U.S. Government (1976)

Project SHARE, *Illustrating Services Integration from Categorical Bases* (HS Monograph Series), U.S. Government (1976)

Project SHARE, *Journal of Human Services Abstracts* (1976-)

Southeast Institute for Human Resources Development and American Society of Public Administration, *Coping with the Demands for Change in Human Services Administration,* Atlanta, Georgia

Southeast Insitute for Human Resources Development, *An Overview of Planning for Human Services in Eight Southeast States,* Atlanta, Georgia

Task Force on the Organization and Delivery of Human Services, *Current Issues in Title XX Programs,* National Conference on Social Welfare (1976)

Task Force on the Organization and Delivery of Human Services, *Expanding Management Technology and Professional Accountability in Social Services Programs*, National Conference on Social Welfare (1976)

Arizona

Department of Administration, *Department of Economic Security: Management Survey and Report Supplement* (Viewpoints of DES from Outside Agencies), State of Arizona (1975)

Guy Spiesman, Gary Hulshoff, Sam McConnell, *Legislative Staff: The Equalizer in State Government*, Final Report of the Human Resources Services Staffing Demonstration of the Arizona State Legislature, Goodwill Industries, Phoenix, Arizona (1976)

Florida

Governors Management Advisory Council, *Report on the Department of Health and Rehabilitative Services*, State of Florida (1978)

Governors Management Task Force, *Report and Recommendations*, Warren King & Associates (1974)

National Academy of Public Administration, *Reorganization in Florida: How Is Services Integration Working?* NAPA (1977)

Office of the Auditor General, *Department of Health and Rehabilitative Services: Special Review on the Progress of Reorganization*, State of Florida (1977)

The Research Group, Inc., *The Organization and Delivery of District-wide Services in the Districts*, prepared for the Florida Department of Health and Rehabilitative Services (1979)

Georgia

Executive Committee on Reorganization and Management Improvement, *State of Georgia Reorganization and Management Improvement Study*, State of Georgia, (1971)

Executive Committee for the Study of State and Local Government Services, *Georgia State and Local Government Coordination Study*, State of Georgia (1972)

Institute of Government, Reorganization Study Staff Memorandum No. 5, University of Georgia, Athens, Georgia (dated August 6, 1971)

Minnesota

Association of Minnesota Counties, *The Human Services Act*, St. Paul, Minnesota (July 1974)

Association of Minnesota Counties, *The Minnesota Community Corrections Act* , St. Paul, Minnesota (July 1974)

Department of Economic Security, *Report to the Legislature,* State of Minnesota (January 1978)

Hennepin County Office of Planning and Development, *Human Services Integration and Reorganization in Hennepin County,* Minneapolis, Minnesota (June 1976)

Governor's Council on Executive Reorganization, *Executive Reorganization for the Improvement of State Government,* State of Minnesota (1968)

Office of Human Services, *Economic Security and Health and Social Services: A Strategy for Change in State Government,* State of Minnesota (December 1976)

Office of Human Services, *Human Service Boards: The Latest Look,* State of Minnesota (May 1977)

Office of Program Development, *Human Services Reform: A Model for Chief Executive Intervention,* State of Minnesota (August 1975)

State Planning Agency, *The Fairbault, Martin, Wantonwan Human Services Board, A Study of the Implementation of the Human Services Act* (January 1978)

Pennsylvania

Auditor General, *Audit Report, United Services Agency,* State of Pennsylvania (1975)

Center for Human Services Development, *United Services Agency Evaluation Project, First Year of Development and Operation,* Pennsylvania State University

Comprehensive Mental Health Planning Committee, *Toward Complete System Integration,* Final Report of Secretary Frank Beale, Department of Public Welfare, Harrisburg, Pennsylvania (1976)

Office of State Planning and Development, *Report on Planning Implementation to Governor Milton Shapp,* State of Pennsylvania (1974)

Pennsylvania Bureau of Systems Analysis, *Plan for the Reorganization of the Executive Branch,* Office of Administration (1969)

School of Social Administration, *The United Services Agency — Process Evaluation,* Temple University, Philadelphia, Pennsylvania (1976)

State and Local Welfare Commission, *A Reallocation of Public Welfare Responsibilities,* Department of Public Welfare (1963)

Washington

Council for Reorganization of Washington State Government, *Survey Report and Recommendations,* Warren King & Associates (1965)

Department of Social and Health Services, *Integrated Services Delivery*, State of Washington (1975)

Institute of Governmental Research, *The Administrative Reorganization Experience in the State of Washington*, University of Washington (1971)

Task Force on Executive Reorganization of the State of Washington, *Report to Governor Daniel Evans*, State of Washington (1968)

Index